IT'S A DOG'S
IN THE FIRE SE

G000041277

Memories of a 'Happy Squirter'
by
Peter St. Bernard

A humorous account of life in the Fire Service, complemented by cartoons, spanning in excess of two decades of experiences by the author, who served in two separate Fire Brigades, which were as different as 'Chalk' and 'Cheese' and in terms of size went from the sublime to the ridiculous.

Many of the stories related will leave the reader with no doubts that the 'Trumpton's' of the world did exist, along with a 'Dad's Army' mentality.

Amongst the chapters which are described in an amusing manner are: 'Accidents', 'Open Days', 'Operational Foul-Ups', 'Radio Messages', 'Sickness', 'Station Life' and 'Visits From The Hierarchy'.

Although the modern day Fire Service has progressed in leaps and bounds over the years, thanks to technological advances, little has changed in many aspects of day to day life within the service, especially in the relationships between the officers and the men.

DEFIANT PUBLICATIONS

A percentage of the profits from this book will be donated to the Fire Service Benevolent Fund.

IT'S A DOG'S LIFE
IN THE FIRE SERVICE

BRIGADES INVOLVED

LITTLE SNOBSBURY
-Small, one station Brigade (efficient and cost effective?)
A haven for popinjays.
-Twinned with KOOGYDELBBOG (Ruritania) English translation
- ALL PRATS TOGETHER.

MAMMOTH COUNTY
-Massive, multi-station Brigade. Gargantuan, monolithic, all devouring, all powerful, cost cutting (except for officers) - A MAMMOTH QUANGO, ultimately led by a TYRANTosaurus.
-Twinned with lots of other MAMMOTH COUNTIES, worldwide, for cultural and fact finding exchanges by the hierarchy, unfairly referred to in the popular press as 'freebies'.

Covers designed by Alison Leavers. © 1990

Cartoons by John O'Hara © 1990

Typesetting by Word Up, Holmfirth, Huddersfield

Printed for Richard Netherwood Limited by Gorenjski Tisk p.o. in Yugoslavia

ISBN 0 946857 30 X   © DEFIANT PUBLICATIONS 1990
                                           FIRST PUBLISHED 1990

IT'S A DOG'S LIFE IN THE FIRE SERVICE

CONTENTS

Foreword

A fire engine is one of the most loved vehicles in existence. Ask any mum and her kids, who stare in awe as the big gleaming red monster passes down the High Street with horns blaring, bells clanging and blue lights flashing. But how many folk stop to ponder and think about where the machine is going? Very rarely do they stop in their tracks and wonder, even in the remotest sense, that it may be going to their house, office, factory or car on fire.

It is always assumed by 'Joe Public' that the fire engine is going to someone else's property. I wouldn't mind a pound for every time a member of the public has stated, "I never thought it would happen to me." Then and only then did they realise from a personal point of view that the Fire Service really existed.

I also feel sure that the majority of the public at large assume that fire engines, whether in full flight or on a routine mission, appear to be travelling from A to B for no apparent reason, are based nowhere and when urgently required are magically transported from heaven knows where to the scene of trouble like vehicles from 'Thunderbirds'.

So we have a situation in which on the one hand the fire engines are loved one minute, as they dash off to someone else's house, hated the next minute because they are the last item wanted at their own property, but loved once again if needed in an emergency by the same person. Using the saying, 'Someone Else's House', is somewhat akin to 'There's Always Somebody Worse Off', both on a par with some of the world's worst sayings, like STOP THIEF and DO NOT THROW STONES AT THIS NOTICE.

Another factor concerning fire engines is that most of the outside community rarely appear to notice that it carries a crew of men (or women) with it. Listen to the people in the street, who point and say, "There goes a fire engine," as if it is driven by remote control.

Apart from attending fires and road traffic accidents, the Fire Service in Britain responds to all manners of emergencies, e.g. a child with its head stuck in railings, people trapped in lifts, trees, aircraft, machinery, boats and floods. In addition, firemen attend electrocutions and suicides, animals trapped in culverts and canals and other bizarre situations. There are many humorous references to these incidents within the pages of this book and in many instances they are supported by cartoons from 'J.O.'.

Firemen all over the world are unique. Danger, destruction and death are their daily bread and in certain circumstances they will give their lives in the course of their duties to the community and will continue to do so without a thought for their own safety or of their wives and children becoming widows and fatherless.

To understand the motives of why people become firefighters is intangible. As a side-note, a colleague once confessed to me, "I was useless at anything else so I joined the Fire Service — it seemed like a good idea at the time." A key factor which helps them to cling together through danger, intermingled with lengthy and often boring hours of duty, is 'humour', a natural safety valve and much of this book is dedicated to this wonderful human talent. In my humble opinion 'humour' helps the world go round — presumably the members of the 'Flat Earth Society' obtain their 'kicks' in other ways.

To put this book into perspective much of the humour is directed at the hierarchy of the Fire Service, both in the uniformed and civilian branches. As in many other walks of life the people in high places who govern our daily lives are more open to humorous criticism than those on the ground floor who merely follow orders. I would like to stress that despite the high content of humour, mistakes and foul-ups at all levels, the operational standards of life saving, protection of property and the dedication of the personnel in the British Fire Service ranks as second to none.

I would like to thank many of my former colleagues, not only for contributing valuable material and for reminding me of humorous situations, but also for their encouragement whilst I was in the process of writing this book. Some of these erstwhile characters have given me permission to use part of their real names, whilst others have requested that I use a pseudonym for them.

I would also like to thank the unknown editor of 'Incognito Press' for the use of some of his excellent material. Long may his 'writings' continue.

This book is dedicated to my long suffering family and to all of the firemen I have met and worked with over the years. Last but not least, the front cover picture is an everlasting tribute to our long since gone, but not forgotten pet, 'Brandy', who 'posed' for and gave me the inspiration for the title 'IT'S A DOG'S LIFE IN THE FIRE SERVICE'.

Introduction

My downfall began in January 1966 when I left the relative comfort of the signalbox in which I had worked for a lengthy period of time. My first love, steam locomotives, had disappeared from the area and with 'Beeching' policies coming to their height there were strong rumours of the eventual total closure of the line, which meant ultimately my becoming redundant or being transferred to a less likeable job. (In fact the line is still open today and the signalbox in which I worked only closed a few years ago.)

My next mistake was to emigrate to Australia, the land of opportunity, as a £10.00 'Pom'. The outward journey was via Geneva, Beirut, Karachi, Calcutta and Singapore. By the time I arrived at the first port of call in Australia, Darwin, I was already beginning to feel home-sick. An everlasting memory of the stop at Darwin was of the appearance of some airport officials, who boarded the aircraft and proceeded with great relish, to 'disinfect' the immigrants with antiquated fly-spray style containers.

Soon after arrival in Sydney I was taken to a hostel and my home-sickness was not helped by the sight of large numbers of grown men who were in tears and burbling that they wished to return home as soon as possible. The seven months I spent in Australia were a catalogue of disasters. I had taken little finances with me and jobs were hard to obtain. Prior to joining the New South Wales Government Railways, I had to pawn the few valuable items I had, in an effort to pay the rent and to avoid starvation.

Once joining the railways I had a succession of onerous jobs, including being a locomotive cleaner, a parcels porter and a shunter in freight yards. The latter job was particularly dangerous and during daylight hours I was accompanied by the seemingly statutory allocation of a dozen or so large blue-bottles buzzing round my head.

It was at a location with the latter function that a strong rumour was circulated concerning my being a prime candidate for National Service and being of 'call-up' age, twenty years old, the immediate future didn't look too rosy. I hadn't been long in 'Aussie' when the first Australian National Serviceman was killed in Vietnam.

At first there were banner headlines and protest marches against the authorities for involving Australia in this bitter and bloody conflict. However, the initial furore soon died down with the advent of more important things such as 'test matches' and the like. Small newspaper articles barely recorded the second, third and so on fatal casualties and being the 'Coward of the County' I didn't want to hang around to find out if the rumour was true or false, and I certainly didn't want the possibility of the last fleeting moments of my young life in some God-forsaken far off jungle being recorded on an inch of newsprint, 12,000 miles from home.

I immediately arranged a loan from my sister, who lived in Canada, and beat a hasty retreat from Australia, eventually returning home via Honolulu, San Francisco, Vancouver and Toronto. Upon arrival at London Airport I was the happiest person in the world and was almost tempted to kiss the tarmac, like the Pope. Soon I was on the final leg home, back to mother, clutching my sparse possessions and a few precious pound notes. The bulk of my belongings, in a trunk, appeared to go on a world tour of their own as I didn't receive them back from Australia, for many, many months.

At least I was home, but there was one slight snag; I owed in excess of £200, which was a small fortune in those days. I was also broke and out of work and the opportunities for a well paid job, with little or no qualifications, were rather remote.

After a while I acquired an appointment as a trainee bar/cellarman at a local pub. Although the week consisted of split shifts over six day periods, it was rather enjoyable. The problem was the pay. Although I was grateful for my employment, the £8.00 a week I earned was hardly likely to make a dent in my huge debt. The most I could afford to pay back in any one given week was about £1.00, and it didn't take a mathematics genius long to work out that it would take me about four years or so to rid myself of the financial millstone.

My 'Saviour' was one of the regular customers, a red-cheeked man, who turned out to be a Station Officer from the local fire station. One of my first observations of this gentleman was his obvious liking for large quantities of beer. He could have competed quite favourably with a camel stocking up for a lengthy desert journey — however, I digress. In amongst the various conversations, he informed me that the Brigade was always on the look-out for strong and healthy candidates and I seemed to fit the bill perfectly. He totally glossed over the fact that I was 5' 8" tall and only nine and a half stone in weight.

Once he mentioned that the starting pay was £14.00 per week, with paid holidays and unlimited overtime I was hooked and so I was soon to embark on an up and down career which was to last in excess of twenty years before I resigned to go into full-time publishing.

When I joined the job, the fire station I was employed at belonged to a one station Fire Brigade. When 1974 came along it was absorbed into one of the huge Metropolitan Brigades and when I look back in time I realise what a joke the 'One Station Fire Brigade' was, with all the trappings of high office — Chief and Deputy Chief Fire Officers. There were Home Office inspections and regular visits from Aldermen, Councillors and Mayors, all of which had to be 'cow-towed' to by the firemen. It was a cross between 'Dad's Army' and 'Trumpton'. The attitudes of the officers were balanced between 'Captain Mainwaring' and 'Captain Flack' and the intelligence of the men was totally ignored or looked down upon.

Today, most of the 'Captain Flacks' of the world have gone, but instead of being replaced by men of more superior ability, both in terms of thinking and practical skills, the modern officer appears to have gone

4

back in time and there are ever increasing legions of duplicate 'Captain Mainwarings' in high places. There are a few exceptions here and there, but many officers find themselves in newly created 'gobbledygook' departments, which appear to do little or nothing except produce vast quantities of paperwork, much of which makes little sense to anybody but themselves.

Once in charge of these departments, they then set themselves up as 'Little Hitlers' and immediately set about the task of plotting to outwit a fellow officer or officers in other 'gobbledygook' departments in such a way so as to impress the Chief and his immediate subordinates into giving them further promotion. Any mention of them being 'operational' again makes most of them blanch and scuttle back within the safe confines of their 'paperwork kingdoms'.

With reference to 'gobbledygook' domains, the perfect description of one of these was produced by 'Incognito Press', an 'underground' organisation within the realm of MAMMOTH COUNTY, under the title of 'NEW DEPARTMENT' and reads as follows:

"A new department has recently been opened at Brigade Headquarters, that will in future be known as the EMPIRE BUILDING DEPARTMENT. It is being created by the popular demand of those ambitious young wizz-kids, who like to watch the 'Tail Wagging the Dog' training video at least one a week. The purpose of the new department is to take over comparatively simple tasks which at present run smoothly and make them as complicated as possible, so that it will require in the future specialists to carry them out and thus relieve the operational staff of part of their duties, in order to give them more time to fill in the increasing amounts of paperwork, created by the EMPIRE BUILDING DEPARTMENT."

When I joined LITTLE SNOBSBURY in 1967, as long as you could read and write, add two and two together, and carry someone on your shoulder for 100 yards, you could have a job as a fireman. In the seventies, mostly due to poor pay, the manpower situation became so critical the powers that be at the time were virtually begging any Tom, Dick and Harry to come in off the street, with the discipline code being all but totally ignored.

In the eighties, mainly due to the aftermath of the strike of 1977/78, pay and hours were improved, but once high unemployment came into being the hierarchy started to tighten its grip and it could afford to pick and choose who joined. Nowadays it is preferable to be highly qualified when joining, with only the young cream of society being considered. As a direct contrast to 1967 the chosen elite have to undergo a short but intensive induction course prior to joining properly. The inventor of this system must have based his findings from the film, 'The Hill', starring Sean Connery. Once into Training School and for many years thereafter until the probation period is finished, the 'lucky' candidates face a mountain of information to be absorbed from Manuals, Standing Orders, Technical Bulletins and the like, most of which would baffle a 'Mastermind' champion.

I have never known a job where so many of the rank and file have wished their lives away, praying for the day of retirement to arrive, with comments like, "Thank God, only eighteen more years to do," etc. For my part, I have been one of the lucky ones. Like the 'Great Train Robbers' of 1963, I also didn't have to serve the full thirty years sentence.

What cannot be taken away over my twenty years of service is the richness of the experiences I accumulated concerning the frailty of human behaviour. Being a keen observer of life in general, I have attempted to translate, as accurately as possible, the best and worst of everyday happenings, on and off duty, into a catalogue of humorous situations which I hope the reader will enjoy. All of these incidents, good and bad, have helped to contribute material towards 'It's a Dog's Life in the Fire Service'.

Finally, I would like to quote a statement from a close colleague of mine, Gordon, who retired a few months before I left in the late eighties. In December of the same year we won a hard fought general knowledge quiz at the fire station we had both spent so many years at. Whilst being presented with our trophies by the Deputy Divisional Commander, whom we both knew, Gordon said, as a passing gesture, "It's amazing you know, when you leave the Fire Service your brain starts to function again," to which there was an amazed silence. We stood smirking at him. It was the ultimate triumph for both of us as this high powered representative of the Brigade had been rendered impotent, and he was powerless to wipe the jubilant smiles off our faces. It had been a long wait, but well worth it.

Many years before I joined, a colleague overheard a remark from a fellow firefighter, who, bemused and disgusted by the antics of some of his comrades and the attitudes of a number of senior officers, said, "Someone ought to write a book about this lot."

Well folks, here it is:

Accidents

During the many years I was in the Fire Service, both at LITTLE SNOBSBURY and MAMMOTH COUNTY, I witnessed a large number of humorous accidents, some of which I was involved in myself. I hope the reader will enjoy the variety of 'accidents' I have selected within the pages of this chapter. It commences with 'sports activities'.

All sorts of 'sports' were played from time to time, but without doubt the most popular sport was, and still is, volleyball. In most games there was a spirit of fair play, but from time to time there would be flare-ups between individuals and near punch-ups would occur. If there was a deliberate foul at the net, like fingernails taking chunks out of an opponents face or a knee in the groin, then the game would deteriorate to one of 'Jungle' rules.

Attempts would be made prior to the start of each game to balance the teams in terms of average height, but if a game was lost it was always the smaller chaps who were blamed. When it came to accidents, however, it was a different kettle of fish. The big six foot plus 'He-Man' types were always the first to get injured, serving them right for being so tall and ungainly.

If you were in the middle of a match which was coming to the boil it was not unknown for an injured party to be dragged to the sidelines, regardless of whether or not it was a serious accident. The unfortunate would be writhing in pain and the only sympathy he would get would be comments like, "What's the matter with you? A broken leg is it? So what? You've got another one." If the victim persisted with his moaning he would be subjected to further comments like, "Big Girl's Blouse" or "Cissy", etc.

Many volleyball players ended up with swollen ankles and would be seen nursing their injuries, with their feet immersed in buckets of water. During one particularly 'violent and noisy' game, a non participant, the Station Officer (a huge bloke with a barrel chest) was working beneath his car in the station yard. Unknown to the players the vehicle jack had slipped and the S.O. was trapped under his car. It was not until the game was over that his cries for help were heard. Fortunately it was only his pride that was injured.

The second most favourite sporting activity was five-a-side football or different variations of it depending on the numbers of players available. From the point of view of station property it was the most hazardous, with windows constantly being broken. In most instances the Brigade paid for the damage, but when it reached epidemic proportions the person causing the breakage had to fork out of his own pocket or the games would have been banned.

By far the funniest five-a-side 'match' I was involved in almost turned into a near tragedy. The game was littered with fouls and obscenities and as I later put in a 'fake' report, 'Most of the fouls and obscenities were committed by the Sub Officer', who was 'Savage' by nature. I also put in this 'report' that we had been forced against our will to go out and play football by the same Sub-O. I had pointed out the obvious hazards, like the drill tower, but he had snarled, "Anyone with half a brain will look out for these things."

The drill tower, a tall metal structure, had at its front a set of parallel vertical bars running from virtually ground level to the top. At the base of the tower, looking side-on, it protruded outwards some five feet or so. On the day we played this particular game a salvage sheet had been placed from the first floor of the tower for drying purposes and it was wrapped around the parallel bars, so hiding them.

During the course of the game the 'Savage' Sub-O was haring along with the ball. Suddenly, for no apparent reason, he stopped in his tracks and slowly slid to the ground on his knees. At first we couldn't understand what had happened. Then we heard a YOI-YOI-YOI-YOI-YOI-YOI-YOI-YOI-YOI-YOI-YOI-YOI metallic noise echoing up the parallel bars.

When we reached him his face was badly cut and he was in a state of shock. He was hastily carted off to hospital where he received a number of stitches. This was nothing compared to the number of blokes who were in stitches once it was ascertained he was not seriously injured. On humorous 'get-togethers' this incident is still often at the top of the agenda. This same Sub-O had a reputation for being accident prone, having fallen down an open water pit at his previous station. Now we knew why.

On the subject of 'accident prone' characters, a number of firemen and some of the officers were accident prone or caused accidents to other people or property. One such character, Fm. 'Tarpaulin', was one of those fellows who used to put his 'brain into gear' after the event.

We were standing in the station yard one day, looking around the cars belonging to various members of the Watch, when he came across one with a small section of rust showing on a wing. He studied the wing and commented, "That wing is starting to rot, so and so will have some trouble with that in future months." At that he 'tapped' it with his foot and a huge hole appeared, much to the amusement of all onlookers, with the exception of the owner.

I was riding as the fifth man on the first appliance, a Pump Ladder, when we were turned out to a 'House Fire — Persons Trapped'. Our 'accident prone' friend was one of the B.A. compressed air wearers and on the way to the job he became so excited with the prospect of wearing a set, that as he slung the mask over his head, he completely ripped the rubber surround from the visor. A replacement was substituted and this time he kept it in one piece.

On arrival his eyes were bulging with expectation and as soon as the order was given for him to don his face-mask he was off like a greyhound out of a trap. Without waiting for his partner he hurtled up the stairs, forgetting to take a hose-reel with him. When he reached the landing it was so hot he about turned and hurtled back down again, flattening his partner in the process. Once we calmed him down the job was dealt with in a proper fashion.

Yet another 'accident prone' chap had the unusual nickname of 'Arbut'. This had come into being when somebody recognised that every time he was involved in an argument, especially one he was losing, he would interject, "Ah. But."

Most of the firemen, at some stage or another, tended to own 'bangers' instead of decent cars, for a variety of reasons, including 'Arbut'. He decided to go 'up-market' and saved up for a Range-Rover. Once purchased, he used to sweep in and out of stations like a swashbuckling cavalier, looking down his nose at the 'bangers'. He was soon brought down to earth with a bump when his pride and joy won second prize in a collision with a double-decker bus. At least it went out in style, rolling over and over to the roars of the crowd.

Talking about coming down to earth with a bump, 'Arbut' also attempted to defy 'Newton's Law of Gravity' when he fell through a window on the roof of one of the out stations in MAMMOTH COUNTY, during drills. Fortunately for him he was able to partially grab some overhanging hose-lines, which slowed his speed of descent.

Not long after I joined the Fire Service at LITTLE SNOBSBURY, I attended a lecture given by my new Sub Officer, 'Glarer', whom I will describe in full later in the book. We were seated round the table-tennis table in the recreation room and during the course of this utterly boring session one of the lads, 'Punchy', a former amateur boxer, commenced rocking, to and fro, in his chair, until the inevitable occurred — he went beyond the point of no return and disappeared backwards.

If anybody else had been in charge of the lecture there would have been howls of laughter, but there was almost total silence, apart from a few muted sniggers which were soon halted by the glares from 'Glarer'. After 'Punchy' was re-seated and had recovered his composure, 'Glarer' looked at him and said, "Quite finished? Alright if I carry on?" Not for one moment did he enquire about 'Punchy's' well being.

Having completed a compressed air B.A. drill, we were in the stages of servicing our sets when something went wrong with the first stage reducing valve of one of the sets. 'Glarer' came to investigate and he was holding the faulty valve when it literally 'blew up' in his hand. There was a loud bang of escaping compressed air and a nut flew across the engine house. Somehow this nut went through his fingers and he escaped without a scratch. If this had happened to anybody else it would probably have caused them serious injury.

The second accident that created a near miss for 'Glarer' occurred whilst I was in the B.A. room on an upstairs floor, which housed stocks of compressed air cylinders, in the company of a Scottish Leading Fireman. As we were stacking the charged cylinders one of them decided to go on a journey of its own. It fell off the stack and by its own accord rolled inexorably towards a window. We tried desperately to reach it, but to no avail.

The cylinder crashed through the window and it seemed an eternity before it reached the ground. The area into which it was falling was a confined one, between the main block of the fire station, the boiler-house and the headquarters block. It landed on its neck and exploded at exactly the same time that 'Glarer' walked into the area. The sheer velocity of the escaping air forced the bulk of the cylinder from wall to wall, like the ricochet of a bullet. Somehow, don't ask me how, this lethal missile completely missed 'Glarer'.

It was strongly rumoured, though no-one ever asked him, that he had been a tail gunner on bombers during the last war. Bearing in mind that most tail gunner's were shot down at some time or another, if the 'rumour' was true, then 'Glarer' must have led a charmed life, which had certainly continued into his Fire Service career. The Germans certainly did us no favours by missing him with their 'Fokkers'.

On the subject of cylinders, an Irish junior officer, sometimes referred to as 'Bravo Tu-Tu', once fed in excess of 3,000 pounds per square inch of compressed air into a cylinder designed to take 1,980 pounds per square inch. It was only when the cylinder became round in shape that he realised his 'error'. Fortunately it didn't blow up for had it done so it would have wreaked terrible havoc. Needless to say he was on the receiving end of a 'bollocking'.

There were countless incidents of minor accidents which were highly amusing to the onlooker, but not quite so funny for the participant.

One fireman, called 'Bertie', was out in the station yard, on a Sunday afternoon, testing his latest acquisition, a 'scramble' type of motor cycle. As most people will know, the high pitched note from the exhaust of these bikes soon starts to 'grate' on the nerves.

Round and round he went, up and over makeshift ramps and inclines. The rest of the Watch were in the television room becoming somewhat annoyed by the screaming engine, but fate was soon to intervene on our behalf. Each time the 'scrambler' shot into the air from one of the ramps, the note of the engine used to change slightly until it was back to earth again. We heard the engine note change as it hit one of the ramps, but this time it was accompanied by a loud scream, followed by a crashing noise and then silence.

We rushed outside to investigate and found the silent bike lying on its side in the appliance bay, where it had come to a standstill after crashing beneath one of the partially open 'up and over' doors. Of the 'rider' there was no immediate sign.

We suspected he had either run off to hide his embarrassment or had gone to a washroom to lick his wounds. It wasn't until some little time had passed that he was discovered lying unconscious beneath the station van which was parked next to an outside wall. He was revived, but the strange thing was he never brought the bike into the station again — I wonder why?

Some of the minor accidents only lasted seconds, but they were often the funniest — straight out of slapstick comedy.

We went to the assistance of a person locked out of her flat, on an icy winter's day. Upon arrival the Officer in Charge (O.I.C.) met the occupier and as they were engaged in conversation I leapt out of the cab. Much to the mirth of my colleagues, passers-by and the locked out member of the public, I immediately slipped on the ice and disappeared beneath the fire engine. Rather embarrassing to say the least.

A close friend of mine, whilst out driving, once approached a retained fire station just as the klaxon went off. Out of interest he stopped to observe what the response would be. Like a scene out of 'Trumpton' a number of cars arrived within minutes, spilling out half a dozen part-time firemen, The Butcher, The Baker and The Candlestick Maker, etc. The station was opened and the appliance bay door raised.

As they were about to set off, a seventh 'Captain Flack' look-alike arrived in his car. He leapt out of his vehicle and hurtled towards the appliance (he didn't want to miss out on his turn-out fee!!!) As he approached it he tried to stop running, but he couldn't. The more he tried, on the polished floor, the worse he became, until eventually he lost his footing and he slithered, in a prone position, feet-first, beneath the fire engine.

His colleagues, almost helpless with laughter, assisted this unfortunate being from beneath their charge and helped him into the cab. They then set off, but my friend was unable to drive away for some little time as he had been reduced to a sniggering, jibbering and dribbling heap.

A number of accidents involved vehicles of all kinds, including fire engines. All but a few were caused through carelessness of some description, usually ending up with an enquiry, if it was serious enough, led by a senior officer (an expert of course!!!). The end result being 'bollockings' all round, verbal or written.

One of the best known characters to come to LITTLE SNOBSBURY, was Gordon, who has already been briefly mentioned, a die-hard Midlander and like many a fireman who had transferred here before him, he began to wonder after a week or so what he had walked into with all of the pettiness that went on at this station.

Not long after his arrival he was instructed by a Station Officer to take the station van out and check some hydrants. During the course of this duty, whilst travelling along one of the main roads, a lady pensioner's poodle, or similar type of beast, ran out in front of the van. Having no time to take evasive action, the dog was knocked down and unfortunately killed.

Upon his return Gordon reported to the Station Officer and informed him of the tragic accident, and of the fact that he had comforted the former owner and done everything he could for her, apart from burying the dog. He was ordered to fill in an accident report form. After completing the written section, he came to a page that contained two blank boxes, which were available for sketches — before and after.

Gordon consulted the Station Officer, enquiring as to whether or not he had to do any drawings, which under the circumstances didn't seem to be necessary. The Station Officer snapped back, "Of course you have to." Inspired by the ludicrous order, Gordon proceeded with his drawings. The first simply consisted of a sketch of this unfortunate 'Harry Growler', as one associate 'Pierre Louise' described dogs, trotting across the road. Not being very artistic, by his own admission, it looked more like a miniature donkey on stilts, rather than a dog.

The second drawing of this 'dog/donk' showed it lying down with its stilts, sorry, legs, reaching to the heavens. The drawings were submitted and much to Gordon's astonishment they were accepted by the hierarchy.

One fellow, who had migrated to LITTLE SNOBSBURY from West Sussex, a Queens Park Rangers fanatic and a fellow hater of 'Glarer', backed a seventeen ton Hydraulic Platform over the bonnet of the A.D.O.'s radio car, much to the latter's chagrin. Although 'Q.P.R.' had neglected to see if all was clear before he reversed, the A.D.O. was partly to blame as he had parked his car too close to the rear of the H.P.

Another immigrant, this time from South-West Scotland, an extremely tall and thin character, often referred to as 'The Stick Insect', jumped into the drivers seat of a fire engine parked in the station yard and failed to notice a standpipe which was protruding out of the ground from a hydrant immediately in front of the appliance.

He drove forwards and bent the standpipe in half before realising something was obviously amiss. I can still see the look of abject resignation on his face when he inspected the damage, before sloping off to the Officer in Charge to report his misdemeanour.

Not long after I passed my Heavy Goods Vehicle (H.G.V.) test, I was deemed to be a fully fledged member of the emergency fire engine driving set, later known as an EFAD. (To think, at one time I thought an EFAD was something a ladybird ate!!!) Shortly after I qualified I was involved in my one and only accident as a fire engine driver.

Both of our appliances were parked at the rear of the mechanically operated up and over doors of the appliance bays of the station at LITTLE SNOBSBURY, by now under the control of MAMMOTH COUNTY. On the day in question I was the driver of the second line appliance, the Pump, which was only normally turned out on its own to the more minor incidents, such as a vehicle on fire or a cat up a tree.

We were turned out to such an incident and as I ran through the appliance bay I checked to see if the up and over door was fully open, which I was satisfied in my own mind it was. We leapt aboard, adrenalin flowing, and at the same time the corresponding front appliance bay door, of similar style to the rear door, but electrically operated, was also opened.

As I drove into the appliance bay I thought the world had collapsed on top of me. The metal door had somehow dropped down just enough for our 45' ladder to connect. The whole of this up and over door was dragged onto the top of the fire engine, en masse. I have never heard a sound quite like it and don't wish to ever again.

The remnants of the door were cleared away and I continued to the incident with my fingers crossed. Needless to say, my colleagues and I were rather shaken up, but the powers that be hadn't the foresight, nor the consideration, to despatch another fire engine in place of ours. What 'Red-Cheeks', the residential Station Officer was going to do to me on my return was nobody's business. Upon our return, however, he had gone home for his tea. I was later charged with negligence and received a written warning.

On a winter's day, during the run up to my last Christmas in the job, we were eagerly looking forward to a hearty breakfast, with our early morning chores all but completed, when the Pump, of which I was the O.I.C., was sent to complete the initial attendance on another station's patch. The wall speaker announced it was a 'Road Traffic Accident — Person Trapped'.

Although bitterly cold, the roads were dry and free of ice, that was until we turned into the lengthy, but little used cul-de-sac where the incident was. The first fifty yards or so were fine and by now we had spotted the R.T.A. in the distance, where a car had ploughed into some railings. Our colleagues were already in attendance, as were the police and an ambulance.

As we proceeded down the road, at about 25 mph, our appliance started to sway gently from side to side — horror of horrors — we were on black ice. None of our comrades, which included a senior officer, nor the police, had had the brains to think about stationing someone at the entrance to this road to warn oncoming traffic of this hazard.

I turned to the driver, the erstwhile Gordon, and asked him if he had tried the brakes. He replied, "I have tried the footbrake, the handbrake, and even reverse. Got any other bright ideas?" Despite all the efforts to slow down the opposite happened and our speed appeared to increase. Between ourselves and the incident was a stationary Ford Sierra, complete with driver, and some twenty yards further on, partially blocking the road, was a police car.

As the Sierra loomed ever nearer I tried one last desperate gamble and ordered Gordon to steer the appliance up the verge and onto a patch of grassland, even if it meant the machine being bogged down. The gamble failed and the fire engine slithered along the verge before careering on to its inevitable fate.

Whilst this performance was going on, our colleagues, along with the police and ambulance personnel had stopped in their tracks to observe our plight. Despite frantically waving their arms in an effort to attract the attention of the driver of the Sierra, he remained motionless in his vehicle, failing also to notice our less than normal approach, with our

headlights and blue flashers in use and the blaring of the two-tone horns. Without wishing to be impolite to this gentleman, he must have been daft, deaf or had two glass eyes not to have noticed what was going on, with eight tons of vehicle heading towards him.

I turned to the other two members of my crew, 'The Corporal' and 'The Gambler' and said, "I think we are going to ...." My words were cut short as WE DID. It was like being on a bumper car circuit. Our appliance belted into the rear of the Sierra pushing it forwards some ten yards. A few seconds later we caught up with it again and one further push shunted it straight into the police car, which did a superb pirouette, after which all three vehicles came to a stand.

The enraged driver of the Sierra leapt out of his car and stomped towards us. I immediately climbed out of the cab and met him half-way, before he confronted Gordon, who had commented, "Just let him say something to me and I will punch him on his f*!*!*g nose." The driver shouted, "WHAT KIND OF DRIVERS HAVE YOU GOT IN THE FIRE SERVICE?" I was sorely tempted to say, "They are okay when they are sober," but resisted the temptation.

Whilst I was calming the Sierra driver down, a fireman from the other crew ran over to us, slipped on the ice and disappeared under our fire engine, much to the great amusement of all at the scene, with the exception of the Sierra driver. Even the driver of the original crashed car, who was not badly injured, having a foot trapped in the pedals, saw the funny side of things and mentioned 'Fred Karno' amidst his comments.

Once calm was restored, having ascertained that nobody else was injured, details were taken and the appropriate radio messages were relayed to Fire Control. Upon our return to the station, with more damage done to Gordon's ego than the fire engine, we were greeted by the smirks on the faces of the day shift personnel, to which Gordon's reply was in the form of a dozen or so 'V' signs.

The finale to this story came in the afternoon of the same day. By coincidence it was the childrens Christmas party. As we were now off duty for four days it gave us the opportunity to fill in the accident report forms and make lengthy statements. As Gordon and I had been prime witnesses we had to get together to ensure that our statements were more or less the same, otherwise questions would have been asked from those on high in MAMMOTH COUNTY.

We had to wait until Gordon's wife arrived at the station to release him from his duty of looking after his two doting grandaughters. We made our way to the seclusion of the station office, whereupon after closing the door, Gordon let out a rasping fart. Once it had subsided he said, "That's what I think of the Fire Brigade." His fart had been accompanied by his legendary double 'V' sign salute, with both arms sweeping skywards from his sides.

Gordon once came on duty, a Sunday day shift, with a chunk of his nose missing. He was immediately pounced upon by ourselves, with demands as to how this had happened. Somewhat embarrassed by the taunting, a by now red-faced Gordon explained that as he was hurriedly backing his car out of his drive onto a quiet main road his progress was checked by the unexpected appearance of a motorist coming towards him.

Cursing under his breath at being held up and worried about a late arrival at the station he impatiently waited for the motorist to pass by so he could continue with his reversal. The errant driver slowed down giving no suggestion he was going to stop, turn left, or turn right.

A by now infuriated Gordon shouted to himself, "COME ON YOU STUPID F*!*!*G PRAT, GET A MOVE ON, I WANT TO GET TO WORK ON TIME." Sweeping his arm in a violent motion from left to right, in an effort to speed him up, one of his fingernails ripped into the bridge of his nose taking a piece out, which was followed by a flow of blood.

To add insult to injury, the other driver stopped close to Gordon's house and politely gestured to Gordon that he was letting him out. Gordon's hidden gesture was somewhat different. What the other driver must have thought when he saw Gordon's half-enraged, half-sneering face, with blood pouring from the cut on his nose, is unknown. Once again, Gordon's pride had been dented.

Gordon sadly retired a few years ago and the loss of him, with his marvellous sense of humour and infectious smile, was a great loss for everyone who had the privilege of knowing him. However, his name crops up many times within the pages of this book.

At one time Saturday and Sunday afternoons were classed as official stand-down periods, provided there was no essential station work and this was considered sacrosanct until a few years ago. Many of the lads used to utilise these free periods to service their cars. Most knew what they were up to, but others tinkered around and often ended up begging a lift or walking home as they had done more harm than good to their vehicles.

On of the funniest stories I ever heard was of a fireman who had purchased a three wheeled car, nicknamed a 'Plastic Pig', and obtained permission to take it over the station inspection pit. The only snag was he forgot it only had three wheels. When he drove it over the pit the front end went down and it swung to and fro like a child's toy.

An incident involving our hose trough was even funnier. The crew of the first line appliance had arrived back at the station for their dinner and as normal had parked the machine at the rear of the bays. Not long after they had disappeared for their lunch, the Deputy Chief Fire Officer and his entourage, who had been on a visit to the H.Q. block, were heard chatting together outside the mess prior to their departure.

The conversation continued for a few minutes and they were then escorted off the station by one of the locally based senior officers. They skirted the entire length of the rear of the appliance bays, got into their cars and drove off. The escorting officer then returned to his section of the station, once again skirting the bays and the station yard.

The wheel of fortune always revolves and every dog has its day at some time or another. Whilst the crews were having their dinner, one of the driving instructors had returned late, arriving immediately prior to the departure of the members of the hierarchy. He looked around the yard and a huge smile slowly spread over his face. Then, without uttering a word, he observed them driving away and noted the local officer walking back to his office.

To go back in time slightly, I was driving towards work on a morning shift when I noticed this same driving instructor, a Sub Officer, who, with his white Brigade cap looked more like a member of the ice-cream selling fraternity than a member of the Fire Service, some distance in front of me astride his tandem cycle. For no apparent reason he fell off it and instantly looked round to see if anyone within the near vicinity knew him. You can imagine his reaction when I pulled up and grinned at him.

He had been *reminded* of this incident many times and now at last he had a chance for revenge. Striding into the mess, with a grin from ear to ear, he said to all assembled, "Is it normal practice to park fire engines in the hose trough?" There was a stunned silence. Each individual's brain was working overtime in an effort to ascertain if they were personally involved in whatever had happened.

"Follow me," he announced, to all and sundry. The entire Watch followed him, crocodile fashion, into the station yard, and there it was for all to see — a fire engine in the trough. To make matters worse it had partially demolished a fence and a wall, with the rear of the appliance jammed on the latter.

The appliance was the Station Officer's vehicle and for he and his crew, especially the driver, it was a particularly embarrassing moment in time. Those not involved breathed a sigh of relief and turned on the unfortunate driver. Statements like, "What's the matter with you, haven't you the strength to put the handbrake on?" didn't help him one bit. It mattered not that a later investigation proved there was a fault in the handbrake system. Thereafter the driver was known as 'Handbrake Mick'. For the triumphant Sub Officer, the humiliation of falling off his tandem had been avenged and his honour restored.

Part of the Fire Service training code is that of observation. However, nobody at LITTLE SNOBSBURY had noticed the appliance slowly rolling from a standing start until it had gathered sufficient speed to crash into the wall, despite the fact that the H.Q. block overlooked the yard.

The real beauty of this story is the fact that none of the senior officers, including the Deputy Chief, had noticed the fire engine in the trough. So much for 'Observation'. I bet no-one in the 'Big House' in MAMMOTH COUNTY grilled *them* about this bizarre affair!!!

On the 'ground floor', however, it was a different story. The Divisional hierarchy were hastily summoned and a host of questions and accusations filled the stage. The Station Officer involved, my ex. 'Gaffer', Roger, had a fantastic habit, when being questioned, of saying, "Errmmm.... Errmmm..... Errmmm," before replying to an awkward question. It was his way of buying time in a tricky situation.

On being closely questioned by a senior officer as to what had happened, his eventual reply, after a row of "ERRMMM'S," was, "Well, it was over here and now it's over there," much to the fury of his tormentor. As was normal after such an incident a mountain of paperwork had to be filled in and wherever possible 'bollockings' were handed out, something the hierarchy were experts at.

Despite the efforts of the station personnel, the fire engine refused to budge and the Brigade 'Wrecker' was summoned to remove it. Once freed, it was dragged unceremoniously off to the Brigade Workshops.

The most vulnerable items on top of fire engines are the blue flashing lights. Many was the time I have seen them swept off appliances by overhanging branches of trees, much to the mirth of the members of the public who witnessed such happenings.

Because of the layout of Hydraulic Platforms, it is rare for the flashing lights to be damaged in similar circumstances, as they are, in part, protected by the booms. They are not, however, 'fireman-proof'. When housing these booms the lower boom has to be in line with special markers so that when housed it missed the blue lights etc.

These lights, however, were quite often broken during drills, usually when the station alarms went off, by a semi panic-stricken cage operator, who, in his haste to make the machine up, didn't bother to line the booms up in the correct manner. There would be a sickening crunch, bits of blue plastic would fly in all directions and the operator would look towards the heavens, asking the Good Lord why it had happened to him. More paper to fill in and another 'bollocking' on the horizon.

Other vulnerable items housed on the top of fire engines are the ladders. There were many instances of these falling off appliances, most caused by a fault of some kind, but others were caused by incompetence. It wasn't unknown for the all but defunct 50' Wheeled Escape ladders to break loose and run amok amongst crowded streets and at least one fire crew had the wonderful experience of watching their own 'Escape' overtaking them.

A crew from my Watch went on a fire call to a large building, where, in the adjoining private road there were a number of 'Sleeping Policemen' ramps, designed to slow traffic down. The driver tended to all but dismiss these hazards and drove over them at a speed far in excess of what he should have been doing. The crew heard a loud metallic crash and there was a set of buckled ladders lying in the road. "Sir, I wish to report . . . . ."

Another crew, again from my Watch, went to a fire in the country, along with a machine from another fire station. After dealing with the incident both appliances went their separate ways, with our lads returning the way they had come. Upon rounding a bend in the road, the O.I.C. 'Pierre Louise', at the time a Leading Fireman, turned to his crew and laughed, "Ha, Ha, the crew from the other station have lost their 30'

ladder. It's lying in the road."

All of his crew were reduced to tears until one of the members realised the other fire engine had arrived and departed on a different route. Laughter was replaced by dismay·when they inspected the rear of their appliance. Sure enough it was their ladder. What a way to score an 'own goal'. Another, "Sir, I wish to report . . . . ." upon their return to the station.

Two of the most bizarre accidents involved two firemen who all but killed themselves by challenging and losing out, by head-butting over-hanging beams within the station at LITTLE SNOBSBURY.

In the first incident a number of men were playing snooker when the 'bells' went down. The snooker room was on the first floor, but it was on a slightly higher trajectory than its counterpart, the adjacent recreation room, the two being connected by a small flight of stairs. One fireman, 'Buzz', a Londoner, was so keen to get to his appliance that instead of simply running down the interlinking stairway he literally took off from the top step. His head came into contact with the RSJ and he fell to the ground in a crumpled heap, being attended to by the firemen who were left on the station, another fireman taking his place on the machine. The next time I saw him he was lying in bed with a massive criss-cross plaster on his head.

The second chap, by coincidence, was also a Londoner (they must have had a head for these things) an ex. Guardsman. He was fooling around in the mess, dancing on a table-top, much to the annoyance of 'Pierre', who was attempting to eat his fish and chips. 'The Guardsman' did one jump too high and smacked his head on a main beam.

All but unconscious, he fell down, planting his backside into the plate of fish and chips. He then partially recovered and crawled on his hands and knees on the table, whereupon he then held his head with both hands, moaning and groaning. Whilst he was performing 'Pierre' was totally unmoved by his colleague's predicament. He calmly proceeded to pick off the chips which had stuck to 'The Guardsman's' trousers and continued eating them.

The most common type of accident in and around fire stations was the breaking of windows and the local glass merchant in LITTLE SNOBSBURY must have made a fortune over the years. Until the station was rebuilt, and the old television room done away with, the little window in the passage leading to this room must have held the record for being broken over and over again.

As soon as we were given stand-down in the early evening, unless we were going to play volleyball, most of us would run up the stairs in an effort to win the race to reach the most comfortable seats in the television room. As a consequence of a dozen or so 'Macho' firemen trying to rush through a door space designed to take only one person at a time, there were many instances, in this crush of humanity, when someone's elbow went through this little window.

Windows were broken in all sorts of ways. By ladders etc., during drills, footballs, cricket balls, firemen accidentally putting their fists and elbows through them, equipment disappearing through the glass (e.g. the compressed air cylinder already mentioned) and people losing their tempers. The end result of a heavily slammed door from someone in the latter category often resulted in a pane of glass dropping out of a door or window.

One 'Macho' fireman called 'Nestor', a tough lad of Welsh/Ukranian descent, tried physically to halt the downward movement of one of the electrically operated up and over doors in the appliance bay. It was only when half a dozen large panes of glass shattered he ceased his actions, all of which he vehemently denied when questioned about the incident.

The most unusual method of breaking a window was at another station I was based at, in MAMMOTH COUNTY. Whilst preparing for an important social function the doors of the appliance bays were covered with salvage sheets, from the inside, partly to stop members of the public staring in at us whilst we were enjoying ourselves. 'Dave Rainbow' decided to use a heavy stapling gun to secure parts of the salvage sheet to the engine house doors. In this he was quite successful until he tried to staple the sheet to a section of glass. I need comment no further!!!

The final story in this chapter concerns one of my former 'masters', a Divisional Officer who took great pleasure in visiting stations out of the blue and administering 'bollockings' in all directions, should anything be out of order. At one station he paid a visit to, the Watch members had been playing volleyball prior to his arrival.

At the time, the hierarchy of MAMMOTH COUNTY were paranoid about accidents involving vehicles reversing without the assistance of a guide at the rear of the Fire Service machine or van and if anyone was seen by a senior officer not employing such a guide he was in for the high jump. To be fair to the hierarchy I have seen fire engines back into all kinds of objects. I have also seen two appliances, back to back, with their 45' ladders entangled, their respective crews engaged in fearsome arguments about whom was to blame.

To return to the visiting D.O., part of his job was to lecture the men on the hazards associated with reversing without assistance. It had even reached a point where the Brigade had issued a video, explaining in clear, concise terms as to the perfect method of guiding somebody backwards, using various hand signals that even the smallest child could understand.

Upon leaving the station after delivering his lecture he leapt into his smart car and promptly reversed (un-supervised, tut-tut) at such a speed so as to bend one of the steel volleyball poles almost in half when he collided with it. One can only hope a 'well-wisher' sent him the 'training video' as a present!!!

Amusing Operational Incidents

One of the first major fires I attended, at LITTLE SNOBSBURY, involved a monastery, where the roof of the church was on fire. It was a three skinned roof and an extremely difficult job to tackle, as the inner skin held the seat of the fire. Despite tremendous efforts by the firemen involved the entire roof was gutted and much damage was caused by burning timbers crashing down into the main body of the church.

There was great confusion, due to the large volumes of smoke billowing out of the roof, with much of the building smoke-logged. Once the initial chaos was sorted out and some semblance of organisation came into being the situation calmed down.

As the flames gradually subsided, the jet I was in charge of, inside the church, was knocked off, and I was ordered to take the branch outside. Once the flow of water ceased I disconnected the branch, tucked it under my left arm and ran towards an exit in an adjacent ante-room.

This ante-room had a number of monks within its walls, who were collecting valuable items to take to a place of safety, such as paintings and candle-holders. As I ran into the room and neared the exit I saw a fireman running towards me with a branch under his arm. I shouted. "IT'S OK MATE, WE DON'T NEED ANOTHER BRANCH, I'M TAKING THIS ONE....." Before I could finish I came to a dead halt. I had come to a standstill before a massive wall-to-wall mirror. (I didn't know monks were into that sort of thing!!!)

You can imagine the look of surprise on my face as I stood there, with both hands on the mirror, looking myself straight in the eyes. As I backed slowly away I suddenly became aware that each monk had ceased working and they were all staring at me. The strange thing was that none of them smiled let alone laughed at my predicament. Each had a curiously puzzled look, as if they felt sorry for me. 'Poor lad, if that's what life in the Fire Service does for you then we shall stay as monks'. I half-smiled at them and backed out of the room. Once clear I beat a hasty retreat.

Similar experiences were related to me from time to time, but nothing on the grandiose scale of what I had done. They were usually in smoke-logged bathrooms, bedrooms, kitchens, and living rooms, anywhere where there was a mirror of some kind, where B.A. wearers would be spotted by colleagues, communicating with themselves, all of which they would deny later.

Although the roof was destroyed and much of the inside was beyond repair, most of the confession boxes were still intact. At opportune moments, with no senior officers or monks in sight, some firemen took advantage of the situation by sitting in the boxes in pairs, one acting as the 'priest', and the other confessing his latest wine, women and song sins. Perhaps the 'Lord on High' also has a sense of humour, for none were struck by lightning.

Not too many months before I left MAMMOTH COUNTY we had a night 'shout' to a 'Lorry on fire, carrying nitro-glycerine'. On the way to the incident, one conjured up visions from the film 'Wages of Fear' where a number of sweating drivers drove lorry loads of the stuff over a rough mountain road in South America, with at least one of the vehicles being blown up, along with the driver.

The lorry had been reported near to a notorious public toilet next to a busy dual carriageway. By stating 'notorious', it was a known fact that it was used as a 'meeting place' for two or more males, if you get the drift. It has since been demolished, so presumably these 'characters' now have to 'skip the light fantastic' through the daisies and 'pansies' in the adjacent fields.

Four or so appliances had been despatched by Fire Control and upon arrival at the site of the incident there was no sign of any fire whatsoever. All machines were assembled together by the duty officer, near to a large traffic island, the junction of four main roads.

All O.I.C.'s were mustered by the A.D.O. including myself, and after a conflab I set off, on foot, with a couple of colleagues to the lay-by outside the toilets. Utilising our torches we inspected all of the parked lorries, with their blacked out cabs and snoring drivers, but there were no visible signs that any of these vehicles had been involved in any kind of fire.

Finally, I approached the only private car in the lay-by and tapped on the window. The occupant, a man, cautiously lowered the window. I asked him if he had seen anything on fire. "No mate, I've seen nothing.

I'm broken down, waiting for the A.A." I thought to myself, 'How convenient — a likely story'. To confirm my suspicions, when the police arrived at the scene, the 'broken down' car suddenly burst into life and disappeared over the horizon.

Despite the call being an obvious hoax and a good one at that (someone must have had a good imagination) the A.D.O. decided to explore all avenues and all machines were despatched down different roads to investigate further, but nothing was found and the 'Stop' message was relayed to Fire Control.

Another night call summoned us to a house fire within one of the new estates in the former Borough of LITTLE SNOBSBURY. In charge of the first line fire engine was a Sub Officer, a duplicate of Eli Wallach, the notorious 'Baddy' in such films as 'The Magnificent Seven' and 'The Good, The Bad and The Ugly'. I was in charge of the Pump.

'Eli's' fire engine wouldn't start, so I was despatched ahead of him. Unfortunately for us the route card was in the hands of the stranded Sub-O. For those not in the know a route card describes the shortest way to any given road on the 'patch'. These had been compiled by firemen and in the main were extremely accurate. One faulty card I came across, read, 'Left out of the station, first right, first right again, another first right, followed by a final first right.' If followed to the letter you would end up back at the fire station. Brilliant!!!

There were four of us in the crew. With one driving and two putting their B.A. sets on this only left myself to locate the address on the map. Being a relatively new road it was not in the A-Z. All I had to work from was a home-made map, with minute writing listing the roads in this estate, with arrows pointing here, there and everywhere. Bad enough to study in daylight and all but impossible in the dark when being shaken around at 50 mph, with only a torch as an aid.

As we neared our destination we heard the Sub-O book mobile and I cursed my luck that it was I who was struggling to find the right road and not 'Eli'. We reached the maze of roads and in a fifty-to-one chance we came to the right road, a cul-de-sac, at the first attempt.

When we arrived a neighbour greeted us and informed me that there had been a terrible row earlier in the evening between the estranged husband and the occupier, his wife, but she wasn't sure if there was anyone in the house.

Upon initial inspection there appeared to be a fire in every room, including the garage. The two B.A. wearers took a hose-reel each and made a forcible entry into the house. With the driver engaged in pumping duties, I set off to find a hydrant, locating one some distance away. (Later I discovered we were parked over one!!!)

When 'Eli' arrived I informed him of the situation and that my crew, apart from being engaged in firefighting, were also looking for casualties, including the possible suicide of the estranged husband, as it was becoming increasingly obvious it was an arson job.

His reply was, "F*!*!*G HELL." More personnel were sent into the house with sets on, but despite intensive searching, no-one was found. The individual fires, in excess of a dozen, were extinguished, but there was extensive heat damage and the rooms were still intensely hot.

The living room had been badly affected and upon closer examination we noticed that someone, presumably the estranged husband, had gone berserk with a sledge-hammer or similar device, as there were large dents in items like the dining room table and piano etc.

By now we had been joined by a Superintendent from the police, the most senior officer at the incident. (Our duty officer, for reasons best known to himself, didn't attend the incident for hours, despite a number of requests from 'Eli'.) As he was discussing events with 'Eli' and myself in the still steaming hot-house of the living room, the telephone, which had all but melted, rang.

An astonished silence prevailed for a few seconds, then 'Buggy', one of the firemen, gingerly picked it up and said, "Hello." A voice on the other end of the line, a woman, hesitantly enquired, "Who are you?" 'Buggy' replied, "I'm from the Fire Service." She then screamed, "MY GOD, HE'S GONE AND DONE IT," and promptly slammed the receiver down.

This information was passed on to us by a trying-hard-not-to-laugh 'Buggy'. The Superintendent, apart from commenting, "Stupid cow. Fancy putting the phone down," suggested that under the circumstances we searched each room again, to make absolutely certain there were no bodies.

We went from room to room, scanning each one carefully with our torches. Whilst entering one of the smaller bedrooms, we stopped in our tracks, there was an arm sticking out from beneath the bed. There was a shocked silence, until it was discovered that the 'body' was nothing more than a tailor's dummy. The remainder of the house was thoroughly searched, but no-one was found.

Some time later it was ascertained that the lady of the house and her children had fled to a friend or relatives home, after the upset of the argument. Once they had departed, the estranged husband had telephoned his sister, making the threat that he was going to burn his wife's home down, a threat she hadn't considered important enough to inform the police about. It was she who had rung whilst we were there.

The following day the errant husband gave himself up to the police and he was charged with arson. The most stupid part of this incident, was, that despite lighting individual fires in each room, with the intention of destroying the house, he had shut all of the doors, the end result being that the fires were, for the most part, starved of oxygen, thus preventing his ambitions being fulfilled.

On the subject of arson, another such incident within MAMMOTH COUNTY involved an Irishman who lived in a high-rise flat. In an effort, presumably to claim insurance money, he piled all of his furniture into the centre of a room and poured paraffin over it. So far, so good. That was until he set fire to it. As the flames leapt to the ceiling he realised

his means of escape was on the other side of the room and he had to be 'rescued' by firemen, being subsequently arrested by the police. A case of 'Out of the fire and into the Frying Pan', a reverse of the norm.

Moving away from arson and on to the subject of amusing operational incidents concerning the running out of hose, there were countless incidents of blokes falling through stairs and into holes whilst running out the same. One fireman fell into a water-filled inspection pit at a job in a bus depot, much to the amusement of his colleagues.

The 'ideal' timing between a pump operator and the person running out a length of hose is for the water to reach the branch operator seconds after the branch has been inserted. This rarely happened on operational duty, only on drills. On one occasion I witnessed the opposite.

The fireman concerned, 'Pierre', was half-way through running a hose-line out at a rubbish fire, when he noticed the water hurtling towards him. The faster he tried to unfurl the remaining hose the slower he appeared to go. Instead of throwing the hose to the ground he grimly tried to carry on with his task. The remaining folded hose came under pressure from the increasing volume of water which was trying to force its way into the hose and it wrapped itself round his arms like a hungry python.

The luckless 'Pierre' had no way of reducing the pressure and he started to go purple, a combination of blood and water pressure, as his temper and body began to rise. Once the pump operator's attention was brought to 'Pierre's' predicament, he released the pressure and the 'rogue' hose was chucked to the ground and kicked in revenge by 'Pierre'.

We turned out to a timber fire at a local warehouse of a well known firm, a 'Co-operative' type of premise. In the days of LITTLE SNOBSBURY there were many such places which had their own Fire Service, either in a full or part-time capacity. Just as we arrived one of the local 'firemen' was running a length of hose out from an internal hydrant. When he reached the flames he shouted to his colleague at the hydrant to turn the water on.

The water rushed down the hose-line, but when it reached the branch it was no more than a dribble. This hose must have been last used after the Luftwaffe had paid a visit, for the water poured out of hundreds of little holes along its entire length, soaking everyone and everything, except where it was supposed to.

Finally, with relation to hose stories, our mutual 'accident prone' firefighter, the 'Savage' Sub-O, was collecting a length after it had been used on a railway enbankment fire. Instead of rolling it up he flaked it over his shoulder. Sometime during the course of this operation he smelt an obnoxious odour — the one we all dread — that of dog muck. Thinking he had trodden in something he inspected his boots, but they were clean. He continued flaking the hose until he realised the muck was on the underside of it, much of which had been transferred to the shoulder and back of his fire tunic. 'It's a dog's life' for some firemen!!!

On the subject of dogs there are a number of stories relating to these creatures under other chapter headings, with the exception of the following:-

We were called to a 'shout' at a local scrapyard in MAMMOTH COUNTY, where entry was gained through the metal gates, common to such premises, by cutting the lock off with bolt croppers. At first there was no obvious sign of the 'standard deterrent', a guard dog or dogs. The incident was only a minor one, but before we reached it two alsations appeared from the other end of the yard.

As is the want of many owners of 'scrapyard canines', they were half-starved, scruffy and apparently ferocious. Barking like mad they headed towards us. We immediately about turned and fled for the gates as fast as our firebooted legs could take us. (It's amazing how you can become an unofficial world sprint record holder, even in fireboots, when you are being pursued by an angry alsation or dobermann.)

Upon reaching safety, the gates were closed and the two 'Baskerville' beasts threw themselves against them. Just as the O.I.C. was considering whether or not to employ high pressure water jets against them the owner arrived.

The O.I.C. told the owner, "We are not going in to deal with the fire unless the alsations are tied up." The owner more or less stated that we were cowards, by saying, "Fancy being frightened by a couple of harmless dogs, they couldn't possibly hurt you, as they have no teeth." When we shone our torches at them, as they sat there panting, all we could see were toothless gums. We felt a right bunch of prats.

During the summer of 1976, which was very hot and dry, we were constantly attending grass and woodland fires, day and night. One incident found us fighting a grass fire near to a railway line and a scrapyard. One appliance, with a Sub-O in charge, was positioned at one side of the fire, having gained access via the railway station. I had been ordered to take the Pump to the other side of the fire, which meant us going into the scrapyard.

As there was no direct route to the yard from where we had first arrived, we had to negotiate several roads before arriving at the main entrance. As we drove in we were almost immediately confronted by a massive alsation. At first we thought it was loose until someone noticed that it was chained, loosely, to a lengthy pipe inserted in the ground, which ran for about two thirds of the scrapyard. Driving past it, our machine was positioned by the fire, out of the dog's reach.

During the course of our firefighting, the alsation leapt up and down, barking constantly at the end of its tether at the limit of the pipe nearest to us. Before we were able to quell the flames our appliance conked out and we had to radio for assistance. As luck would have it the other crew had finished with their end of things and were despatched to assist us.

When they arrived, instead of driving up to us, all of the crew, with the exception of the driver, decided to go on a walk-about. As they strolled casually up the yard the alsation noticed them and took off like a rocket. The other crew didn't realise it had a limited run and in their panic all of them tried to board the fire engine (which was still out of reach of the dog) through the same door, resulting in a number of bruises to all concerned. They felt right idiots when they saw the alsation come to an abrupt halt, some yards away. Another classic case of 'It's a Dog's Life'.

'Pierre' was at home one day with his wife and mother-in-law, who was visiting them, complete with her 'Harry Growler' pet, in the shape of a Jack Russell terrier. A fellow fireman from LITTLE SNOBSBURY, known as 'Omo' or 'White Strength', because of his constant pale features, decided to pay 'Pierre' a visit at the same time.

'White Strength' was seated on the living room sofa, with his legs crossed, chattering away to 'Pierre', his wife, and mother-in-law, with the Jack Russell some distance away. Without realising it, 'White Strength' was rocking the one leg, to and fro. 'Pierre' noticed that the dog had gone to the alert position and was dribbling, but said nothing to warn 'White Strength'.

Eventually the dog could take no more and launched itself at 'White Strength's' waving leg, sinking its fangs into his foot. His immediate and natural reaction was to kick the dog. He booted it across the room and after a couple of yelps it retreated to another part of the house.

After 'White Strength' had departed, 'Pierre's' mother-in-law said to him, "Don't let that nasty man inside the house again, kicking the poor dog like that."

Whilst still harking on the subject of animals, we turn to the flying variety. We were turned out to a gas explosion at a high-rise flat in MAMMOTH COUNTY. Upon arrival, there was no fire, but all of the windows had been shattered and the metal frames were hanging out in all directions.

Inside the kitchen was the occupant, a badly shaken man, awaiting transportation to hospital for a check-up. We discovered from him, that for some unknown reason the pilot light on his cooker had gone out, and during the course of the night gas fumes had built up. Upon getting out of bed he had gone into the kitchen and decided to light a cigarette. Bearing in mind that we all should know what gas smells like, he either had no sense of smell or was totally daft.

He lit up his fag and the next thing he knew a huge fireball exploded. Fortunately for him it instantly blew all the windows out and was gone in seconds. The only injury he suffered was the loss of his eyebrows and his hair had melted in the fierce heat. The most humorous part of this incident was his pet canary, which despite losing its feathers, was still jumping around in its cage, chirping away merrily.

Another amusing operational incident involved a former LITTLE SNOBSBURY fireman, an Irish chap, who later in time achieved fame by appearing in the local 'rag' after being head-butted by an irate motorist at a fire in the country, for which the motorist was subsequently found guilty in court and fined.

Our 'Head-Butted' friend attended a fire involving a car in an integral household garage. If the car cannot be easily removed, this type of fire can be awkward in a confined space. Quite often the flames are driven forward by the water from hose-reels or jets.

'H.B.' decided to get into the car and release the handbrake. Somehow he caught his foot under the clutch and within seconds he was all but overcome by smoke and had to be rescued by his comrades. He was propped up against a wall and one of the firemen ran to the nearest appliance, returning with an oxygen cylinder. Instead of stopping to think and turning the valve on slowly, in his haste to assist, he turned it fully on.

'H.B.' was on his way to recovery when the blast of oxygen whipped his head backwards, smacking it into a wall, putting him back in the same boat. Fortunately, most firemen are hardy customers and he soon recovered from both experiences.

Firemen, generally speaking, are not racist, with the odd exceptions here and there, who, for the most part, keep their thoughts to themselves, in the public eye at least.

Two tales were related to me from 'Dave Rainbow', who had been in the 'Big City Brigade', prior to the take-over. The 'racist' involved, was, at the time, a Leading Fireman. He was the human double, in looks, of 'Animal', from the 'Muppet Show'. The nickname of 'Animal' also suited him for he was constantly picking his nose and in the dormitory he used to wipe his 'gilberts' on the wall next to his bed.

When a car is involved in a fire or a road traffic accident, it is normal practice to disconnect the battery leads, if possible. The first 'racial' incident involving 'Animal', found he and his crew in a situation where they were about to remove the leads, when, after noticing the occupants were of West Indian origin, he ordered his men in a loud voice, "CUT THE BATTERY LEADS."

The owner of the car, a rather large chap, strode up to 'Animal' and said, "I don't want you to cut my battery leads." The instantaneous reply was, "F*!K OFF — CARRY ON LADS." The West Indian then said, "If you cut the leads, I will have to punch you on the nose." 'Animal' hesitated, took a look at the size of his adversary, and responded by saying, "*Disconnect* the battery leads."

The second occurrence involved a group of Asians gathered round a car which had been involved in a traffic accident. 'Animal' told them to clear off, in no uncertain terms, to which they refused. Using his authority, he said, "If you don't clear off, I'll call the police and have you removed." The spokesman for the group said to 'Animal', "If we let go of the car it will crush the person underneath." "DON'T LET GO," was 'Animal's' instant response. 'Afro/Asians' 2 — 'Animal' 0.

A particularly funny story was related to us around the bar one night by a Divisional Officer, 'Smoking Joe'. At the time of the incident he was an operational firefighter and was helping to deal with a fire in a 'Brothel', in an infamous 'Red Light' district.

Whilst searching a heavily smoke-logged 'bedroom', he put his hand into something 'he couldn't describe', moving away from it to continue his search. After the house had been thoroughly searched, the fire put out, and the rooms vented, he returned, out of curiosity, to find out what it was he had put his hand in. He found it alright — it was a bucket containing used condoms!!!

Normal Breathing Apparatus procedure stated that you were not allowed to enter smoke-logged premises alone. Also, a control board had to be set up, manned at all times, and your own personal tally had to be handed in to the control board operator. This procedure was drummed into each and every fireman.

One of the first incidents, at LITTLE SNOBSBURY, in which I had the opportunity to wear a set, involved a fire in the living room of a house. Two of us were ordered by Sub-O 'Squirrel' to don our face-masks and enter the building. He refused, in his panic, to set up a board, merely snatching our tallies and ordering us to get to work.

The mains electrical current had been isolated by a thoughtful occupant, or so we had been assured, and we made our way into the smoke-filled room. Instead of leaving us to fulfil the simple task of quelling the small fire with a hose-reel, Sub-O 'Squirrel' and the duty Station Officer, who had just arrived, decided to crawl in after us.

I glanced round upon hearing them and was aghast to see that neither had sets on and our personal tallies were clipped on 'Squirrel's' fire tunic. So much for B.A. procedure! If, in the unlikely event of the house blowing up around us, it was a possibility that no-one would know for some little time who was in the building.

As the smoke began to clear there was a tremendous scream, making me almost jump out of my skin. The first thought that flashed through my mind was, 'Oh God, the power hasn't been turned off after all and someone's touched a bare live wire'. I whipped round to see where the scream was coming from, fully expecting to see 'Squirrel's' or the S.O.'s eyes being lit up, as 240 volts surged through one of them.

It wasn't any electrical current that was making 'Squirrel' scream, it was the Station Officer. As the smoke had thinned he had stood up and was standing on one of 'Squirrel's' hands. What a fiasco!!!

Next to LITTLE SNOBSBURY Fire Station there used to be a small railway marshalling yard. After closure it lay empty and derelict for many years until a massive office block was built on the site, belonging to another MAMMOTH state enterprise, this time the car industry.

It was in use for a few years, then, like the railway yard before, it too demised. It lay empty until more recent times, since when it has been half-knocked down, and is now in the process of being rebuilt (at the time of writing) into an even fancier dwelling, no doubt owned by yet another MAMMOTH conglomerate, like the 'BIG BALL, BETTER BALL, BALL BEARING COMPANY'. What a waste of ratepayers money in the first place.

During the time it lay empty the fire alarm used to be triggered off now and again, usually by 'gremlins'. Both fire engines would turn out, but once it was established that there was no obvious sign of fire, the crew of the Pump would be left behind to await the arrival of the key-holder.

We were in such a position, one early Spring morning, awaiting the key-holder, when a police 'Panda' arrived. The sole occupant, a very attractive W.P.C., came across to join us. Without making it too obvious, I thought to myself, 'I wouldn't mind giving you one, just the tonic at this early hour'. Fate was soon to intervene, in my favour.

Due to the close proximity of the fire station, coupled with the fact that all of the calls we had been to at this premise, had been false alarms, I hadn't bothered to don my fire kit. All I was wearing, on the top half of my body, was a thin pullover and although it was a nice morning, it was not exactly over-warm. I shivered involuntarily and the W.P.C. commented, "It's alright for you, I've been out in the cold for most of the night. All you have had to do is leap out of bed and jump into the nearest warm thing."

At that, we all looked at her and smirked. We didn't say a word. Realising what she had said, she went bright red and muttered, "Well.... Um.... Um.... Err.... Um.... Err." etc., and tried to change the subject. What a coup.

Switching to one of the colder seasons, the Winter, the Pump, with 'Pierre' in charge, responded to a secondary call way out in the sticks in the early hours after a heavy fall of snow. When they were almost at their destination they took a wrong turning and ended up in a narrow little lane. After they had travelled some distance they were confronted by an immense snowdrift.

'Pierre' was unaware that they were in the wrong road, but instead of using his brains and trying to find another route, he ordered the driver, Gordon, to charge the drift. "You must be joking," Gordon replied. "Do as you are told," ordered 'Pierre'. "It's your funeral," Gordon muttered. He then reversed a number of yards and accelerated forwards.

The machine ploughed into the drift, but instead of breaking through, as 'Pierre' had intended, they became marooned, with some of the snowdrift as high as the cab windows. The appliance wouldn't budge in any direction and to make matters worse the radio aerial had snapped off, making it impossible to contact Fire Control to inform them of their predicament.

It was 3 o'clock on a moonlit icy morning and all of the members of the crew clamboured on to the top of the fire engine. Gazing round the bleak, snow covered, lunar type landscape, they observed an isolated farmhouse. Colin, 'The Gambler', was sent on foot, like Captain Oates, out into the wilderness to summon assistance.

Meanwhile, back at the ranch, when Fire Control were unable to contact the 'missing' crew, a couple of machines were further despatched, one to the incident and the other to search for 'Pierre' and his men. Whilst 'The Gambler' was doing his 'Captain Oates' act, Gordon and his remaining colleagues were having the time of their lives, taking the 'Mickey' out of the luckless 'Pierre' for having got them into this ridiculous situation.

By now, the searching appliance had arrived in the near vicinity and the 'trapped' crew observed it traversing adjacent roads in the distance, its blue light flashing round and round, in a vain attempt to locate them. It was not until 'The Gambler' raised a far from happy farmer out of his warm bed and relayed a telephone message through to Fire Control that they were 'rescued'.

Not all members of the public are grateful for the attentions of the Fire Service, even in an emergency. One women held the police and firemen at bay for quite some time by shouting abuse and hurling slates at them from the roof of her terraced house. Another woman, not over enthralled by the presence of the police, as well as firemen, when her house caught fire, really got stuck into the coppers. "WHY DON'T YOU F*!K OFF," she shouted at them. Station Officer 'Red-Cheeks' intervened and tried to calm her down. All he received for his pains was, "AND YOU CAN F*!K OFF AS WELL."

One dark evening, we were turned out in the Pump to a house fire on the borders of our 'patch' and that of another station in a different Division. In the days of LITTLE SNOBSBURY and the adjacent 'Big City Brigade' this particular road was divided between the two Local Authorities.

On the one side of the road were the 'Council House Peasants' and on the other were the good citizens of LITTLE SNOBSBURY, in their larger, privately owned dwellings. Fire does not discriminate between the two, but some firemen do, especially one particular Station Officer, 'Alf', renowned for dropping clangers, who once commented on the way to a job, "Take it easy driver, it's only a council house."

To return to the story at hand, both appliances involved arrived at the scene of the fire (the council house side) virtually at the same time. B.A. wearers with high pressure hose-reels were sent in to douse the flames. It was immediately ascertained from a neighbour that no-one was inside the house, the first priority of any fireman.

The mother and daughter had been taken out by her two sons to a house further up the road, as they were suffering from the effects of smoke inhalation. I was despatched to locate their whereabouts and had the presence of mind to take an oxygen resuscitation set with me. Upon finding the two females, who were half-choking to death, oxygen was administered to calm them down prior to the arrival of an ambulance.

After they had gone to hospital I returned to the scene of the fire. It was now out, but an upstairs room had been gutted. I was helping to make the gear up, when the 'man of the house', a little Scotsman, rolled up on foot from the local 'boozer', quite the worse for wear through drink.

He was so feared by his family (his two grown-up sons had moved away from home due to his violence) that no-one had gone to the pub to inform 'Daddy' of the fire. Only the sons had been contacted. So when he arrived home he was totally unaware of the fire until he saw us. Although he was only about 5' tall, he appeared to put the fear of God into the police, as the constables present at the scene took one look at him, made for their 'Panda' and drove off.

Any normal, loving parent and husband would have immediately been concerned as to the safety of his family. Not this bright 'Herbert' though, he was something else. He marched, or rather staggered towards us and said, "What are you f*!*!*g bastards doing in my house?" in a slurred Scots dialect.

Despite our efforts to explain what had happened and to calm him down, he became more aggressive, insulting and obscene towards us. Eventually he was persuaded to look at the damaged upstairs room. Upon seeing the extent of the damage he almost exploded with rage, as if it was our fault the fire had happened. Restrained by his sons, he launched into a lengthy verbal tirade against us.

Not once did he ask about the whereabouts or condition of his wife and daughter. Our 'Gaffer' had reached the point where he was going to knock him out with his torch, when the sons persuaded us to leave. I for one, was extremely grateful to go, and we left under a barrage of, "F*!K OFF'S", which gradually diminished as we disappeared into the distance. He certainly brought new meaning to the excellent Cliff Richard song, 'Daddy's Home'.

On the subject of uncaring people, I went to a first floor flat on fire, in MAMMOTH COUNTY. When we got there it was a real corker. Flames and smoke were pouring out of the windows and curling up to the next flat above. We managed to save the upper flat, but the other one was all but destroyed by the fire.

The fire had accidentally been caused by a teenage girl who resided at the flat with her boyfriend. Sometime during the proceedings he arrived at high speed on his motor cycle, having been informed about the fire whilst at work. Without bothering to stop completely, he leapt off his still moving machine, which crashed to the pavement with its engine still running.

He ran past his girlfriend, who was sobbing uncontrollably, and entered the burnt out flat. He muttered and swore out loud and like our Scotsman in the previous story he too never asked once about his girlfriend's well being. You cannot please all of the people all of the time, as the saying goes!!!

Benevolent Home

Due to my young daughter having a succession of various operations, my family and I qualified, through the generosity of the Fire Service Benevolent Fund, for a series of annual breaks at the Fund's Home in Devon.

It is a fabulous site, with a large number of superb bungalows for families and facilities within a rambling house for single persons and married couples with no children. The house and estate once belonged to the owner of a well known cigarette manufacturer. Although he didn't mind flogging his lethal wares to the population at large, he himself didn't smoke and all the workers on the estate were banned from smoking — rather hypocritical to say the least. To add to the general irony, the outside swimming pool was built in the shape of a coffin!!!

The first year we went there, there were no bar facilities and as a consequence we didn't really get to know the manager and his wife socially, apart from the odd meeting in one of the local pubs in the nearby village, not dissimilar in name to 'Chigley'. The following year saw the opening of a bar within the house making social evenings far more pleasant for all concerned. Firemen of all ranks, from all over Britain, visited the Home for a multitude of reasons, injury, family illness, folk recovering from operations or through the death of a loved one.

Although we were all equal — 'no rank on holiday' — it soon became obvious that the senior officers, for the most part, kept themselves to themselves, keeping away from the 'lower ranks', thereby retaining the 'Them and Us' criteria. Many of their wives would remain aloof and only mix with their own kind.

In the bungalows it was entirely self catering, whilst in the house meals were available via the dining room. It was hard to understand why, when at a Benevolent Home, how some people behaved. There were instances of officers' wives complaining about the most trivial of things and expecting the staff to wait on them hand and foot, with vociferous complaints about being placed in a room without the most perfect view.

One could understand if the people involved were paying a fortune for the holiday, instead of it being free, complete with travelling expenses. They seemed to forget that most of the staff worked on a part-time basis and would try and treat them as servants. We all like to look smart in a dining room, but the way some of them dressed you would think that they were going to the Lord Lieutenant's Ball of the Year.

From the second year onwards we came to know the manager, Clive and his wife Heather extremely well and became firm friends. Clive, the image of Lionel Blair, was a character and a half. He was an ex. Red-Coat from a well known holiday combine and an unrepentant practical joker, always ready to exploit a situation. A rugged, hard working, hard

playing, live-for-today, die-tomorrow type of person.

In total contrast, Heather was tall and slim and looked every inch an ex. 'St. Trinians Old Gell'. At times she adopted a haughty and 'La-De-Da' approach, without realising she was doing so. An extremely pleasant and polite lady, but naive and gullible, a real sucker for set-up situations, as will be described later.

They had two pet dogs, a placid golden retriever called 'Cassy' and a vicious, especially if provoked, Jack Russell terrier, which went by the name of 'Sandy', who never thought twice about nipping you whenever an opportune moment arrived. Heather, in her 'Haughty' moments, used to call them 'Sarndy' and 'Carssy'.

For a period of time, Clive was pestered by a persistent door to door salesman, who wouldn't take no for an answer. On one of his 'visits', his last, Clive saw his opportunity and whilst the salesman was at the front door he engineered a method of placing the Jack Russell into the salesman's car without being seen.

Backtracking, he made his way to the front door and confronted the salesman. "Look mate, I've already told you many times that I'm not interested in buying anything from you, now clear off," he drawled in his native Berkshire/adopted Devonian accent. The salesman tried to protest, but to no avail, the heavy wooden door being slammed in his face. Clive then nipped to an upstairs room to observe the next act.

The disconsolate salesman returned to his car. As he was about to open the door he was confronted by 'Sandy', growling in a more than menacing manner, revealing two rows of razor sharp teeth, the canine equivalent of a 'Wolverine'. The harder he tried to shoo 'Sandy' out of the partially open window the worse the dog became, fixing him with

39

the kind of mad stare that only a dog such as this can do, prior to launching an all-out attack.

He beat a path back to the house and pounded on the door — for over twenty minutes. Clive eventually answered the frantic knocking, opening the door and saying "What's the matter mate? I thought I told you to clear off half an hour ago." The once smartly turned out, but by now, totally frustrated, panicky salesman, covered in sweat, blustered out his tale of woe to Clive, who replied, "I can't understand how the dog got into your car in the first place. If I was you I should ensure that your car windows are shut when on private property in future." The angry terrier was retrieved and the salesman, possibly by now a completely broken man, was never seen again.

Other members of the staff, consisted of a gardener, Steve, and his wife, Teresa. They both helped out in the bar from time to time and Teresa also helped with the cleaning of the bungalows, the house and worked in the office. There was also a chef, a massive bloke who could have competed quite favourably with a Japanese Wrestler. Although he generally answered to the name of 'Bruno', one of his Christian names was 'Milford', the type of name normally associated with a 'Woofter', which was probably why he preferred to be called 'Bruno'.

For a period of time 'Bruno' used to have a regular visitor, a semi-tame bird in the shape of a chaffinch. It used to hop in and out of the kitchen and he fed it so many scraps it must have become twice its normal size and when it was hopping round its legs all but disappeared. He nicknamed it 'Orville'. "Come here 'Orv', come and see your Uncle Bruno." It became so overweight it required its own runway to take off, like a heavily laden bomber — poor thing.

Most of the heavy maintenance on the estate was carried out by Clive, assisted by teams of volunteer firemen on working parties from all over the country, on their days off. Some of these latter characters would 'play' first and think about work afterwards, but once caught by Clive they would end up with the worst of all possible tasks, digging latrines in the fields, soon learning the errors of their ways after being at the top end of the scale of, "We are all in the shit lad, it depends on the depth."

Sharon, one of the part-time workers, who helped to serve meals etc., had known Clive and Heather from their days of living and working in Berkshire. She had followed them to 'Chigley' and was described by Clive as a 'man hunter', stating that she had arrived there with a mattress strapped to her back and only wore a bra for appearances sake and not for practical reasons as her breasts were too small to be noticed. Nevertheless, she was often glared at by jealous wives when seen chatting to their husbands.

I was standing in the foyer of the house, chatting to Heather, when a large consignment of beer barrels arrived. The front door was wedged open and the barrels were rolled through the foyer and into a corridor. Whilst this was going on, Clive appeared at the front door with the Chairman of the Benevolent Fund, an extremely high ranking officer, who was accompanied by his wife. At the same time as they arrived Teresa came out of the office and proceeded to turn right into the corridor. Her attention was focussed on Clive and the Chairman, so she wasn't concentrating on where she was going. As a result she didn't notice the stationary beer barrel at the entrance to the corridor.

Much to her horror she tripped over the barrel and partially flew into the air, legs a'kimbo, before landing on the other side of the barrel, upside down, in a most unladylike position with her dress draped over her face. Clive, who often referred to her as 'Your Wideness', sniggered and commented to the amused Chairman, "You will have to excuse some members of the staff, only, good ones are so hard to find." An extremely red-faced Teresa struggled to regain her composure as she straightened herself up, and, with a half-hearted sheepish grin, fled from the scene. With tears streaming down my face, I too had to leave.

Not all of the 'inmates' had a happy time at the Home. There was one couple, who were staying in one of the bungalows with their children, who generally kept themselves to themselves and were only seen in 'public' in the bar during the evenings, usually sitting on their own.

She was an attractive girl and was constantly the subject of many admiring male glances, due to her wearing extremely short mini-skirts. Half-way through their two week stay, we saw her in the bar with her husband and she had a beauty of a black eye. Once they departed a 'neighbour' from a nearby bungalow related how he had heard a fearsome row going on between them as he passed by. He then heard a dull thud and the argument was over — hence the black eye.

One poor unfortunate was on holiday with his family, not at the

Benevolent Home, but elsewhere in Devon. He was out walking one day when he fell off a cliff, which, once heard about at the Home, provoked comments like, "Excuse me mate, which is the quickest route to the beach?"

He broke several bones, including an arm, and after being discharged from hospital arrangements were made to send him and his family to the Benevolent Home. He duly arrived, swathed in bandages, plaster and a sling. Within a matter of hours he was back in hospital again. During the course of his short time in the bungalow he had leant on a window frame with his good arm, not knowing that someone had carelessly left a sewing needle sticking upwards out of the wood. It snapped off and entered his arm, poor fellow. I know not if he ever returned. Perhaps he now sells lucky charms!!!

Of the entertainment facilities available to the 'inmates', the most popular was the tennis court, especially if it was too cold to go in the swimming pool. Not a very good player myself, I never dressed up for the occasion, mostly wearing jeans instead of shorts. My wife, a far worse player than I, used to go the whole hog, imagining she was at Wimbledon.

She never blamed herself for losing points even though on most occasions I used to hit the ball back to her for an easy reply. It was always the fault of her racket, or the net was too high. (As if it was lower on my side.) The balls wouldn't bounce high enough, or they would bounce too high. "I missed the ball because I was distracted by a falling leaf."

She always became infuriated when I referred to her as 'Maria Bueno', because of the outfit she wore. She was even more infuriated by the fact that she was running all over the court, whilst I, with my jeans pockets full of keys, fags, matches and other items, managed to get by with the minimum of effort.

Towards the end of one stormy game, with the score at 6-0, 6-0, 3-0 in my favour, I had had enough of her constant moaning and really went to town. The last three games were polished off in a succession of drop-shots, which crept over the net, with others which went to the far corners of the court, well out of her reach. With the game now over, she had reached boiling point, when a friend, a fellow sufferer and part-time 'fire-eater' from MAMMOTH COUNTY, 'Simon', arrived with his racket. He obviously thought I was on my own or he wouldn't have asked, "Want a quick thrashing?"

Now 'Simon' was quite a stocky and muscular chap, but he was frightened to death of his wife. She was pleasant enough, but rather strong, both in mind and in body. Not the sort of lady to be on the wrong side of an argument. We males are generally the 'Masters of the House', outside the four walls, but she was the 'master' both on the inside and the outside of 'Simon's' house.

Returning to the tennis, 'Simon' realised with horror what he had said, as he recognised the all too familiar symptoms of an enraged wife, as, in the middle of a tantrum, she stormed off the court with a face like a female Russian bus driver, glaring at 'Simon' on the way past. My 'beloved' didn't speak to me for two days. Fortunately she has a good sense of humour and it wasn't long before she saw the funny side of the 'tennis' episode.

During the course of our various visits we met countless folk, one of whom was 'Neville', who, because of his 'posers' outfit of flip-flops and outrageous shorts, became known to the locals as 'Supergrock'. (All tourists in Devon are known as 'Grockles', a lowly tag.) He was at the Home following an operation, accompanied by his wife and kids.

For a while we played tennis as mixed pairs and one day we noticed Clive and 'Bruno' chasing a sheep which had escaped from a nearby field. They eventually cornered it by a tree, near to the tennis court. In its panic the sheep tried to climb up the trunk of the tree and it jumped up and down until it fell on its back. It was then pinned to the ground by the brave duet of 'hunters'. 'Neville' shouted to them, "It's not every day that you see a sheep fall out of its nest." Clive and 'Bruno' were so amused by this comment they hadn't the strength left to hold the sheep. It escaped again, being rounded up later in the day.

The local hostelry within 'Chigley' that we frequented was called 'The Ship', known by many firemen as 'The Dog-House Inn', a safe haven of retreat from the better half. Drinking after closing time was rife and it wasn't uncommon to leave at 2 o'clock in the morning, again incurring the wrath of the *gentle sex,* especially after making blasé statements like, "I will be home early tonight my dear."

It was a different kettle of fish when *they* went there though. It was okay for them to get *drunk,* sorry, 'tipsy'. Ladies do not get drunk, only men. Mind you, it seemed at times, especially when the weather was rotten, that we spent half of our holiday in there. We once left at opening time — work that one out!!!

There existed in 'Chigley' a character called 'Bill the Butch', not because he was 'queer', you understand. Clive, 'Neville' and his wife, with my wife and I were in the bar of 'The Ship' having a lunch-time session. Both of the girls were drinking cider, but neither realised it was the local 'hooch'.

'Bill the Butch' had just closed his shop and he walked into the bar with some sausages and other meat. My, by now, half-cut wife said, "Oh, I have just remembered, I've got nothing for our evening meal. Can I have some of your delicious cooked ham please?" He muttered, "I've just closed the shop — oh never mind," and off he went. 'Bill' went through the ritual of opening and closing his shop, duly returning armed with the ham.

When he returned to the pub 'Neville's' wife piped up, "Oh that looks nice. Could I have some?" Raising his eyes to the heavens, 'Bill' commented, "Why didn't you ask a few minutes ago?" "I didn't think," came the response. "Is there anything else that you want?" My wife then said, "Could I have four pasties whilst you are over there?" 'Neville's' wife also made a similar request. Off 'Bill' went again, through the same routine, no doubt cursing his luck that he hadn't gone to another pub in the first place.

Now 'Bill the Butch' was a true-blue Englishman who hated all foreigners of any description. Upon his final return to the pub he was engaged in a lengthy chit-chat with the two wives. During the course of the conversation mention was made about a particular type of 'foreigner' whom 'Bill' absolutely detested. It certainly touched a nerve, for a torrent of abuse and swear words came out of his mouth, including, "I WOULD SHOOT THE F*!*!*G LOT OF THEM IF I HAD MY WAY."

Clive, 'Neville' and I were a little distance away and we were staggered when we heard the flood of swear words from 'Bill's' mouth and thinking the girls would be shocked and upset, we stepped forward to intervene. Then we noticed that far from being offended, such was the state of their 'hooch' soaked minds, they hadn't even noticed he was swearing and were nodding in agreement at his comments. We left them to get on with it.

On one occasion, at night, 'Simon' joined us on a trip to 'The Ship', and despite his 'cross my heart and hope to die' promise to his good lady that he would keep out of 'Bad Company' (Clive, Steve and myself) and not be home too late, he too arrived back at the Home in the early hours.

After dropping us off he drove up to his bungalow, which he observed was in darkness. Praying that he wouldn't awaken his wife, he switched off his engine and lights as he approached the bungalow. 'Almost there' he thought to himself. Then there was a sickening crunch as he drove over a metal chair, dragging it for several yards before coming to a halt. Lights came on inside the bungalow and all hell broke loose, as you can imagine. 'Simon' was all but banned from further visits to 'The Ship' for the duration of the holiday.

All in all, the vast majority of the 'inmates' at the Home, were down to earth, and the humour in and around the same, especially in the bar, where many hilarious stories were recounted, was second to none.

There was the story from Heather of a family which were booked into the Home from the Liverpool area. An easy enough task for the driver — on to the M6, M5 and A38 — a piece of cake. By late afternoon on the day they were due, all the new influx of residents were booked in, with the exception of the family from Liverpool. The hours dragged on and there was still no sign of them. Around midnight the phone rang, it was them. The phone call was from *Southampton* of all places. As if that wasn't bad enough, Heather was further informed that they had become lost in *London*. They eventually arrived the following day.

I related the tale about my 'Gaffer', Roger. His wife, 'Edith', had been through a major operation and they, together with their family, were allocated a place at the Home. 'Edith' rang my wife when they returned home, saying that they had enjoyed a marvellous holiday etc. She then went on to say, "I thought to myself, Roger's a big boy now (around fifty) I will let him pack his own suitcase. When we arrived in Devon and unpacked, the only pair of socks he had were the ones he was wearing."

The last section of this chapter is devoted to deliberate (or otherwise) set-ups at the Benevolent Home.

The first involved Steve, the gardener, who, not having been employed at the Home for long, was approached by Clive, who requested him to do a 'stock-take' of the plants and bushes. Not for one moment did he dream it was a set-up, but the other members of the staff knew. It took him hours to complete. He was noted by all involved, marching up and down the rows of dahlias and roses etc., armed with a clipboard, like a sergeant-major counting his troops. It wasn't until Clive dropped a hint of some kind that Steve realised he had been had.

Clive told us that many years before he moved to Devon he had worked in a slaughter-house and one evening he was asked to do some overtime as they had a 'special', in the shape of a massive bull to deal with. Once the beast was despatched from this earth and hung up, he noticed it was sporting a huge pink and black spotted 'chopper'. With no-one else being within the immediate vicinity, he lopped it off and placed it into a bag to take home.

Once home, he hatched a plot to outwit two 'Romeos', who were always chatting the girls up in his local. He went to the pub and bided his time until they were in the company of two girls and further waited for one of them to go to the toilet.

He hadn't too long to wait before 'Romeo' number one left his seat. Clive followed him into the toilet and as they stood side by side, he unfurled his 'monster', which was so long it almost touched the trough.

46

Clive chatted amiably to him, until the latter, out of the corner of his eye, noticed Clive's 'weapon'. A look of total astonishment and utter disbelief came over his face, which made him feel rather small to say the least.

Clive waited for a couple of minutes after 'Romeo' number one had departed, allowing him enough time to return to his companion. Coming out of the door he pretended to adjust his flies, noting number one 'Romeo' tapping 'Romeo' number two's shoulder and pointing towards Clive, saying, "That's the bloke." Clive strode off in triumph.

Whilst on the same subject, 'The Corporal', on my Watch, said that when he was in the army, his platoon was challenged to a 'largest chopper' contest, by a rival platoon. As soon as their 'champion' took one look at the 'Hampton' belonging to 'The Corporal's' champion, he refused to get his own out and slunk from the room, tail between his legs so to speak, a thoroughly beaten man.

Heather attempted to frighten me with a mug of tea which contained a 'china frog', but having seen one before, I simply drank the contents and placed the mug on the table, saying, "Oh, look, there's a frog in it," and calmly walked away.

Later the same day we were in the kitchen yard, chatting to Clive, whilst a perspiring working party were enjoying a 'cuppa'. I said to my beloved, "Cup of tea my dear?" to which there was a positive reply. I went to the kitchen and there to my immense glee, was the mug with the 'frog' in it. Now, some people have a fear of spiders, others snakes, but my wife's particular weakness is frogs. I duly made the tea and took it outside, handing it to her. A MUG for a MUG.

The contents were slowly despatched until the top of the frog's head

appeared. She brought the mug over to me and whispered, "There is something in my tea." I glanced at it, trying hard not to laugh and commented, "I'm sorry, I must have left the tea bag in it." She gradually tipped the contents out and looked once more into the mug. "Aagh, there's a frog in it." (Frogs normally sit in croc mugs!!!)

There then commenced a piercing scream as she threw the mug high into the sky and fled through the gate, still screaming. The mug crashed to the ground, but amazingly it remained in one piece. As her screams disappeared into the distance, one member of the work party, who hadn't heard the initial outburst, calmly commented, "She must have had the mug with the frog in it."

I am, by nature, a late night person, and as a consequence I have a job to get up in a morning and it is usually an hour or so before I am completely alert. (As one fireman 'The Old Recruit' once said, "Keep a lert — the country needs lerts.")

One morning, I trundled down to the house to collect the paper, still suffering from the effects of a hang-over from the night before. Next to the main entrance was Clive, on a scaffolding gantry, dressed in protective clothing, sand-blasting the stonework. Immediately above him was the balcony of his private quarters.

Upon noticing me, he said, "Morning." Switching off the sand valve, he then sprayed me with water, but at that stage I was barely wet. Without my realising it, behind me, 'Bruno' had arrived on the scene. As I backed out of range, giving Clive a 'V' sign, two huge arms wrapped themselves around me. Now, when you are trapped by a fellow the size of 'Bruno', you go where he wants to take you. He carried me back into the firing line, much to Clive's pleasure, whereupon I received a full jet of water from my head to my toes. Once soaked, 'Bruno' released me and said, "Cheerio, have a nice day."

I splish-splashed my way into the office, Clive's and 'Bruno's' laughter echoing in my ears. Heather and Teresa were present and were highly amused as I stood there dripping. I stated that I would like to get my own back, but it had to be straight away, as Clive wouldn't be expecting instant retaliation. I asked Heather if I could go through her living room and get to Clive, via the balcony, with a bucket of water.

Heather instantly agreed, as she always wanted to get one over on Clive. Once I was ready it was agreed that Heather would ring down to Teresa and that she would go outside and distract Clive. With the Jack Russell locked firmly away, I filled a bucket with water. Heather opened a window and then sent the signal to Teresa. I waited for a few seconds until Clive switched the sand-blaster off and had turned to find out what Teresa wanted.

I stealthily climbed out of the window and tip-toed across the balcony. At the last second Clive sensed something was wrong, but it was too late. The entire contents of the bucket went down the inside of his protective clothing, at the neck. In a flash, I was back in the room, with the window firmly shut, answering his stream of swear words with a succession of 'V' signs. Revenge was sweet.

Afterwards, Clive collared hold of Heather, saying, "You stupid woman, you missed an ideal opportunity. Why didn't you shut the window after he had climbed out of it, or alternatively placed 'Sandy' on the window sill? He would have been trapped with an empty bucket of water." Back came the weak reply, "I never thought about that."

Another fellow who was employed at the Home, a northerner, "Tha nose tha does," earned himself the nickname of 'Trapper'. He had bragged to Clive and 'Bruno' that he was an expert at laying a trap to catch rabbits. Clive and 'Bruno' knew where the trap was set, but it was weeks before one was caught.

Filled with triumph, 'Trapper' marched into the house, chest puffed out and found Clive. "Ee lad, put ma bunny in't freezer," smirking as he walked away. During the evening Clive returned the same rabbit to the trap and the next day was a repeat of the first. This went on for a week, towards the end of which the rabbit was becoming more than stiff. Using techniques once employed by the Gestapo, Clive had to break the rabbit's bones, without marking it too much, making it supple once more.

After the week passed by, 'Trapper' went to collect his 'bag'. Beaming from ear to ear, he said to Clive, "I've come for't rabbits lad." "What rabbits?" Clive retorted. As the true story unfolded, the smile disappeared from 'Trapper's' face. Another sucker went into the annals of history.

The best set-up of all time at the Home was 'hatched' in the bar of 'The Ship', in May 1985. It was aimed purely and simply at Heather. Clive mentioned that from time to time complaints would filter back from the Benevolent Fund's H.Q. in London and copies of the letters would be forwarded on to him. They were so pathetic they didn't bother Clive, but they really touched a nerve with Heather.

Thus the scene was set. A 'bogus' letter. Although false, it had to be seen to be realistic. Everything in 'The Letter' bordered on the truth and special mention was made of 'dirty grill pans', Heather's pet hate.

It took several days to compile, but once completed it was a masterpiece. My wife had 'tut-tutted' as it was being formed, but eventually she threw her lot in with us and even compiled the last part of the letter, all of which was written in her own handwriting. After completion I read it from beginning to end, in the early hours. I laughed so much my sides ached. My wife thought I was going to have a seizure.

The idea was to present Heather with 'The Letter', via Clive, late on a Friday afternoon, after the H.Q. had closed in London. Appropriate headed notepaper was acquired, complete with a forged Chairman's signature. It stated, "Dear Clive, please find a letter of complaint enclosed. I would appreciate your comments at your earliest convenience."

All of the 'inmates' were informed of 'The Letter', with the exception of a rather large and fearsome lady, called 'Polly', from the 'Black Country', whom we had deliberately left out for unwitting participation later on. All were invited to put in an appearance at the bar the following night.

7 o'clock came and the bar was opened. Clive came downstairs and with thumbs up said, as he passed by, "Hook, line and sinker, we've got her mate." After some brief consultations with a few early participants, he returned to my wife and I.

An hour or so earlier he had been seated on his living room sofa, brooding, with a deliberately angry expression on his face, whilst Heather was doing the ironing. Sensing something wasn't quite right, she asked Clive, "What's the matter?" "Nothing," came the sullen answer. This went on for several minutes until Heather said, "Oh, come on Clive, I know when something is wrong."

Clive retorted, "If you insist. We've had another letter of complaint, but if you read it, it will upset your weekend." Heather *insisted,* so Clive *reluctantly* threw it at her and Heather proceeded to read the contents of 'The Letter'.

126 Sherbourne Road
London SW10

26th May 1985

Dear Sirs,

Although myself and my husband enjoyed our stay at Harcombe House, I feel it is only right and proper to point out that the management of the same may or may not be aware that people are on convalescence and should be treated with the respect due to them.

Despite being treated most warmly upon our arrival by the manager, Clive, his wife Hazel never once introduced herself properly to us. This gave us the immediate impression that she was biased against senior officers. Although we do not encourage the wives of firemen to attend Coffee Mornings back home, we always try our best on holiday to mix with others on an equal basis.

Although the chalet was generally clean and tidy, soot was perpetually falling from the obviously unswept chimney and the grill pan was dirty. I realise that Mrs. Laurence has her hands full and has problems of her own (which I will expand on later) but one has to draw the line somewhere and try to set proper standards.

Amongst my husband's various problems is a nervous disorder which demands peace and quiet as much as possible. We thought that the peaceful countryside around Harcombe would be ideal. However, due to incessant yapping of a small mongrel (which I believe went by the name of Randy!) from the balcony above the entrance to the house, it contrived to upset my husband and he in turn tended to take it out on myself and the children, Rupert and Amanda.

In addition to the yapping mongrel a begging retriever appeared constantly at our patio window. Although I myself have no objection to animals, my husband is allergic to both dogs and cats and my shooing away of this stray animal again had him on edge.

We thought the scenic view around Harcombe was excellent but felt that the gardens could be a lot tidier and the external condition of the blue van, used apparently for transport, left something to be desired.

We felt that Clive in many ways seemed to run Harcombe House etc. on his own and was covering for Mrs. Laurence on many occasions. Although I hate to point it out Mrs Laurence had an excess liking for white wine. Perhaps this latter problem helped her to cope with the stresses of an unusual life style.

I wanted to bring these matters directly to Clive's attention, but did not want to have a confrontation as it would have upset my husband even further. Friends of ours have complained in the past but to no avail which seems to point to the fact that the management of Harcombe House have friends in high places. One can only hope that if enough complaints are registered, someone will HAVE to sit up and take notice.

Although several months have passed since our stay at Harcombe, it has taken me until now to relive the awful memory and put pen to paper.

In marked contrast we thoroughly enjoyed our stay at Littlehampton in 1983 where we could not fault Maureen and her staff and we look forward in future to returning there again.

Yours faithfully

Clive described her reaction to us. She was gently ironing one of his shirts when she started on the contents and by the time she had finished, her arm was swishing the iron furiously, taking it out on the shirt. Her mutterings and mumblings were interspersed with — "How dare they" — "What a nerve" — "This is dreadful Clive" — "Fancy complimenting that bitch at Littlehampton" — "You cannot make out the signature" — "Cowards" — "No full address either" — "I intend to go through all the files in the office until I find a family with two children called Rupert and Amanda."

She continued, "I'm going to ring London, I want their full address." Clive interjected, "You can't, it's closed. I'm off for a bath." He retreated to the bathroom, his sniggers drowned out by the noise of the running water.

Emerging from the bathroom, Clive noticed Heather pacing furiously up and down the living room, muttering and chuntering. He said, "I told

you I shouldn't have shown you the letter, for heavens sake calm down, there's nothing you can do about it until Monday anyway. I'll see you downstairs in a few minutes and if I was you I shouldn't mention the letter to anyone." He hurriedly departed, almost in agony from restraining himself from laughing.

Some thirty minutes had passed since Clive first came into the bar and a rather larger than normal contingent of customers were present when Heather haughtily swept into the room. It was obvious that she had consumed some wine to help restore her battered composure. We immediately plied her with more.

Instead of keeping quiet, as Clive had suggested, she whispered to my wife and myself, "We have had another *letter,* a really rotten one, Clive's furious." We sympathised with her and told her not to worry as it was probably from a crank of some kind, who had nothing better to do. She went on, "Keep it a secret, Clive's told me to keep quiet about it, but I just had to tell someone." She then gave us 'The Letter' to read, which gave us an excuse to rid ourselves of the pent up laughter within us.

Whilst we were attempting to read it, Heather went on to complain about the complaints, which included, "They have more or less accused me of being a drunkard," as she slurped her umpteenth glass of wine.

Heather then moved on to other groups, being sociable and trying hard not to say any more about the 'forbidden' subject. Meanwhile, we had to keep going out of the room for 'snigger-breaks'.

Once the wine she was consuming got to work, the 'secret' had been relayed by her to everyone in the room. By now 'Polly' had joined us and when she found out the basics, she was furious. "IF OI CUD GER OLD OF THE WRITER OI'D WRING ER SCROWNY NECK," she remarked boomingly, in her genteel 'Black Country' accent.

It was coming towards closing time and most of us were slightly the worse for drink. (In a 100 yards race we were 50 yards behind Heather as she swayed from side to side.) The bar was jam-packed and I realised we had planned no 'Finale' and that many people were waiting for the end of the saga, in excited anticipation.

I conferred with Clive and said, "We will have to end this shortly. I have an idea. Keep quiet and do as I say." I then instructed him to go behind the bar and serve until last orders were called. At the appropriate time, I went behind the bar and told Clive to clear off, as I had an announcement to make. (Under normal circumstances Clive would have ignored my foolhardiness or given me a bunch of fives, but he slunk off and sat in a corner of the room.)

I rang the bell and all went quiet and I said, "We all know Heather and we all know how hard she works to make our stay a happy one." (Round of applause.) "Some less than nice person has sent a rather nasty letter of complaint to London, who have passed it on to here." (*Shocked* silence and mutterings of 'How ungrateful'.) I continued, "I intend to read the contents out, unless someone objects."

Heather lurched across the room, fell against the bar and slurred, "You're not going to read it to anyone, it's confidenshal." (You're not going to read it to anyone, it's confidential.) She then tried to snatch 'The Letter' out of my grasp, but failed miserably. "I'm coming behind to get it." (I'm coming behind to get it.) As she made her way towards me, Clive intercepted and forced her to sit down, taking not one bit of notice as she said. "Clive, stop him" (Clive, stop him.)

'Polly', not one for being kept quiet for long, was seated at the end of the bar, occupying a space meant for three people. She swelled up with anger, her face going purple with rage and shouted at me, "A YOW, YOW ERD WHA EATHER SED, DOUNT YOU DER RADE THE LERRER." At that a huge right arm, accompanied by an equally large hand, reached out for me, but I just managed to evade them. A good job too, for she would have torn me to shreds if she could have got hold of me.

I proceeded to recite 'The Letter', trying to ensure I didn't slur my words too much and keeping well out of 'Polly's' reach. As the various 'complaints' were reeled off, there were appropriate 'Ooh's' and 'Aaah's' and other comments from the highly entertained, previously primed, 'audience'. From time to time I glanced at 'Polly' (steam coming from her ears) and Heather (almost crying.)

When I had finished reading, 'Polly' hammered the bar top with her enormous fists and bellowed, "OI OPE YOWER SATISFIED." I totally ignored her and reached into my pocket for a pre-written letter of explanation, an apology and a donation to the Benevolent Fund. It was

handed to Heather, who had somewhat sobered up due to the shock of my reading 'The Letter'.

She flushed with embarrassment as she studied the contents, which she read out. Even 'Polly' was lost for words, quite an achievement according to her husband. It had been a classic evening, which really should have been recorded for posterity on a video.

A copy of 'The Letter' was left with Heather and over the years hundreds of folk, from Chief Fire Officers to firemen have scoured its pages, with equal comments of, "How Disgusting," to, "First Class," once informed of the truth.

More about Clive, Heather and company later in the book. Many of the central characters have since departed from the Benevolent Home and with respect to their replacements, somehow the place will never quite be the same again.

Confrontations came in many guises. Most were over in minutes, others not. Many were minor, but on some occasions they came to 'fisticuffs'. I will describe the LITTLE SNOBSBURY ones first.

The first involved a former railway stoker, nicknamed 'Foghorn-Leghorn', because his loud, raucous voice was similar to the strutting rooster in the cartoons. "AH SAY, AH SAY, BOY." On his very first day of duty 'Foghorn' witnessed Sub-O 'Squirrel' being attacked by an irate fireman, Bob 'The Apprentice', who hailed from Scotland. When I say 'attacked', 'The Apprentice' had simply had enough of 'Squirrel's' childish behaviour and swung a punch at him, which barely connected. 'Squirrel' screamed at 'Foghorn', "YOU SAW THAT!" 'Foghorn' replied, "Sorry, I never saw a thing." The matter went no further. Lack of witnesses I think.

'The Apprentice' also had a go at 'Glarer', a real good one. As previously mentioned, 'Glarer' was a Sub Officer, a rank in those days which was extremely powerful. He was the classic 'Bully Boy', hiding behind his rank at the slightest sign of dissent, and at times he made Adolf Hitler look like a Red Cross worker. (Apologies to the Red Cross.)

He constantly picked on the younger members of his Watch, particularly the probationary firemen, including myself, and I knew at least one young lad who was driven out of the job because of him. When firemen stuck up for themselves, usually the longer serving men, he steered clear of them. One Leading Hand, a huge, normally placid Scot, 'Jock', once lifted him into the air by his reefer jacket and hung him on a coat peg, saying, "Sub Officer or not, if you ever speak to me again in that manner, I'll wring your bloody neck." He never spoke to him in that manner again!!!

'Glarer' originated from the London area and was universally loathed by the firemen at LITTLE SNOBSBURY, often being referred to by the older men as, 'That Greasy Cockney', after they had fallen foul of him. He had thick blubbery lips with a profusion of awkwardly shaped and discoloured teeth and constant bad breath. Most of all though, he had bulbous, staring eyes, thus his nickname of 'Glarer'. We used to sing, behind his back of course, "Jeepers, Creepers, where did you get those Peepers," and I still chuckle to myself whenever I hear that song today.

Returning to the story at hand, on the day 'The Apprentice' had a go at him, 'Glarer's' health and temper had been made even worse due to a large, weeping sore on one of his cheeks. In the evening, when there were no officers present, he frequently kept us on parade for well over an hour at a time, lecturing (bollocking) us on this, that and the other.

During this 'Punishment' routine he had verbally attacked 'The Apprentice', so much so that he could take no more. He interrupted 'Glarer' in the middle of his tirade, and in a calm, controlled voice, said, "Sub

Officer, your teeth are rotten and your breath smells." 'Glarer' was so stunned he stepped back a few paces from his 'opponent'. Almost lost for words, he muttered, "Your teeth are not exactly marvellous either." "We are not talking about me," 'The Apprentice' interjected, "We are talking about you."

The rest of us were as stunned as 'Glarer' and we waited with bated breath as to what would happen next — a fight perhaps! No, 'Glarer' was too big a coward for that. Humiliated, he fell back on his rank and ordered us into the drill yard, where he ran us ragged.

Another fireman who had a go at him was 'Q.P.R.' There was a discussion taking place in the mess, in which 'Glarer' wasn't an active participant. Part of this discussion was about having talent, ability and qualifications. 'Q.P.R.' said, "If any of us had any of these three, we would be in a better job." 'Glarer' burst into the conversation, saying angrily, "What's the matter with this job? You are lucky you are in it." Back came the instant retort, filled with venom after months and months of being goaded by 'Glarer', "If you were talented and had plenty of qualifications, you wouldn't even dream of joining the Fire Service. Anyway, no-one was talking to you, so mind your own f*!*!*g business." Next duty shift, out we trooped into the yard for a prolonged session of drills.

Each time we turned out to a job, his face was filled with panic. If HE made a mistake that was okay, but if anyone else did the same he would be in for a 'bollocking'. On the drill ground, if you made a mistake, it didn't matter how far you were into a particular drill, with ladders, hose-lines and other gear strewn all over the place, it all had to be made up and the drill commenced from scratch again. This could occur several times and eventually, to 'Glarer's' immense satisfaction, the other firemen would turn on the unfortunate miscreant and revile him. 'Divide and Rule' was 'Glarer's' maxim. The day he transferred to another Brigade was truly a red-letter day indeed.

Not long after joining I was trying to work out where one particular fireman, with a West of England type of accent came from. I gave up guessing in my own mind and asked him outright. "Mind your own business," he sneered out loud. I was so incensed by his reply that I said, "You are a yokel then." He went red with anger and confronted me, fists clenched, and snorted, "WHAT DID YOU SAY?" I replied, "You are from Yeovil, are you not?" He instantly calmed down, stating, "That's alright then, for one minute I thought you had called me a yokel." It had been a near miss.

'Jock', the huge Scotsman who had hung 'Glarer' on a coat peg, had two of the largest hands I have ever seen. From time to time he would place one of his hands over the top of your head and squeeze the pressure points below the ears — the 'Death Grip' as he called it, an excrutiatingly painful experience, believe me.

The third time he did this to me I had had enough and attempted a right arm uppercut. Before I made contact with his jaw, it was held in a vice-like grip with his free hand. It did the trick as far as I was concerned, for he let go of my head. He said, "If you ever try that again 'Laddie' you will be in some real trouble." From then onwards he desisted from his 'Death Grip'. Mind you if my fist had connected with his jaw, it would have been a case of, 'I can prove to you, in one almighty blow, that I can break every bone in my hand'.

His fellow Leading Fireman on the Watch was another Scot (no wonder the grass was greener in Scotland, than in England, they were all down here, tramping on ours) who went by the name of 'Skin'. He was extremely proud of his 'Scottish' heritage and used to ridicule the English. (Although he didn't mind working in England living in a house supplied by the Local Authority, and having an English wife.) He constantly bragged about 'Bonnie Scotland' and its superior way of life.

I once mentioned that I had seen a comedy sketch on the T.V. from 'The Goodies' show, or something similar, which featured a 'Bagpipe Spider' and he almost went berserk. He soon kept 'Mum' when I met his father, an out and out Londoner — so much for his 'heritage'. He used to return to his 'homeland' foir holiday breaks and on one such trip he had his driving licence confiscated for drinking and driving.

There was a heated argument in the dormitory one night, between 'Skin' and another fellow, Fm. 'Angry', who was renowned for having an extremely short fuse. Fm. 'Angry', although still a young man, had lost most of his hair, which partially explained why he was so bad tempered. The argument reached fever pitch and before 'Skin' knew where he was, Fm. 'Angry' was hanging him out of a window by his ankles two floors up. "F*!*!*G APOLOGISE, OR ELSE," was the demand. The apology was instantaneous. He was hauled back into the room and the situation defused.

At LITTLE SNOBSBURY there was an efficient and well organised system for the routine maintenance of appliances and other vehicles at the close at hand Council Workshops. (In MAMMOTH COUNTY it was just organised chaos.)

One particular morning I was in the rear of the cab in the Hydraulic Platform, with 'Skin' and the driver in the front. The H.P. was being used as a mode of transporting myself to workshops to pick up a car or a van. When we arrived at the depot a Land-Rover was parked in our way. 'Skin', using his authority, said, "That is workshop's Land-Rover, I will move it," giving me a look as if to say, 'you are not good enough to do the same'.

He swaggered to the Land-Rover, opened the door and smiled smugly at us. As he was about to get into the vehicle his face changed com-

pletely and he turned ashen. He then ran, as fast as his legs could carry
him, away from us. At first we couldn't understand the reason until the
H.P. driver said, ''I don't think that Land-Rover belongs to the depot
as there is a massive alsation in the back looking at us.'' Sure enough,
there was. When 'Skin' had prepared to jump into the Land-Rover, all
he had seen was a jaw full of teeth heading towards him. I don't blame
him for doing a 'runner', I would have done the same in his place.

When we came off duty, I was giving 'Q.P.R.' a lift home, when we
spotted 'Skin', homeward bound on his cycle. As we drew level, 'Q.P.R.'
leaned out of his window and 'barked' at him. 'Skin' wasn't amused and
all but fell off his bike. It had been a day to remember.

Part of station life is devoted to showing members of the public
round, usually in organised groups, like Cubs and Scouts etc. A group
which turned up one night consisted of about twenty or so under-
privileged youths. What one would describe today as 'yobs', with their
'skinhead' appearance and hobnailed (bovver) boots.

At this stage in time it was a relatively 'new look', before their more
infamous acts of violence became a cult. They were, for the most part
well behaved. In charge of the Watch at the time was 'Derek', yet another
'immigrant', this time from a coastal resort in Lancashire, who held the
rank of Sub-O.

When the group of assorted 'skinheads' had been shown round, 'Derek'
said he would show them how to operate a branch, as some of them
had indicated that they wished to have a go. A pumping appliance was
set up in the yard and a roll of hose laid out. He told them to gather
round, but instructed them to stand back a little as he didn't want any
of them to get wet.

He then showed them how to insert the branch, a hand-controlled one,

without actually doing so. Raising his arm, he further explained that this was the the signal for 'water on'. Seeing the raised arm the pump operator got to work. All too late 'Derek' realised the water was upon him and he frantically tried to connect the branch.

Because of the increasing pressure, 'Derek' found it impossible and he was knocked to the ground by the force of the water coming out of the hose. He was soaked from head to foot. I looked at him as he screamed at the pump operator. It was as if his body had disappeared, being replaced by a huge head. His wide open mouth, which stretched from ear to ear, bawled, "YOU F*!*!*G STUPID PRAT, TURN THE F*!*!*G WATER OFF, I DIDN'T ORDER YOU TO TURN THE F*!*!*G STUFF ON" — forgetting that he had raised his arm.

As if to pile further humiliation on him, all of the 'skinheads' were doubled up with laughter. If they didn't know how to swear before they arrived for their visit, which was doubtful, they certainly knew how to do so by their departure.

My first impression of the inhabitants of the fire station at LITTLE SNOBSBURY was that half of them hated the officers and the other half hated each other. One chap in particular was known as 'Nosy', for obvious reasons. 'Nosy' was a law unto himself and would mete out a verbal bashing to firemen and officers alike, pushing them to the limits of their patience. His motto in life was, "F*!k em. Don't apologise, it's a sign of weakness."

He was the master of 'set-up' situations, not so much the comical variety, but the 'load the guns, pass them to two warring factions, then stand back and watch the fireworks'. He once stirred up trouble between two blokes, one of whom was well over six feet tall, the other being five feet eight. They agreed to meet in the station yard after going off duty, to 'settle' things.

The tall one, Fm. 'Sealed Knot', had a large club in his hand when they met, a little unfair to say the least. The smaller chap looked like he had had it before they started. However, being a former member of the Parachute Regiment he had a distinct advantage. Fm. 'Sealed Knot' took a mighty swipe at 'The Parachutist', but missed completely and his opponent immediately nipped into the void and punched him on the nose. This went on several times, before the taller protagonist, with a bloodied face, gave up. Of 'Nosy', there was no sign.

Whilst operating the Hydraulic Platform it was a cardinal sin to rotate the booms without first taking the cage out of its fixed road driving position, making sure the lower boom was raised enough, so that when rotating, the boom wouldn't sweep the blue flashers, radio aerial and sirens off the roof of the cab.

During the first part of the practical side of an initial H.P. training course, the instructor and two trainees, 'Foghorn-Leghorn' and Martin 'Forker' were in the cage together. The instructor, a junior officer, explained the various controls, stressing in particular about the importance of not touching the rotation lever, for the previously mentioned reasons. "Clear in your mind Martin?" Martin nodded and the instructor said, "Right. Get to work."

Martin released the cage from its anchor point, a jaw coupling, and raised the third boom outwards and away from the rear of the vehicle. His hand then went towards the rotation lever. He never got the chance to touch it. The instructor threw himself at Martin, almost knocking 'Foghorn' out of the cage. In an instant he was on Martin, hands round his throat, bending him almost in half backwards over the safety bar, shouting at him, "I TOLD YOU NOT TO TOUCH THE ROTATION LEVER." He didn't make the same error again.

LITTLE SNOBSBURY Fire Brigade always participated in the local annual carnival, usually despatching the H.P. to join the procession of floats as they snaked round the town. The machine and its crew were crawling along the High Street, when they noticed a former LITTLE

SNOBSBURY fireman coming the other way in his lorry. This fellow, a man of Welsh extract, was, at times, 'not all there', a prime candidate for the 'Funny Farm'. He had resigned from the Brigade under a cloud and as a result he had a massive chip on his shoulder. He literally hated the Fire Service.

The crew of the H.P. knew this and as he approached and recognised them, they goaded him with comments like, "How would you like to join the Fire Brigade? We are on the look-out for good blokes." The 'Welshman' stopped his lorry, then, leaning out of his cab window, almost beyond the point of no return, eyes blazing, he did a succession of double handed 'V' signs, shouting at the top of his voice, "F*!K THE FIRE BRIGADE" — "BOLLOCKS TO THE LOT OF YOU" — "YOU CAN ALL GET STUFFED."

He then drove off, leaving a section of the community of LITTLE SNOBSBURY in no doubts as to his thoughts of the Fire Service.

Moving on to 'Confrontations' within MAMMOTH COUNTY, I was based for several months at another station within one of the newly formed Divisions, under 'Animal', by now a Station Officer. There was a barman from a different Watch, a rather large fireman, who had been on the day shift and due to a row of some kind he told his colleagues that they could stuff his barman's job and after locking the bar he threw the keys into a partially filled beer glass.

When we came on duty we discovered that the bar and recreation room were in a right mess. They were cleaned up and later in the evening the former barman arrived for a drink, wearing a huge hairy pullover. When 'Animal' found out he was on the station he stormed into the recreation room and confronted him, face to face. The fact that the ex. barman had been in the Marines, where it was rumoured he had spent more time in the 'glass-house' than on active service, didn't deter 'Animal' one little bit, as he often boasted he was a 'karate' expert.

'Animal' growled, "What the f*!*!*g hell do you think you were playing at, ditching the bar keys in a glass of beer and leaving the room in such a state?" The next thing 'Animal' saw was a huge fist smacking into his face and he sank to the floor, with his arms wrapped around his opponents ankles.

The ex. Marine, in true 'Incredible Hulk' fashion, seemed to double in size as his temper got the better of him, with the hairy pullover adding to his dimensions. Watching this 'fight' was a young recruit from Devon, a former 'Rock Sampler', who couldn't believe his eyes and he went white with shock. As the Marine dragged 'Animal' from the floor and was about to beat the living daylights out of him, some of the lads intervened. It took half a dozen large firemen to restrain him, whilst 'Animal' was escorted back to the office.

When the Marine had calmed down he left the station. 'Dave Rainbow' administered first aid to a cut on 'Animal's' forehead, dabbing Dettol on it, to which 'Animal' screamed in pain. He muttered, "I could have

killed him if I had wanted to.'' The Marine was later placed on a charge, but little came of it and shortly afterwards he was *promoted* and sent to a station on another Division.

We once had on our books a fireman called 'Moggy', who was quite a nice chap until he had a couple of pints of cider inside him. A classic 'Jekyll and Hyde'. He was a little the worse for wear one night and was playing 'knuckles' with 'Animal', a fight to the death, so to speak.

'Moggy' was so accurate that 'Animal' rarely had a turn and his knuckles began to swell. 'Animal' said, "I'm not bothered, it's only pain. My mind can control pain." (He hadn't seemed to have controlled it when the Dettol was applied to his head!!!) I will give him his due though, he refused to give in and 'Moggy' ceased in frustration.

He left the bar area, along with 'Animal' and a few seconds later we heard an almighty crash. We thought, 'Oh no, he has floored the Station

Officer', and went to investigate. As it happened he hadn't touched him. To release his frustration, 'Moggy' had punched a metal roller towel holder so hard, it had fallen off the wall.

A few days later, with 'Moggy' not present, an off duty 'Animal' came to the bar and proceeded to consume quite a few 'bevvies'. Just as he was leaving, the subject of the 'knuckle' fight came up. He half-turned, still walking, and said "I would have put him in his place with my karate if he had gone too far." (Where had I heard that one before!) He then promptly walked into one of the concrete pillars, almost knocking himself out.

Another bar incident involved a 'late night' session, where there were only three participants left. The barman 'Pat', a Sub-O (a rather brusque Liverpudlian) and 'Eli Wallach', who, at the time was lower in rank than the Sub-O. All night long 'Eli' had called him 'Sub' and the various conversations had been nothing but polite. Then, just once only, 'Eli' called him 'John'. The mood changed instantly to one of confrontation. At the top of his voice 'John' shouted at 'Eli', "JOHN? YOU DARE TO CALL ME JOHN? IT'S SUB OFFICER TO YOU," and a furious row developed. At that 'Pat' shut up shop and promptly went to bed, leaving them still arguing.

Yet another 'bar' confrontation involved an ex. Post Office messenger boy and another former Marine, 'Chalky'. If you were to believe everything 'The Messenger' told you about himself, you would have been a right sucker. You name it, he had done it, and he knew everything about anything. A 'Walter Mitty', or rather a 'crap' or 'bull-shit' merchant. He once told me that the main reason he was leaving his wife was because she couldn't conceive children. At a later date I discovered she had produced four children in as many years, by another man. How's that for a barren woman!!!

A game of three card brag was in progress and two of the participants were friends of mine, on their one and only visit to the station. The O.I.C. was a standby Sub-O, known to some as 'The Caped Crusader'. He had two visitors — his girlfriend and her sister. 'Chalky' and 'The Messenger' both decided to chat the latter up, plying her with drinks until she could hardly stand, let alone join the 'Performing Arts' society.

Judging it to be the right moment and noting that 'The Caped Crusader' and his 'Moll' were absent from the room, they both made their play for the 'Nether' region at the same time. One was standing in front of her, and the other, behind. As each thought his moment of triumph had arrived, both met a hand coming the other way.

Withdrawing from the girl, who was so sloshed she hadn't noticed what was going on, they squared up to each other. 'Foghorn-Leghorn', never one to miss out on an opportunity where 'loose' females were concerned, 'rescued' her and took her in hand, or rather his hand, and sat her on his lap.

Whilst this rumpus was going on, my two mates had been staring

boggle-eyed at the antics. One asked me, "Is it like this all of the time?".
I replied jokingly, "This is one of our quieter nights." On hearing the
row, 'The Caped Crusader' burst into the room and parted 'Chalky' and
'The Messenger', much to the disappointment of most members of the
Watch, for it was almost a certainty that 'Chalky' would have had 'The
Messenger' for breakfast.

After the hue and cry had calmed down, the drunken girl complained
that she wasn't feeling too well (surprise, surprise!!!) and 'Foghorn'
quickly pushed her off his lap. She staggered, or rather fell, onto a row
of casual chairs, falling on her back. It became increasingly obvious that
she was going to be sick, by the gurgling noises she was making. I said
to the other card players, "I can't help her, I have a good hand." The
fireman seated next to me stated something similar and my two mates
looked on in total disbelief. She became violently ill and in the end the
gallant 'Foghorn' came to her assistance.

A group of firemen were amongst a party on board a ferry during an
organised 'booze-up' to Hamburg. One of the participants was an
attendant from MAMMOTH COUNTY Fire Control, 'CATTAHOLIC', a
fellow renowned for his almost bottomless drinking capabilities. Also
included in the party was a mutual friend, a non fireman, 'Big Steve',
who had spent many an hour at the station bar.

Both were sharing a cabin with two other chaps. 'CATTAHOLIC',
having returned from the closed bar was throwing a tantrum, beating

his fists on the table, demanding another drink. Now 'Big Steve', great bloke that he is, has an extremely short fuse, with regards to the temper stakes and within seconds he was on 'CATTAHOLIC', holding him by the scruff of his neck, shouting, "HAVEN'T YOU HAD ENOUGH ALREADY? IF YOU WANT ANOTHER F*!*!*G DRINK, I'LL STUFF YOU THROUGH THE F*!*!*G PORTHOLE, YOU CAN THEN DRINK AS MUCH AS YOU F*!*!*G WELL LIKE, THERE'S MILLIONS OF GALLONS OUT THERE, WE WANT TO GET SOME F*!*!*G SLEEP." At that he threw him on his bunk and silence prevailed.

'Big Steve' would have been totally unsuitable, from a temperament point of view, to serve in the Fire Service. The first officer he crossed would have been laid out by a right hook. He was once assisting a friend in dismantling an exhaust off a car. Try as he might, he couldn't get the tail-pipe to budge. He wedged himself into a suitable position and tugged and tugged, going purple in the process. "COME OFF YOU EFFING, EFFING, EFFING BASTARD." All of a sudden it came off — whoosh — burying itself into his forehead. Another round of F*!*'S poured forth.

His brother once told me of the one and only time he went shopping with him to a department store, for a pair of trousers. A young girl was informed by 'Big Steve' that there wasn't 'much room' for his 'bollocks'. "What does sir mean?" asked the embarrassed assistant flushing. "My bollocks," he said, "I cannot get my f*!*!*g bollocks in." His brother then disassociated himself from him as a further, larger, pair of trousers were produced.

Returning to the Fire Service proper, there was another confrontation which almost ended in a punch-up, which again involved 'The Messenger', this time with 'Nestor', who had tried to stop the electrically operated appliance bay doors, as described earlier in the book. It was at the commencement of a breathing apparatus drill, the B.A. shack being the venue. 'Upon Arrival', 'Nestor' was given full details of the 'pretend' incident, by 'The Messenger', which involved the emission of 'Gamma' radio-active rays — the most deadly ones. (You need to sit in a lead-lined box to be safe from those.) 'The Messenger' then ordered 'Nestor', who was acting as the Officer in Charge, to get to work.

'Nestor' asked him if he was sure they were 'Gamma' rays and not 'Alpha' or 'Beta', the former of which was confirmed. 'Nestor' then said, "Right then men, we are not going in there — far too dangerous — drill over." "Get in," snapped 'The Messenger'. 'Nestor' refused point blank. "If we go in there we would all be dead men, so we are not, so there." I suggested that the radio-active particles be down-graded, as a compromise, but neither would give way and they squared up to each other. We split them up, with calm eventually being restored and the drill was abandoned.

Another incident involving 'Nestor' began after a quite innocent statement from another potentially 'violent' member of the Watch, 'Snozzle', during an afternoon tea break. Having nothing better to do at the time, the latter asked the rather obscure question, "What is the difference between a plank and a piece of wood?"

An immediate row blew up with half of the Watch backing up 'Nestor' and the remainder siding with 'Snozzle'. 'Nestor' shouted, "THEY ARE EXACTLY THE SAME — THERE IS *NO* DIFFERENCE. A PLANK *IS* A PIECE OF WOOD," to which 'Snozzle' sneered back, "OF COURSE IT F*!*!*G WELL ISN'T. YOU WALK THE PLANK FOR INSTANCE, YOU DON'T WALK A PIECE OF WOOD." "BOLLOCKS," came the angry reply. "DON'T YOU SAY BOLLOCKS TO ME, I'M RIGHT," bawled 'Snozzle'. "NO YOU ARE F*!*!*G WELL NOT," screamed 'Nestor', "YOU KNOW F*!K ALL." — "I DO KNOW F*!K ALL." And so it went on and to this day the problems associated with the difference between a piece of wood and a plank have never been resolved.

One of the Divisional Commanders we had was 'The Tasmanian Devil', a brusque, stern man who frowned on the enjoyments of life on fire stations and volleyball etc. was all but banished during his reign, usually on the pretext of his, 'There is still station work to be completed' attitude. He once brought one of the rare games of volleyball to an end because he found a single empty bottle of coke in the television room.

During a 'purge' on the driving log books he found six miles recorded under the 'Social and Leisure' heading. Despite the fact that the entry was almost twelve months old, he demanded to know why this gross wastage of ratepayers money had occurred. I was able to identify the signature as 'Taffy's', from my Watch. 'The Tasmanian Devil' ordered me to ask him where he had been. Upon being asked, 'Taffy' remarked, "I cannot remember what I did yesterday, let alone several months ago." I rang 'T.D.' and informed him of 'Taffy's' reply and suggested, as an alternative, that the six miles may well have been entered under a wrong column heading. Not being a man to tolerate any kind of excuses, he said, "Either way Leading Fireman, you and your Watch are incompetent," and slammed the receiver down.

His attitude towards the older men bordered on the ridiculous. Upon glancing into the drill yard, from the comfort of an upstairs office, he noticed the three elder members of my Watch, 'Billy J', Gordon and 'Taffy', strolling, rather than running during drills. He ran from the office and confronted all three and with a tone of, 'I'm alright Jack, I don't have to run round drill yards anymore', he asked, "Why are you not running during drills?"

'Billy J' said, "Come off it sir, we are all around the fifty mark." He cut 'Billy J' short and and snarled, "YOU SHOULD BE AS FIT AS THE DAY YOU JOINED THE JOB. IF NOT, THEN YOU SHOULD BE OUT OF IT." The reposte from 'Billy J' was, "If you sign the chit stating we are not fit to carry out our duties, so we can retire early, that will do for us." Realising he had been outmanouvered, 'T.D.' turned on his heels and was gone. No further silly remarks about fitness and no retirement chits either.

During one particular night shift, without prior warning, 'T.D.' popped in when we should have been doing drills, which we were not. He confronted our 'Gaffer', Roger and demanded to know what we had done in the way of training. Roger thought for a few moments and replied, "Well......Erm.....Erm.....We have done a little bit of this and a little bit of that." 'T.D.' almost exploded, "WHAT DO YOU MEAN, A LITTLE BIT OF THIS AND A LITTLE BIT OF THAT?" Streams and streams of "Errmmmm's," came from Roger and 'T.D.' stormed off the station, muttering under his breath.

'The Tasmanian Devil' had to retire early because of poor eyesight. It was strongly rumoured that the 'quack', whilst giving him a routine medical, discovered that not only was he wearing glasses, but also contact lenses, aimed at helping him to pass the eyesight test. Once the contact

lenses had been removed he was asked to read the card. "What card?"
"On the wall over there" "What wall?" came the puzzled reply.

Prior to retiring he visited one of the stations on his Division, where
a fire crew hadn't long returned from an arduous job. The Leading Hand,
'Baz', himself not too many years off retirement, was a man, who not
only didn't mince his words, but hated 'Bull-shitter's'. Being an ex.navy
man, he once told me, "When H.M.S. Hood was sunk in 1941, there
were less than a handful of survivors. I have met fifty of them!!!"

He went into the station office, huffing and puffing, through his recent
exertions. 'T.D.' said, "You are not fit Leading Fireman," to which the

instant retort was, "At least I can see where I am going." There was no further comment from the Divisional Commander.

I was at a union meeting, where a large number of members were present, due to there being some important issues on the agenda. The usual amounts of 'bull' and 'woffle', were used by the union hierarchy in attempts to 'fob off' awkward questions. As is the want of some union officials who get carried away with their positions in life (power mad), one of them gave a 'rabble quelling speech', ultimately reaching fever pitch, like a Nuremburg rally.

Amidst a barrage of heckling and booing, this by now purple-faced man leapt to his feet, wiping the sweat off his brow, and shouted at the top of his voice, "IF ANYONE IN THIS ROOM IS PREPARED TO CALL ME A LIAR AND CAN BACK IT UP, I WILL RESIGN." One member stood up and said, "I will call you a liar and I can prove it." He was totally ignored and there was no resignation!!!

Gordon and 'The Old Recruit' were chatting one day in the mess. Somehow they got onto the subject of 'Hot Air Balloons'. (There are plenty of them in the Fire Service!!!) 'The Old Recruit' got himself into a corner by stating that if you get into a balloon and raised it off the ground, the rotation of the Earth would bring places to you, rather than the other way round. Gordon sneered and commented, "Come off it, are you trying to tell me that you can go a few thousand feet into the air and wait for Torquay to come to you?"

'The Old Recruit' realised that somewhere along the line he had dropped a clanger, but couldn't fathom out why, until Gordon further commented, "You would have to go up to the stratosphere to be able to do that." Instead of realising his error and admitting to it, 'The Old Recruit' tried to save face by saying, "How do you know that? Some kind of expert are you?" to which the reply was, "Because I'm f*!*!*g telling you, that's why."

One young recruit, who lived some distance from our station, took to wearing a 'Harry Lime' mack and whenever I saw him with it on, I used to say, "Hello Harry," and hum the theme tune. Being too young to remember 'Harry Lime' he hadn't a clue what I was on about. At the time he was first wearing the mack he used to hitch-hike to and from home to work and one day an off duty A.D.O., who was at a filling station, saw him on the opposite side of the dual carriageway, in full uniform, complete with cap, trying to thumb a lift. As if this wasn't bad enough, he was also wearing his horrendous 'Harry Lime' mack.

The following day the A.D.O. came to the station and hauled him into the office, giving 'Harry' a right going over, terminating with, "If I ever see you thumbing a lift in future in uniform or wearing uniform with your white mack you will be for the high jump." The shamefaced young fireman slunk out of the office, followed by a still fuming officer. Whilst the lad was still within earshot, I said to the A.D.O. "Have you seen a mack like that before?" He thought for a moment and replied, "It rings a bell.

Why?'' I hummed the first few bars of the 'Third Man' and the A.D.O. laughed out loud, ''Of course, the 'Harry Lime' mack.'' The 'mack' was never seen again.

At a later date, 'Harry' purchased a motor cycle and on his way home one evening he was travelling along the same dual carriageway where he had been spotted by the A.D.O. His speed was up to the maximum permitted for this road and out of the corner of his eye, in the outside lane, he noticed the bonnet of a car which was about to overtake him. 'A race' he thought. Without bothering to look round he accelerated away and the occupants of the car, two policemen, must have thought, 'This

is our lucky day — what a prat'. All too late, 'Harry' realised he was 'racing' against a high performance patrol car, as he heard the two-tones. He was then booked for speeding by the smirking officers.

Towards the end of my career there appeared a newly promoted Sub Officer on another of the Watches on my station, a humourless, rarely smiling, 'drill-pig'. For a while he was based on the same colour Watch as myself, but on another station within our Division. During each night shift a fireman from our station was delegated to do transport duties around the Division. Part of his duties were to deliver small, fully charged batteries for use in the walkie-talkie radios which were carried on all pumping appliances.

'The Old Recruit' arrived at the station where the 'Happy' Sub-O was stationed and walked into the office with the mail and batteries. The Sub-O said to him, "Have you tested the batteries for faults?" 'The Old Recruit' replied, "What do you mean?" Grabbing the box of batteries, the Sub-O continued, "You flick the top of them and if they are loose or cracked, then there is something wrong with them." 'The Old Recruit' muttered under his breath, "I have got better f*!*!*g things to do than flick the tops of batteries." "WHAT DID YOU SAY?" demanded the glaring Sub-O. "Nothing," 'The Old Recruit' replied and departed to his van.

A few days later 'The Old Recruit' observed the same Sub-O gazing disconsolately under the bonnet of his car. "What's the matter?" he enquired. "I think there is something wrong with the battery," was the reply. "You know what the trouble is," said 'The Old Recruit' (about to destroy the look of hope on the Sub-O's face), "You haven't flicked the top of it recently," and he waltzed off, fully aware of the withering look of hatred following him.

Control Rooms & Watch Rooms

Possibly the most odious duty for an operational fireman at LITTLE SNOBSBURY Fire Station was in the Control Room. This was the nerve centre of the Brigade and provided a direct link to the public, both in emergencies and general run of the mill situations.

It contained the usual paraphanalia which was the want of such an important post: maps, pre-determined attendance cards, lists of high risk buildings, dangerous substances, chemicals, standing orders, Chief Officer's instructions, routine notices and the like, most of which were designed to baffle rather than assist.

Accommodated within the confines of this little room was an ancient PBX golf ball type of telephone exchange, with plug in leads. When heavily in use, the criss-crossed leads looked akin to a family of small octopuses having a tentacle wrestling fight and it was not uncommon to pull out the wrong lead, at the wrong time, incurring the wrath of the person who had been cut off — usually a senior officer.

On the console there was an array of Automatic Fire Alarm (A.F.A.) lines, all of which had to be tested once a week. By the time the amalgamation arrived, these A.F.A.'s had bred like rabbits and almost every available space on the console, in the by then new Control Room, had been invaded by these devices.

Three of the most important items in the Control Room were the radio/telephone link, which was immediately available twenty-four hours a day for use with the fire engines and officers' cars, all of which had their own call signs, the turnout bells switch, which was located in the centre of the console, and in front of the Control Room operator was the 'Red Phone' — the direct '999' emergency line.

Almost immediately upon my return from Training School I was seconded to this duty, day shift after boring day shift, until I was fully conversant with all that was entailed with Control Room duties. LITTLE SNOBSBURY was a quiet Brigade, but despite this fact there were constant movements of fire engines, officers' cars and personnel on out-duties. Each and every one of these movements, along with many other aspects, had to be carefully recorded in the station log book.

This log book was constantly checked by the duty Watch Sub Officer and residential Station Officer, being carefully scrutinized by both in a search for spelling mistakes and other misdemeanours. If such a fault came to light, the unfortunate fireman who had committed such a foul deed would be hauled into the Station Officer's office for a 'bollocking'. One fireman, 'The Guardsman', had particular problems with his spellings and carried a dictionary with him so that he could check all words with more than three syllables — "Cawblymie — no wot I mean bravvar."

To add to the general boredom there was a retired fireman who was employed on the telephone system, from 9am to 5pm, Monday to Friday.

Although he was a nice old stick, he had the dreadful habit of reciting long winded stories, in a slow, droning fashion. Apart from hardly being able to get a word in edgeways, it was almost enough to send you to sleep. Despite the many and sometimes lengthy interruptions from the telephone calls he had to intercept, he always, without fail, remembered exactly where he had left off and continued with his tale.

The day shift was from 9am to 6pm, with one rostered fireman and his relief. The night shift was one of fifteen hours from 6pm until 9am the following morning. For this, the hours of duty were split between two firemen from the A and B rota lists. The A shift man did from 6-8, 11-3 and 7-9, with the B shift man doing the other, least popular hours. This latter chap was provided with a camp bed in an ante-room, and if he was really unlucky he would be woken up smack on the hour of 3am.

To complete the misery of the Control Room operator, the reading of non Fire Brigade material was banned from 7am until 11pm, as was smoking, and apart from meal breaks you were entombed in this little prison, with the clock appearing to tick by ever slower, until the end of the shift came.

To fall asleep on a night shift in the Control Room was considered a crime, but it was often done by many of the men. One thing was certain, no duty officer was going to rise from his warm bed to travel to the station to find out if the man on Control Room duty was awake or asleep.

I only fell asleep on a few occasions and in two I was caught out by circumstances out of my control. The first occurred at around 4am when the 'Red Phone' started ringing. I had dozed off with my head on my arms and hands on the console. When the phone rang I immediately

sprang into action, but both of my arms had gone numb. How I managed to take the call without constantly dropping the receiver, I will never know to this day.

The second time I fell asleep, a little after dawn, I was awakened by a loud banging on the internal front door. I struggled to my feet and rubbing my eyes I opened the upper hatch. There, to my complete suprise, was an extremely posh and severe looking lady, dressed in tweeds and jodphurs.

Between the external front door and the Control Room hatch was a flight of stairs leading to the snooker room. This formidable lady had a huge boxer dog at her side, not on a leash. She proceeded to ask, or rather demand, where a certain road was and as I about turned to consult the map, her dog thundered up the stairs for no apparent reason. Before I could catch my breath she shouted at the top of her voice, in a military fashion, "COME BACK BRUTUS YOU BASTARD,"to which the terrified beast performed a back-flip and fell down the stairs.

Once calm had been restored (thankfully none of the men had been wakened) I was able to supply her with the details she required. As she was about to leave, she thanked me and said, "Sorry to have woken you up," something I could hardly deny, and I was scared to death for quite some time in case she had contacts with any of the senior officers. — "It was such a shame to wake up that nice young man in your Control Room," etc.

One of the prime duties of the 3am to 7am man, apart from staying awake, was to polish what was left of the well worn lino, on hands and knees of course, and to apply brasso to the external brasses, including the public fire alarm button. Woe betide any fireman who failed to complete these tasks, come rain or shine. Other duties included the stoking up of the fire in the boiler-house, which heated the hot water system, and putting the kettle on for the early morning tea.

Many practical jokes were tried out on newly spawned attendants, especially when enduring their first night shifts. One such trick was to attach pieces of used chewing gum on to a billiard ball and stick it to the top of the stairs (where Brutus had gone) at the rear of the Control Room. Once the adhesiveness wore off (around 2am) the ball would plop from step to step, picking up its speed and intensity of noise within the close confines of the lino equipped stairs before crashing to a halt against a wall. When I was subjected to this terrifying experience I almost had to have a change of underwear.

Other rotten tricks included tormentors who piddled on the boiler-house fire, which was almost directly underneath the Control Room, thereby creating a foul smell around the immediate vicinity, which pervaded through the ever open Control Room toilet window, much to the discomfort of the occupier. Sometimes the fire was deliberately

quenched by a person or persons unknown. The unfortunate shift fireman, upon checking the fire, would have to rake the wet ashes out, whilst listening for the 'Red Phone', restart the fire and pray to God, Allah or Odin that the water would be hot enough by 7am. Another trick was to hide a kipper between the most inaccessible hot water pipes in the boiler-house.

There were a host of amusing incidents connected with Control Rooms. One great joker, already mentioned, 'Pierre Louise', once knocked on the hatch door and in a disguised voice demanded something in an urgent manner. Thinking it was a running call from a member of the public, I rushed to the door and flung open the hatch. I was confronted by 'Pierre', who leered at me and grinned from ear to ear. Without wishing to insult him, when he grinned like that, he looked like a cross between a Cheshire cat and one of the members of the 'Banana Bunch', an American pop group of the sixties and seventies who dressed in furry animal skins.

He produced a box of matches and in a haughty BBC type voice said, ''My man. As a member of the public, I would like some fire prevention advice as to how to look after my matches safely.'' Was he in for a fall!!! Out of sight of 'Pierre', on his hands and knees inspecting the lino, was 'Glarer', who reared up and launched himself at him, snarling, ''If you don't get back to work at once the only advice you will be seeking will be from the Labour Exchange.'' I have never seen a face change so dramatically, nor a fifteen stone frame move so quickly, as 'Pierre' fled from the scene.

One item of equipment which was located in the Control Room was a crude, two-way Bakelite speaker. This was linked directly to the Chief's office. So long as you were aware of its existence and had a keen pair of ears to hear the soft click as it was switched on, you were on solid ground. The Chief often turned it on in the hope that you were running he and his fellow officers down, so that you could be hauled in front of him to explain your adverse comments.

One of my comrades, 'Pat', hadn't long been at LITTLE SNOBSBURY, following a transfer, and no-one had informed him of this device. He was sitting on his own in the Control Room, enjoying the peace and quiet, when a voice out of the blue said, ''What's the time?'' 'Pat' was amazed as to where this 'voice' was coming from and when there was a repeat request he began to think the Good Lord was trying to contact him. A third and louder request was heard. By now 'Pat' was beginning to panic, imagining all sorts of things. When the question was asked even louder, for the fourth time, by what was now an extremely agitated Chief Officer, 'Pat' realised where the voice was coming from. Instead of simply reading the time out he leaned as close to the apparatus as was possible and informed the Chief of the same, to which the reply was, ''There's no need to shout.''

'Pat' had the awful experience of dialling the 'wrong number' in the early hours of the morning after he had turned the machines out to an emergency. He thought he was ringing the duty Station Officer to report the call. A man's sleepy voice answered and 'Pat' said, "Fire station here sir. I have just turned the two pumping appliances out to a fire at . . . ," giving the address. The gruff voice on the other end of the line said, "What the f*!*!*g hell are you telling me for? I am not the slightest bit interested. Why don't you try ringing the right number?" The phone then went dead as the angry recipient slammed the receiver down, leaving a somewhat embarrassed 'Pat' to reflect the error of his ways.

As previously mentioned, smoking in the Control Room wasn't allowed, only during certain hours. Whenever the Chief was leaving the station he would invariably tap on the window of the Control Room and you had to lip-read his remarks. Normally he was going to the village or the town, which really meant he was going to the town or the city. He would then get into his 1950's American style limousine and drive off.

'Foghorn-Leghorn' was in the Control Room one day shift, sucking on an empty pipe. The Chief went through his usual routine, which was acknowledged by 'Foghorn'. As he was about to climb into his car the Chief suddenly realised what 'Foghorn' had in his mouth. He returned to the Control Room window and beckoned him to open it. He then demanded to know why 'Foghorn' was smoking in the Control Room, to which he was informed that not only was his pipe unlit, but there was no tobacco in it. The Chief appeared satisfied and once again returned to his car. He stopped in his tracks and stood there thinking. To complete this saga, he again returned to the window, which 'Foghorn' once again had to open. This time the Chief remarked to 'Foghorn', "I know your pipe is not lit and you know it is not lit, but the members of the public (as if they cared) do not," and he ordered 'Foghorn' to put it in a drawer, out of sight.

All in all, apart from the amusing incidents, the Control Room was a dreadful place to waste your life away. The only real pleasure you had was when you put the 'bells' on for a 'shout', especially if it meant disturbing the sleeping crews and the duty Officer in the early hours on a bitterly cold winter's day.

Several months prior to the take-over, the senior officers made some changes in an effort to please, what was going to be their new 'masters' from the adjacent 'Big City Brigade'. Although these changes did help to improve the lot of their existing firemen, the changes were obviously designed and instigated to impress the forthcoming powers to be and so enhance the chances of future promotions for certain officers. One of the improvements was the employment of civilian Control Room attendants.

A Monday day shift arrived and upon walking into the Control Room to take up my duties I noticed a civilian seated next to the telephone operator, but at first thought nothing of it. I duly performed my initial tasks and filled in the log book with the names of the oncoming personnel and the appliances they had been designated to ride. Once these tasks were completed I then checked the duty roll board. At the foot of the board, on a name tally in bold lettering, were the initials CATTAHOLIC. I commented to the switchboard man, "What on earth is a CAT-TAHOLIC?" thinking it to be some new devilish scheme which had been hatched from 'next door', designed once more to catch us out. The reply came back, "CATTAHOLIC means simply, Control Room Attendant A.Holic." I couldn't believe it, at long last we were getting rid of this dreadful job.

CATTAHOLIC

Within a matter of weeks, three or four of these erstwhile characters had been taken on and fully trained, leaving us only to fill in as reliefs and to cover for holidays and sickness. Unfortunately one of these gents didn't last too long. During the early hours of one particular morning, an A.F.A. showed 'FIRE' momentarily and then cleared. Standing Orders were explicit and no matter how briefly an A.F.A. flashed for, the normal turn-out procedure had to be strictly adhered to. Instead of turning us out into the darkness he contacted the affected premise and had an assurance from the security guard that all was well.

Instead of letting 'sleeping dogs lie' this foolish attendant recorded all the details of this incident into the log book, which was as good as cutting his own throat. A few minutes before he was due to go off duty the log book was examined by a Station Officer, who couldn't believe his eyes. He was instantly escorted upstairs to see the Chief and explain his actions, to which he stated, "It was a cold night sir and it seemed a shame to disturb the men." The Chief's comments are unknown, but the unfortunate attendant was compelled to resign immediately.

Shortly after these attendants were recruited and trained, the new Control Room was commissioned and the old one pensioned off. Its replacement was spacious, modern and complete with a new, up-to-date exchange telephone system. Even after the take-over it continued for a while as a fully fledged Control Room, until it was demoted to the status of a Sub-Control, no longer taking '999' calls, but still being used to turn out men and appliances to emergencies upon the instructions from the new Central Fire Control. Eventually it was relegated to a run of the mill Watchroom, no longer being involved directly in emergency duties, apart from the odd running call. Once this happened, all the existing Control Room staff were transferred to the new Central Fire Control and fresh Watchroom men were recruited.

Before the latter situations arose we were still required to do the odd shifts due to the shortage of full-time attendants and relief duties. Before we were taken over by MAMMOTH COUNTY, like many other occasions in the past, a 'super-salesman' had called into LITTLE SNOBSBURY

H.Q. and persuaded the Chief to purchase the latest, guaranteed, twenty-four hour, electric digital clock, for use in the new Control Room. It not only recorded the time, but also the day, date and month. Being self correcting, it could also adjust itself in an instant if there were only thirty days etc., in any particular month.

During the hustle and bustle of the day shifts, and with heavy traffic to contend with outside the Control Room, I never noticed the noises this clock made. It was only in the early hours of the morning, when all was quiet, that I first noticed its strange behaviour. One could get used to the ticking of a clock, but *this* was something different.

When each minute went by a new time would appear, as if by magic, like an up and over door being closed. It would be silent for about fifteen seconds and would then commence whirring like a stalled electric toy locomotive. For the remaining forty-five seconds the whirring would build up into a crescendo, before sighing to a halt once a further minute had passed by and then the whole process would be repeated. If the Gestapo had been able to obtain such a device during the last war they would have been able to extract confessions much sooner.

When midnight arrived it was a sight to behold. The clock strained and whirred, then all at once everything changed together — time, day, date and month cards flipped over, in such a mysterious manner, it would have made Paul Daniels a proud man. Although midnight was shown as 0000 hours, official dictat stated that it didn't exist. If a call came through at midnight it had to be recorded as either 2359 or 0001 hours — how ridiculous.

81

Like one of the earlier Control Room men, this innovation of modern day technology didn't last long either. It broke down in a rather spectacular manner. Its demise occurred during a change of month, February I think, when it couldn't cope with the leap from the 28th to the 1st. All the individual times and dates etc., were jammed into an indescribable mess. Frantic efforts were made to trace the salesman and his Company, but to avail. It lay in bits on a shelf after attempts were made to repair it, all of which failed, and eventually, like so many other saleman's products, it was dumped unceremoniously in a dustbin.

For years, efforts had been made to prevent the men from making free phone calls, but with little success. There was a clipboard kept in the Control Room and every call which was made privately had to be recorded by the individuals who made the calls and these were paid for at the end of each month. The total sum collected was probably about one tenth of the true amount.

When the new Control Room was opened, the officers thought they had solved this problem by installing a tape recorder which automatically recorded all incoming and outgoing telephone calls over a set twenty-four hour period. The time of every call also had to be recorded on the tape. At the end of the twenty-four hour period, usually at 9 am, it was taken away and listened to by the duty officer, being replaced by a clean tape.

The officers must have thought they had succeeded in stamping out the illicit practice of un-recorded private telephone calls, as they rarely, if ever, came across one. It was obvious to them that this modern day deterrent had put the fear of God into the men, who after all were not as intelligent as them. What hadn't occurred to the officers was that we simply removed the tape when wishing to make our own calls. Far from stamping out this menace it was costing the Brigade more than ever before, and *they* were supposed to be the intelligent ones!!!

One of the funniest events that happened in the new Control Room involved this tape recorder. The telephone rang at about 4 am and was duly answered by the duty attendant, who said, "Fire Brigade." Out of the blue from the other end of the line came a torrent of abuse. — "OF COURSE IT'S THE F*!*!*G FIRE BRIGADE, I WOULDN'T BE F*!*!*G RINGING YOU IF I DIDN'T F*!*!*G WELL KNOW. YOU BASTARDS, YOU W*NK*RS, LYING ASLEEP IN BED WHILE I AM OUT IN THE F*!*!*G COLD. F*!K THE LOT OF YOU." At that he replaced the receiver, leaving the attendant speechless.

Later the same day the contents of this obscene phone call had to be typed out for a possible report for the police. There was only one typist available in headquarters, a middle-aged, rather sheltered lady. One can imagine how embarrassed she must have felt. I hope she didn't have to enquire as to how some of the explicit words were spelt, if so one can imagine the reply — "Well.....Errmmm.....Errmmm.....I'm not too sure.....I will consult so and so.....Perhaps he can help you," etc. Whoever it was that rang up, and why he did so, always remained a mystery.

One of the Control Room fellows, 'George', was of Far Eastern origin, from Burma, and being only slight of build he used to cat-nap on the console on nights. He once asked the Officer in Charge of the day shift if he could bring his 'fiddle' wagon, which he used for his side-line job, into the fire station for the next night shift, which was the following day, for which permission was duly granted. The O.I.C. must have been under the impression that the 'fiddle' wagon was a small van of some description.

Shortly before the night shift commenced, a huge fully laden forty foot articulated lorry trundled into the yard and came to a stand with a hiss of air brakes. The oncoming Officer in Charge gawped in amazement as a diminutive man leapt from his giant cab. At first it was thought by the O.I.C. that the driver had lost his way and was stopping to ask for directions, then he realised it was the Burmese Control Room operator. He approached 'George' and stated, ''You cannot leave that contraption here overnight,'' to which the reply was, ''Of course I can, you gave me permission yesterday,'' and he waltzed past him and disappeared within the confines of the station. The O.I.C. must have spent many a nervous hour during this particular shift in dread of what might have happened if a senior officer had popped in and noticed this juggernaut on the premises.

This same character was an avid fan of animals and kept a mini-zoo at his house — dogs, cats and parrots etc. In addition, his wife ran a pet shop and from time to time he used to 'borrow' a small chimpanzee and take it for walks. During one of the 'walks' the chimp was stolen and 'George' went to the local police station to report its theft. When asked by the duty police officer where he had last seen his chimpanzee, 'George' replied, ''In a pram outside Sainsbury's.'' I know not if it was ever recovered.

When Control Rooms on stations were rendered obsolete and the operators moved on, less qualified men were employed to do the more mundane tasks associated with Watchroom duties. One such employee was Irish, with a broad accent to match. He informed us that his previous job had been as a 'Tail-Gunner' on a bread van in Belfast. There were no flies on him, however, for one pay day a couple of extra noughts had been added on by mistake. His cheque was cashed in before the 'error' was discovered and he was never seen again.

Another man used to spend most of the time on day shifts organising his market trading business and Sunday football league matches, with Fire Brigade matters being of secondary importance. Yet another fellow, a retired Control Room operator, weighed about seven stone and constantly looked at death's door. We all expected to find him lying dead on the Watchroom floor during the night shifts.

One final Watchroom attendant who is worthy of a mention, would never have, by his own admission, won any beauty contests, and without being cruel, for he was a great bloke, graced any oil paintings either. He wore treble lensed glasses which were perched on top of the biggest 'hooter' I have ever seen, which reminded me of the 'Potato Men' I used to play with as a child. In addition, his nose, face and neck were a mass of pock-marks and it was rumoured that he used to breathe through the back of his neck.

For a while he wined and dined one of the local ladies, who was much older than him, possibly in the hope that when she snuffed it she would leave him lots of her money. In fact the boot was on the other foot and it was she who appeared to be taking him for a ride. His pay from the Fire Service wouldn't have been very good and once she had 'milked' him dry she disappeared from the scene.

During the early part of one night shift, he was the subject of a 'set-up' by the duty Watch. It commenced once darkness had fallen. One of the firemen donned his motor cycle gear, including a blacked-out crash helmet and went outside the station. He then knocked on the external sliding window, which was there for public use. 'The Potato Man' opened the window and the 'stranger' in the helmet said gruffly, in a disguised voice, "Where's such and such road?" The attendant went to the opposite side of the Watchroom to consult the map. Within seconds the disguised fireman shouted, "F*!*!*G HURRY UP MATE, I HAVEN'T GOT ALL F*!*!*G DAY," to which 'The Potato Man' said, "There's no need to be offensive." This was followed by further abuse from the man at the window.

Just then (by pre-arrangement) a Leading Fireman appeared at the internal Watchroom door and he asked 'The Potato Man' what was going on. "It's the bloke at the window, he is getting stroppy." "Leave him to me," said the junior officer, and he marched outside. A harmless punch was thrown at the Leading Fireman and he fell to the ground in mock agony. Again (by pure coincidence) a second Leading Fireman appeared at the Watchroom door and he was confronted by the extremely agitated attendant. Obtaining brief details off the nigh on hysterical 'Potato Man', the second junior officer remarked, "I'll sort this out." He too was subjected to a fake punch and fell to the ground clutching his face.

Enough was enough as far as 'The Potato Man' was concerned and he banged the alarm bells on to attract the remainder of the Watch. By the time 'help' arrived, the 'violent' motor cyclist had done a 'runner' from the scene of his 'crimes'. Whilst the so called 'victims' of the unprovoked attacks were being 'comforted', the wretched attendant was all for calling the police. Once hearing this remark the two 'attacked' Leading Firemen suddenly made miraculous recoveries and although they both agreed with all and sundry that the 'motor cyclist' was some kind of 'nutter', there was little point in involving the police as the chances of him being caught were negligible.

'The Potato Man' was persuaded to leave his post and go to the bar for a drink, to help soothe his shattered nerves, with an appropriate relief taking his place in the Watchroom. He was half-way through his pint and in the midst of reciting the drama to a 'keen' audience, when out of the corner of his eye he noticed the 'motor cyclist', complete with helmet, peeping round one of the columns in the recreation room.

Fearing more violence, he half-choked on his pint and all but threw the remainder over the barman, as he spluttered and pointed with shaking fingers, "THAT'S HIM, THAT'S HIM, THAT'S THE BASTARD, GRAB HIM." The 'offending' fireman stepped fully into the room and revealed his identity — the 'Potato Man' had been well and truly had.

Flushing with embarrassment 'The Potato Man' tried to ignore the laughter directed at him by staring into his pint and muttering, "You rotten bastards."

Although the civilian Control and Watchroom men were not with us for long, they certainly added a new dimension to our lives and today they are sadly all but extinct as a breed.

Cooking and Food

At LITTLE SNOBSBURY, from when I first joined and for many years thereafter, there were no civilian cooks and all of the meals had to be prepared on each Watch by a rostered fireman/cook and his assistant. Amongst their duties, these men had to wait on the officers and the administration clerk at break and meal times during the day, from Monday to Friday. It was a Dickensian practice, loathed by all concerned. The officers even had the nerve to provide 'waiters' jackets, as if they were being served in a top hotel.

If only they had known some of the antics the 'kitchen' men used to get up to before they received their refreshments, they would never have consumed the same. Knives, forks and spoons used to be licked, as did items of food. On his way from the kitchen to the offices, 'Pierre' would hold a potato or a piece of meat in his mouth until he reached his destination, releasing it onto the plate prior to knocking on the door. If there was plenty of food on the plate he was not averse to eating some of it before he delivered the same. Yet another foul deed was to take a mouthful of tea and spit it back into the cup — ughh. As 'Pierre' used to say, "I didn't want to spill any tea before I served them."

He became so cheesed off one day he mentioned to the admin. clerk what was happening to their food and drink before the same arrived in their offices. He did more good for the firemen's cause in one statement than the Fire Brigades Union could have done in months of haggling. Within a matter of hours the order came down from on high for the men to cease waiting on the officers.

87

Eventually civilian cooks were employed, all female, and these had to turn a 'deaf' ear to the bad language which is always present in a male dominated job. From time to time agency cooks, sometimes male, filled in for holidays and sickness etc.

The first cook we had confessed she hadn't worked on a fire station before and she was a little dubious about cooking and working in an environment which had no other females. She once asked a fireman, in all innocence, if there were any 'funny' men amongst the ranks. This of course led her right into a 'set-up'.

Excusing himself on the pretext of having an urgent task to fulfil, he rushed off before he could answer her question. Having primed the fellow members of his Watch, he returned to the kitchen when all were assembled for their tea and toast. As they were sitting down he called her over and said, "In answer to your question, before I had to disappear, yes, there are one or two 'chaps' who are a trifle effeminate." "How will I know which ones they are?" she asked quizzically. "When they commence drinking their tea, have a peep round the door into the mess. The ones who are 'queer' will have their little fingers pointing in the air."

At that he left her on her own and joined his colleagues. A few seconds later she peeped into the room and to her horror, every fireman, including the one who had 'advised' her, had their little fingers curled in the air as they drank. She would have probably resigned on the spot if the men hadn't burst into laughter. It was a baptism she never forgot.

Individual cooks came and went and towards the end of LITTLE SNOBSBURY Fire Brigade the hierarchy went mad and employed two cooks in tandem. These were the equivalent in size to 'Laurel and Hardy'.

They both had a liking for potted plants and the collection of the same gradually turned into a fanatical obsession. Eventually we could hardly move in the mess, there were so many of them. Despite repeated requests to cut their numbers, 'Laurel and Hardy' steadfastly refused. Then one day they all 'mysteriously' died, something to do with being fed bleach by a person or persons unknown. The hint was taken and they were never replaced.

'Laurel and Hardy' were still employed at LITTLE SNOBSBURY Fire Station when MAMMOTH COUNTY came into being and one particular Sub Officer who was drafted there took an instant dislike to them. Eventually his dislike culminated in him going to see the Divisional Commander, giving him an ultimatum. "Either the two cooks go, or I do." He did — he was transferred to another station.

One former LITTLE SNOBSBURY Leading Fireman once had a large 'Mr. Kipling' type of cake stolen from his locker and I discovered him, fuming, writing a note about the same. It read, 'Will the th*ei*ving bastard

who stole my cake own up, if he has the guts to'. I waited until he finished his masterpiece and pointed out he had spelt thieving wrong. He almost went berserk. "Anyway," I continued, "He probably won't be able to own up at the moment, not with his stomach filled with your cake." I hurriedly departed before he decided to hit me.

I tried to think up a method of placing an identical cake, with one mouthful removed, into 'Animal's' locker, making sure that the aggrieved Leading Fireman would get to know about it, but the idea didn't come to fruition. The junior officer never discovered who the thief was. A perfect case of someone 'having *his* cake and eating it'.

'Pierre' rarely ate a Sunday lunch which was cooked by the rostered fireman, because he reckoned they were too puny. Instead, his wife used to bring him his 'Meal on Wheels', a gigantic plate of food, including several pounds of spuds, all of which were consumed with great relish. He was the equivalent of a giant piranha fish when it came to voraciously wolfing his food down. He was so fast, his pudding was gone and he was off for a snooze long before the remainder of us had eaten the main course.

He once gobbled his food down so quickly, the plate was still red hot and he had to take it for washing with the aid of a tea cloth. When asked for a challenger to an 'eat your food the quickest' competition, by someone from another Watch, I asked him if their 'champion' had to take his empty plate back with a towel. "Forget it," was the reply.

Round the bar in the evening, it was nothing for 'Pierre' to consume several packets of crisps, nuts and chocolate bars, and if anyone couldn't finish their sandwiches etc., he would polish them off, stating, "It's a shame to waste them." I once had a private bet with 'The Old Recruit' that 'Pierre' could make a giant size Mars bar disappear within four bites. His bet was five bites. He would have been correct if I hadn't shoved the remainder down his throat, after the third bite, almost choking him in the process.

In the days of LITTLE SNOBSBURY, breakfast was cooked by two rostered firemen, with no-one else allowed in the mess until 8am, or woe betide them. As a result, the eggs, anything up to sixteen or more, were not placed in the fryer until about five minutes before breakfast, otherwise they would have been rock hard.

Quite often the eggs wouldn't be finished on time and the remaining hungry firemen would pound the kitchen table top impatiently. 'Pierre' used to say, "Hurry up my man, but don't forget I cannot stand runny eggs — I hate eggs like bogey's." If there were just the right amount to go round and more than two were broken (the first two had to go to the cooks) the recipients of the broken ones would each give the cooks a mouthful of abuse, usually ending in, "We will get our own back next time we are in the kitchen on breakfasts, you pair of w*nk*rs."

I once cooked myself a splendid fry-up, much to the envy of some firemen who were present in the mess, with their sandwiches. Such was the aroma, some of the lads begged me to let them have a little piece of bacon or a fried potato, but I refused point blank. I took my plate, a pyrex glass one, from beneath the grill and placed it on the cooker, not realising that the ring I had placed it on was faulty and it was hot — very hot. I piled my succulent fry-up onto it and made for a plastic covered table, dribbling in hungry anticipation.

Placing it on the table, it immediately exploded, due to the difference in temperature, much to the amusement of my colleagues. The food jumped an inch or more into the air and landed in a pile of glass, totally ruined. There were thousands of chunks of glass all over the mess, which took ages to clear up. There were smirks all round me, smirks that said, 'Don't you dare ask any of us for a sandwich, for there will only be one answer, — 'BOLLOCKS'.

Sub-O 'Squirrel' used to give explicit instructions as to how his boiled eggs should be cooked. "No less and no more than five minutes, or you are for the high jump." When served, he would ask, "How long have they been boiled for?" — "Five minutes Sub-O." — "Excellent," would come the the reply, although more often than not they had been on the boil for over thirty minutes, but he never knew the difference.

'Squirrel' was similar to 'Pierre' with his eating habits, though not in the same league. He thought he was popular, but in reality he was despised, basically because he was an idiot. I was told, when I first joined that 'Squirrel' had been promoted immediately prior to the station at LITTLE SNOBSBURY becoming an independent Brigade. His former masters in the County Brigade saw this as an ideal opportunity of shedding this burden from their books. In this they totally succeeded!!!

He often used to get his words mixed up and came out with things like "Pacific" (Specific) and "Reconnanance" instead of "Reconnaissance". As previously mentioned, he was a 'hungry' man, to the point of being a glutton, for he was almost as round as he was 'short', eating anything in sight. Bones would be retrieved from dustbins and left on a plate in the kitchen for him to devour. Men would offer him sweets, "Yum-Yum-Yum, these are my favourites," not knowing they had been deliberately placed in the toilet trough, retrieved and wrapped up again. Others would splice large pieces of cake with mustard or laxatives. All would be devoured in 'Billy Bunter' fashion and he never once noticed they had been 'fixed'. Far from poisoning him, which was the intention, 'Squirrel' used to thrive and rarely went sick.

Walking past the mess one day there was a strong smell of burning wood. I poked my head round the door and there was my 'Gaffer', Roger, chatting idly to one of the cooks, with his arms folded. Behind them was a plume of smoke, which neither had noticed. I said, "There is something burning behind you." Roger casually glanced round and remarked, "It's only the breadboard." He picked it up off a glowing ring, which had left a deep burn mark in the board, and threw it into a water filled sink, where it sizzled and steamed for a while. He then laughed and said, "And I am the Station Officer," needing no further comment.

'Baz', the former sailor, was a close friend of 'The Guardsman' and it was for that reason alone he decided to throw a firework (a banger) into the latter's dinner, as he knew there was no way that 'The Guardsman' would blame him. Apart from leaping in the air with fright, 'The Guardsman's' dinner flew in all directions. Just like the firework, he too exploded and sure enough all and sundry were blamed for the 'misdeed', with the exception of his 'Pal'.

At one of the stations in the Division where I served, one of the cooks used to fry the eggs almost an hour before they were due to be consumed and as a result they were like rubber. This was in stark contrast to one of the lads from the same station, who, when on breakfast duty, used to place rashers of bacon under the grill, count to ten, turn them over, count to another ten and place them, almost raw, onto the plates in the oven.

I will finish this chapter with the story of the 'Night Feast' at the former LITTLE SNOBSBURY Fire Station, which almost had disastrous results on the night in question. Being a lover of English food, I hate the thought of 'foreign dishes', let alone having to eat one. All of my Watch, with the exception of myself and 'Foghorn-Leghorn', who also disliked 'foreign' food, got stuck into a massive 'Chilli'. Much to the amusement of 'Foghorn' I poured scorn on the 'foreign food lovers' saying, ''I hope it poisons the lot of you. Eating this sort of crap only encourages the foreigners to stay here.'' All I got for my pains was a round of, ''Why don't you f*!k off.''

The 'poison' bit became extremely close to the truth. Because the beans hadn't been prepared in the correct manner, all but one of the 'restauranteurs', which included an off duty fireman from another Watch, became violently ill during the course of the night. The exception was the Station Officer, a recent appointment, who had a cast-iron stomach.

All night long, 'Foghorn' and I heard firemen moaning and groaning, leaping out of bed and toilet doors being slammed, as they spoke to 'Hewi' or emptied their bowels. We half expected to find them dead or dying the following morning, for which the three surviving members of the Watch would have been prime suspects. Even the visiting fireman had been up for most of the night, as he confessed later. It served them right as far as we were concerned. It certainly knocked the 'home-made' foreign food 'extravaganza' feasts for six, for a while.

94

Deliberate Set-ups

'Deliberate Set-Ups' are very much part and parcel of the Fire Service. Sometimes they took weeks to arrange, but others were done on the spur of the moment. Some of the more specialised 'Set-Ups' are included under other chapter headings.

Some of the 'Set-Ups' were associated with dual-drive station vans. After partaking in a five-a-side football match at one of the stations we piled into the van we were using which was parked facing a wall on a downward slope. The 'Savage' Sub-O was in the driving seat and I was seated in the passenger side. Knowing he had a short fuse I pressed down hard on the dual-drive brake. No matter how hard he revved the engine the van wouldn't move for obvious reasons.

The other members of the team had cottoned on to what was happening and did little to alleviate the 'Savage' one's health and temper by goading him with comments similar to, "Are you sure you have a driving licence?" In a rage he kept slamming the gears in all directions convinced the reverse gear was up the creek. "WHAT'S THE MATTER WITH THE F*!*!*G THING?" he bellowed. Before he blew a fuse I released the footbrake and we shot backwards. He then realised what had been going on by the smirk on my face and not for the first time I was subjected to a torrent of abuse.

One 'Set-Up' associated with fire engines could only be done when we still had appliances with manual gearboxes. Most drivers, including myself, used to make a hash of the gear changes from time to time and each 'crunch' was ridiculed by the other crew members whenever it happened.

To compound the aggravation some crew members used to position one of their feet so when the driver attempted to change gear (pushing the lever away and to the rear) the foot would halt its progress just as the cogs engaged. Having lost the mechanical impetus of the 'double-de-clutch' there would be loud grating noises from the gearbox and much laughter from the men in the rear.

One of 'Pierre's' favourite 'Set-Ups' was to approach one of his colleagues who was leaning out of an upstairs dormitory window and if a senior officer happened to be passing by on the yard below, he would then dip out of sight and jam the poor unfortunate against a wall by the window and shout at the top of his voice, "OI, YOU BIG-HEAD — YES YOU — YOU DOWN THERE." The Chief Officer or whoever happened to be passing would whip round and glare at 'Pierre's' victim who could do little but protest his innocence.

Whilst out with a fire engine on catering duties the appliance was parked near to some shops where the catering man had gone. In charge of the machine was 'Eli Wallach' who was seated in the O.I.C.'s seat. Immediately behind 'Eli' was 'Pierre'. Near to them was an articulated lorry which had its cab tilted so that the driver could attend to a problem associated with the engine.

The driver spotted the fault, a near empty radiator and disappeared into one of the shops. He emerged with a large jug of water, but when he returned to his wagon he was unable to get the jug between the cab and the trailer as there wasn't enough room. The driver had little alternative but to try and throw the contents into the radiator from several inches away, most of the same splashing onto the ground.

'Pierre' observed 'Eli's' close interest with the by now more than frustrated driver who was rapidly losing his temper. 'Pierre' unwound his window and in a more than loud fashion went, "HA, HA, HA, HA, HA," before rapidly ducking out of sight. The angry driver swivelled round to find out where this derision was coming from and laid his eyes on 'Eli' whom he assumed was the person tormenting him. He more than glared at 'Eli' who turned purple with embarrassment. He in turn whipped round to 'Pierre' and shouted, "YOU BASTARD, YOU ROTTEN BASTARD. I'VE GOT THE BLAME FOR THAT." 'Pierre' simply laughed at him.

Station Officer 'Alf', who had passed the comment earlier in the book, "Take it easy driver, it's only a council house," was a sucker for 'Set-Up' situations. 'Alf' used to leave his brolly in the office and whilst he was off the station one wag emptied the contents of a hole puncher into it. The next time he used it (hopefully in public) he would have been showered in confetti.

He took part in a Brigade video, but didn't realise his men kept altering the inner lining of his helmet and tightening the straps. One minute his helmet was positioned tightly on top of his head and the next it all but covered the same!!!

There were a host of small 'Set-Ups', one being when a condom was placed on the tail-pipe of a fireman's vehicle, but the plan back-fired. Instead of there being just a bang, after the explosion, half of the exhaust system fell off. Needless to say the 'victim' was unimpressed by this prank.

Prior to going off duty we used to hover as near as possible to the appliance bay. Once dismissed, a dozen or so blokes would rush through a space designed for two in an effort to be the first off the premises. Some would be held up by others hurling their caps onto the tops of fire engines or fire kit would be hidden. 'Pat' always seemed to be the first off the starting grid and no matter how slyly we tried he always spotted the person attempting to hide his kit. We got him one day when he failed to notice a number of heavy lead weights being slipped into his fireboots. He rushed out as usual, grabbed the boots, but was unable to lift them and by the time he had removed the weights he was the last out of the engine house.

Until purpose built underground water tanks were installed at LITTLE SNOBSBURY we had to make do with a relatively small galvanised metal tank (above ground) for open water pumping drills, known affectionately as 'The Bosh', situated in the drill yard.

Prior to going off duty one evening a bunch of lads grabbed L.Fm. 'Skin' and held him, squealing, above 'The Bosh'. 'Skin' shouted, "IF YOU DROP ME INTO THE WATER YOU WILL ALL BE ON A CHARGE." This casts doubts amongst the men involved as to the wisdom of their actions and they backed off.

One of the participants (inevitably) was 'Pierre' and as the men withdrew 'Skin' knocked 'Pierre's' cap into the water. Instead of using his brains (assuming he had any!) and waiting until the area was clear before retrieving his cap. 'Pierre' made the mistake of bending over 'The Bosh' with the invevitable result after a 'gentle push' from one of his colleagues.

'SPLASH' he went, head-first into the tank. He floundered around like a stranded whale before clambering out with a glare which would have melted the Polar Regions. His reefer was dripping wet and he chased men all over the yard before cornering 'White Strength' and giving him a 'Bear-Hug' — scant revenge.

Even the dormitory wasn't sacrosanct. The most common 'Set-Up' was the making of 'French Beds'. Firemen would climb into bed, usually in darkness, only to find the sheets ended half-way down. There would be mutterings at first, followed by a torrent of abuse. "Which one of you f*!*!*g bastards fixed my bed? I will get you back." (Sounds of muted sniggers.)

Other stunts included the placing of Scottish thistles and stinging nettles into beds which quite often ended up with near punch-ups if the victim was able to identify the villain or villains. On one occasion during a water fight 'Pierre' rushed out for a bucket of water after receiving a soaking from 'The Stick Insect'. Upon his return he threw the contents over what he wrongly assumed was 'The Stick Insect's' bed, only to discover the latter had switched beds and he had slung the water over his own bed.

One fellow had the habit of falling asleep with his arms cradled beneath his chin. One 'joker' placed a toilet brush between his arms whilst another put an empty metal bucket on his bed. As soon as the victim moved the bucket fell off with a resounding clatter waking him up. He wasn't too pleased when he awoke to discover he was caressing the 'humming' item from the urinals and it was hurled maliciously across the room.

Soon after 'The Gambler' joined 'Pierre's' Watch, 'Pierre' studied how he made up his blankets etc., after the night shifts were all but over and observed where he placed his bedding in the blanket room. The next time 'The Gambler' made his bed and had disappeared from the dormitory, 'Pierre' carefully remade the same and placed it back in the blanket room.

As soon as 'The Gambler' made it obvious he was going to bed 'Pierre' shot into the dormitory and was beneath his sheets before the former arrived. The look on 'The Gambler's' face was a sight to behold. He was of course clear in his own mind he had put his bedding down, but once he discovered his gear was in the blanket room doubt crept into his mind. After a couple of repeat performances 'Pierre' abandoned his actions in case 'The Gambler' was driven insane.

At LITTLE SNOBSBURY we had a device (crude speaker) which was installed to advise us in the event of an impending nuclear attack. It was situated high up on a wall in the appliance bay and every so often we would be notified of a test announcement. All the designated person had to do during the test was to simply listen to the message and the clarity of the same, marking his comments on the test card.

For this test we would select the youngest 'sprog' on the Watch and instruct him to climb up a step-ladder until he was within inches of the

speaker. As this test was usually carried out on the 9.00 am change of shifts on a Monday morning, the bulk of two Watches would be gathered within the near vicinity of the speaker at the appointed hour.

The unsuspecting victim would also have been instructed to mention a 'password' into the speaker after the dialogue from the same had ceased. If the 'sprog' only whispered the password 'Pierre' or the 'Savage' Sub-O would say, "SPEAK UP MAN, THE OPERATOR CANNOT HEAR YOU." Eventually, usually due to the amount of sniggering going on around him, the 'victim' would realise he had been had and descend from the ladder shamefaced before making a rapid exit.

One young recruit was ordered by the 'Savage' Sub-O to put his bedding down on his bed in the dormitory in the middle of the day. The purpose of this exercise was to test the 'sprog's' reaction from the station alarm going off and to time how long it took him to rise from his bed until he reached the appliance he was riding. It was of course a bogus test dreamed up by the 'Savage' one. For his 'plot' he recruited the co-operation of a Staff Sub Officer.

As the youngster waited in excitement for the 'bells' he was 'discovered' by the Staff Officer, who, by 'sheer coincidence' happened to pass through the dormitory. "What the hell do you think you are doing in bed at this time of day?" he asked the shocked recruit. Before he had a chance to explain the Sub-O hauled him out of bed and said, "This is a good way to commence your career. You are coming with me to explain your actions to your Station Officer and you had better have a good answer or it may mean the sack for you."

On the way to the office the 'sprog' tried to explain what was going on to the Staff Sub-O, but he was silenced when the Sub-O said angrily, "I'M NOT INTERESTED IN YOUR EXCUSES."

The 'sprog' was duly marched into the S.O.'s office and he stood there with his heart in his mouth as his 'Gaffer' was informed of the lad's idleness by the Staff Sub-Officer, who somehow managed to keep a straight face. To add to the poor recruit's dilemma, the 'Savage' one hadn't bothered to inform the Station Officer of this 'Set-Up'. It was only after an almighty 'bollocking' was administered to the recruit by the S.O. that the 'Savage' one cracked. He fell about laughing and the 'sprog' was let off the hook.

One of the older firemen was promoted from the ground floor to the rank of Sub Officer within a short space of time. Although he had been a good fireman he was often bamboozled by the vast amount of office work he had to get through after his promotions to a dizzier height. In order to improve his efficiency he took to using the station typewriter to fill in fire reports. One clown on his Watch noticed how laborious his new Sub-O was at using it and at an opportune moment swapped some of the detached letters on the keyboard.

The next time the Sub-O used the typewriter he methodically plodded along not noticing at first that something was amiss. It was only when he checked the first part of his work he noticed something was very wrong. Instead of a particular line reading something similar to, 'Fire caused by . . . . .', some of the vowels had been replaced by q, x and z and read, 'Fzrx cqusxd by . . . . .'

Instead of stopping to think about the problem and checking that the letters on the keyboard matched or didn't match the appropriate lettering on the keys themselves, he produced a screwdriver and commenced dismantling the typewriter in an effort to put the 'cart before the horse'. Fearing the typewriter was going to be reduced to a pile of scrap the perpetrator of the 'Set-Up' owned up before too much damage was caused.

During the afternoon of a day shift 'Eli Wallach', our Sub Officer, who was in charge, fell ill and went home after booking sick. 'Pierre', as the senior Leading Fireman, assumed command and took charge of the first line appliance with myself taking his place as O.I.C. of the Pump. Immediately after he had placed his kit on board I noticed him in the general office, chatting to 'The Old Recruit'. At that particular time the feared 'Tasmanian Devil' was the Divisional Commander and like many others, including myself, 'Pierre' was terrified of him.

Spotting an ideal opportunity to 'gob' the gullible 'Pierre' I rushed to the vacant Station Officer's office and put through a call to the general office. 'Pierre' answered the phone and I snarled at him, in a manner only 'The Tasmanian Devil' could have done, "GET ME SUB OFFICER 'WALLACH' ON THE PHONE." — "Errmmm . . . . Errmmm . . . . He isn't here sir, he has gone home after falling sick." — "WHO'S IN CHARGE THEN?" — "I . . . . I . . . . I . . . . am sir, Leading Fireman 'Pierre'. — "GET INTO MY OFFICE STRAIGHT AWAY." — "Yes sir, yes sir."

I slammed the receiver down and went to watch the results. 'Pierre' ran out of the office and went round and round in circles, fearing the worst from 'upstairs'. I said, "What's the matter?" His panic-stricken reply was. "I've got to go and see the D.C." and he continued running hither and thither. As he was about to disappear through one of the inner doors I pointed out he had no tie on — more panic. He set off once more but I hadn't the heart to let him be confronted by the humourless 'Tasmanian Devil' and informed him it was a joke. He wasn't amused, but had little choice to accept it when 'The Old Recruit' said, "It's different when you are setting others up. There's nothing like a taste of your own medicine." Silence!!

For a while we had a Sub Officer at LITTLE SNOBSBURY who could well have been cloned from 'Desperate Dan' (complete with cow pies) a greedy, arrogant, avaricious and self-opinionated man. Two Leading Firemen, one of them 'The Messenger' decided to teach him a lesson and created a 'Set-Up' by faking a heavy drinking session.

They filled a couple of empty gin bottles with water, placing one on the optic shelf in the station bar and putting the other on one side as a reserve. Prior to the bar opening the other members of the Watch were primed and they proceeded with their plan as soon as the bar opened, making sure 'Desperate Dan' heard they were going to have an off-the-cuff celebration. Every so often he poked his head into the room to observe if anything untoward was going on.

Eventually he joined them, becoming more and more disturbed as their behaviour deteriorated. One of the visitors to the station was another Sub-O and he too had been forewarned of the fake drinking spree. 'Desperate Dan' sidled up to him and whispered, "How would you handle this situation?" His fellow officer said, "I think one of them is celebrating his birthday. Mind you I wouldn't stand for it on my station." This did nothing to ease 'Desperate Dan's' dilemma and for much of the remainder of the evening he watched them guzzle drink after drink of 'neat gin'.

He was still undecided as to what to do when they started on the second bottle. By now they were falling all over the place. Having apparently had enough of the disgraceful goings on he marched off to his office where he was observed by one of the firemen slumped over his desk, near to the phone, head in hands. 'The Messenger' and his mate were given the nod and they made their way, arm in arm, singing and swaying to 'Desperate Dan's' office.

When they arrived the hubbub continued as they slurred at him and fell over items of furniture. "THAT'S ENOUGH," shouted the tormented 'Desperate Dan', "I'M GOING TO REPORT YOU PAIR TO THE DUTY SENIOR OFFICER FOR BEING DRUNK ON DUTY," and reached for the phone. "What do you mean, drunk on duty?" exclaimed 'The Messenger'. "How can we possibly be drunk when we have only consumed two bottles of water?" — "WATER?" — "Yes, water." 'Desperate Dan' then tried to convince not only them, but also himself that he had known all along, but to no avail. "BOLLOCKS," they taunted him, "YOU HADN'T A F*!*!*G CLUE," leaving him foaming at the mouth with humiliation.

'The Corporal' had his name put forward for a Heavy Goods Vehicle course and he made it more than obvious he felt insulted due to the fact that he had obtained a Class One licence during his time in the army and the course he was being sent on was only Class Three. A group of us managed to obtain an official form used by the instructor to make his comments. We really went to town on it and a photocopy found its way via 'official channels' (dumped in a tray in the office) into 'The Corporal's' hands.

Almost all of the 'instructors' comments were of a derogatory nature, culminating in 'Due to the arrogant nature of this pupil, who made it rather plain he shouldn't have been on this course by pointing out he was more qualified than myself, I feel he should never be considered for heavy goods driving in MAMMOTH COUNTY Fire Brigade'.

Whenever he thought he was on firm ground 'The Corporal' employed a half-smile, fully expecting one of us to crack when he thought he was being 'Set-Up'. Convinced it was a 'gob' he half-smiled as he read the report, but doubt began to creep into his mind when we neither took any notice of him, nor laughed at his predicament. To make matters worse, after he commented he was the victim of a 'Set-Up', I remarked, "This is no laughing matter. You have gone over the top this time and upset the driving instructor." It was hours before someone confessed.

A regular visitor to LITTLE SNOBSBURY Fire Station, an outsider, decided to try and get his own back on the antics of 'Eli Wallach' after they had clashed many times round the bar by sending him a spoof letter, which reads as follows:

NATIONAL DISASTER INSURANCE SERVICES LIMITED
Insurance Brokers   Your ref: JAWS
                                                     Our ref. DED/LOSS
To The Sub Officer In Charge,   Date 29/10/82
Red Watch.

Dear Sir,

We have noticed an abnormally high increase in the number of applications for insurance cover in respect of fire risk in the LITTLE SNOBSBURY and surrounding areas for the night of 5th November 1982.

Our suspicions were aroused when it was discovered that the applications included a number of senior fire officers living within the area covered by your station, particularly as under their ALL RISKS policies each has quoted 'Red Watch' as the reason for the increased cover.

Naturally we have no reason to doubt the efficiency of the Fire Brigade or the other Watches at your station, although the lack of publicity in the local press regarding jobs undertaken by your Watch suggests that you only deal with false alarms, the other Watches regularly achieving much notoriety with their heroic deeds.

We would therefore appreciate your comments on the following points which have recently been drawn to our attention.

1) An unconfirmed report that a certain Sub Officer has had to attend Moreton-In-Marsh Training College to brush up his breathing apparatus skills and progress was at a rate necessitating an extension of several weeks to his course. Can you confirm that he can now put a set on the right way up without the need to stand on his head.

2) There have been reports that your men have been unable to locate fires at night unless the incident is well alight. What procedures are laid down to spot buildings not on fire (false alarms) and in particular unlit bonfires after dark.

3) Some of your machines regularly break down or catch fire on route. To facilitate arrangements with the Parks Department could you please provide details of the average distance travelled before an appliance fails so that out of control bonfires can be set up or moved to parks within the radius of the failure zone. For those machines unable to leave the station is it possible to set aside part of your practice yard for the building of bonfires which will get out of control.

4) We understand some of your men are trained in riding bicycles and on occasions have actually overtaken your front line vehicles on the way to incidents. We have access to a number of old Home Guard/air raid stirrup pumps which could be carried with buckets on the handlebars. We would also welcome your suggestions as to how to transport 4,000 gallons of water as this may impair the speed of response by the cycling crews.

5) Regarding Bonfire Night, as incidents often involve trees and hedges

being set alight, may we suggest you post your men amongst the branches at likely incidents to prevent ignition and also to catch wayward rockets. We have observed your foresight in this new area of firefighting whereby the expert can be seen on the job in the hedge.

6) Perhaps a last minute publicity campaign could be undertaken whereby your Fire Prevention experts show the public how to light one side of the bonfire and when that part has burnt down, light the other sides in turn thereby keeping only part of the bonfire going at any one time.

7) The Borough bonfire is to be lit by our insured, The Mayoress, from an 85 foot dias. Should the stairs collapse, can you guarantee that the Watch will be able to push the Hydraulic Platform down to LITTLE SNOBSBURY park to prevent the guy and the Mayoress suffering a similar fate.

8) Our Claims Department welcomed the zealous efforts of your colleagues last year whereby every bonfire in the area had been thoroughly extinguished five minutes before your Benevolent Fund bonfire was due to commence.

Our representative will call shortly to discuss your proposals regarding the above points. May we thank you for your brave efforts on behalf of the community none more so than the writer who has been experiencing considerable difficulty over bonfires for many years.

Yours faithfully,

R. Catesby,

pp G. Fawkes
Fire and Explosives Overseer

'Eli' went potty when he read it as it devalued his so called professionalism and his response was to pour forth a deluge of ''EFFINGS''.

As a finale to the 'Deliberate Set-Ups' chapter I will leave the last act to 'Frankenstein' (what about the honey, mummy?) who will also feature later in the book. All he needed was a couple of bolts through his neck and half the population of LITTLE SNOBSBURY would have fled in panic.

Despite his nickname, 'Frankenstein' was very nervous and shy and when asked questions he would shuffle from foot to foot, tugging anxiously at his clothes — a fidget. Unlike our 'Gaffer' who mumbled, ''Errmmm .... Errmmm .... Errmmm ....,'' whilst thinking of a reply, 'Frankenstein' would mutter, ''Tut .... Urrmmm .... Tut .... Urrmmm''. Going through his repertoire of fidgets, ''Tuts and Urrmmmms,'' after receiving a 'bollocking' in the Station Officer's office, he left the room and slammed the door by accident for which he was hauled back for a second 'bollocking' which all but destroyed him.

He was also extremely gullible and during a spell that 'Eli' was posted to the same Watch as him, 'Eli' decided to subject the poor fellow to

106

a 'fake transfer' order. To all intents and purposes the transfer letter was genuine, with official notepaper and a forged signature of the Divisional Commander to complete the equasion. As the evening parade was dismissed and the crews were about to place their fire kit on the appliances one of the junior officers stepped forward and presented the 'transfer' to 'Frankenstein' in a buff envelope.

Not only had he been 'transferred' to a station he disliked, but it was to a Watch whom he hated. He sat inside his appliance and tore the envelope open. After digesting the contents he disappeared into a melancholic state of trauma. So depressed was he at the thought of this dreadful transfer he didn't bother to check the equipment on his appliance. He just sat there staring at the letter, mumbling, "Tut .... Urrmmm .... Tut .... Not f*!*!*g fair .... Tut .... Urrmmm .... Why me?" and so on.

After the drill session he was noted wandering around the station as

if eking out the last hours of his life prior to being executed. In between his wanderings he would slump into a chair and shake his head in disbelief. From time to time he showed it to 'Eli' and questioned the validity of the Divisional Commander's signature, but to no avail, 'Eli' wasn't to be moved.

During the course of the evening the Divisional Commander put in an appearance at the station and as was passing the bar area 'Frankenstein' tried one last desperate gamble and thrust his 'transfer' in front of him. Fortunately for 'Eli' this particular D.C. had a sense of humour, for he of course knew nothing about it.

"Is this correct?" demanded 'Frankenstein', as he shuffled from foot to foot and fidgeted. The D.C. read it and after noting the forged signature he turned to the unfortunate 'Frankenstein' and said, "That's right lad," and walked away. 'Frankenstein' all but committed suicide that night before some 'kind soul' informed him of the truth.

Discipline Hearings, Dismissals & Resignations

The 'Discipline Code' within the Fire Service is akin to a 'Lawyer's Almanac', with page after page of offences, ranging from being untidy to theft. It doesn't mention 'murder', but presumably this is covered by 'being in custody'. As one Divisional Commander stated to me, after a violent incident on a fire station, in which I described one of the participants as being insane, "I can recommend a charge being brought against him if his hair is too long, but not for insanity."

At LITTLE SNOBSBURY, charges were few and sackings extremely rare. Men usually departed after being 'encouraged' to resign. One such character made his exit after he was caught attempting to 'flog' stolen Christmas trees and another went the same way after it was discovered he was respraying 'nicked' lorry trailers. The latter even had the nerve to 'recruit' other firemen to assist him. Those who did, would comment, "But why are we painting out words like 'Cadbury's' and 'Typhoo'?"

Another 'Bright Herbert', 'Rodney', a sullen-faced, spotty and argumentative young man, went on sick leave for several weeks with a bad back. Although this 'bad back' prevented him from reporting for duty at the fire station, it obviously didn't affect him enough to hinder him from continuing with his part-time job as a window cleaner, for he was spotted by a senior officer, carrying a multitude of ladders on his bicycle. He too was sacked.

One particular fireman, was, to all intents and purposes, the epitome of a 'butter wouldn't melt in your mouth' type. We couldn't believe it when we found out he had been dismissed for attempting to blackmail a 'queer' cafe owner, after being 'trapped' by the police who had been lying in wait for him at the 'drop'.

One stalwart, cheesed off with the Fire Brigade at LITTLE SNOBSBURY, broke into the Chief's office during a night shift and typed out his own reference on the Chief's note-paper and forged his signature. He had applied for a job with a security firm and would have probably succeeded, but his (the Chief Officer's) report about himself was so glowing, that the firm concerned rang the Chief up to confirm if the contents of 'his' reference were correct. "WHAT REFERENCE!" Another fireman down!!!

'Baz' the former sailor and I were all but placed on charges of 'Neglect of Duty' and 'Damage to Brigade Property' by the Chief, after a plastic swivel chair was badly scorched whilst we were on two early morning shifts in the Control room. It had become extremely cold during the night and the only form of heating we had was a large convector heater, which unfortunately only had a short lead.

To enable the plug to reach the socket, the heater had to be placed on a chair and due to a combination of us both dozing off illegally, neither of us noticed the chair slowly cooking. 'Baz' was the first to discover it and after waking me up, he said, "What the f*!*!g hell are we going to do about this?" We thought about ditching it in the nearest canal, but as there were only two such chairs on the station, we thought better of it, for there would have been a 'witch-hunt' for sure, once it was discovered missing. Instead, we decided to face the music.

We were hauled in front of the Chief. Also present in his office was his second in command and 'Exhibit Number One' — the burnt chair. The Chief had a right go at 'Baz'. "You should know better with your years of service," but whilst he was 'bollocking' him, he constantly glared at me. 'Baz' explained about the short lead and of the fact that to use the heater it had to be placed on the chair. Eventually, the Chief appeared to be satisfied, but then the Deputy intervened.

He leapt to his feet and approached the damaged chair, and in his regional 'Northern cum LITTLE SNOBSBURY' accent, said quizzically, "What I cannot understand is why neither of you smelt the fumes?" (We could hardly admit to having been asleep.) He then virtually threw himself face first on to the burnt section of the swivel chair, repeating his first statement, but adding the rider, "I can still smell the fumes now." It was all I could do to restrain myself from laughing at this ludicrous action. We shrugged our shoulders and looked blank, the latter being a natural attribute of firemen.

Both of these officers must have suspected that 'Baz' and I had been asleep, but they were unable to prove it. Realising we were not going to crack, the Chief summed up by saying, "At this moment in time, neither of you are on a charge, but you will be if you do not agree to pay for the cost of having the chair refurbished." We both instantly agreed to pay for the damage and a few days later we had to fork out thirty bob between us. It had been a near miss!!!

The former 'Parachutist' who had been involved in the fight with the 'Sealed Knot' merchant in 'Confrontations', had been in charge of a fat fire at a fish and chip shop, where things had gone badly wrong and water had been turned on the fire, instead of foam. The water-stream caused a 'flash-over' and he and another fireman, Mick 'The Mumbler' were burnt around the head and hands.

Instead of despatching them to hospital as soon as they returned to the station, the Chief had them brought to his office. As they stood there with blood dripping on to his carpet, flesh hanging and melted hair, he insisted on having his penny piece, giving them a right verbal bashing, before they were able to go and dress their injuries. 'The Parachutist' was never the same after this incident and soon afterwards he resigned. It was later rumoured he had 'flipped his lid' and become a recluse in the middle of nowhere.

One recruit who came to us from Training School, 'Arnold Palmer', was an obnoxious little runt who rarely washed and was frequently involved in arguments. For a time he led a charmed life under the 'umbrella' protection of the Fire Service. In those days, if the 'coppers' found out you were a fireman, they generally turned a blind eye to minor misdemeanours, like speeding etc. He even survived prosecution after being caught with no tax disc on his less than roadworthy vehicle and knocking a pedestrian over on a zebra crossing.

His 'Waterloo' came, when he was out 'on the town', in the big city. Although off duty, he was still wearing his blue shirt with his civvy clothes, a move deliberately designed to put the 'frighteners' on people in various clubs and pubs, giving them the false impression he was a police officer.

In the early hours he was involved in a scuffle outside a night club. A passing pedestrian tried to intervene, but 'Arnold' said, "It's okay mate, I can handle this, I'm in the police force." At that his opponent fled from the scene. The pedestrian then said, "Are you indeed? Here is my warrant card (C.I.D.) where is yours?"

Instead of saying, "Look mate, I was in a spot of bother, so I had to give him the impression I was a copper," and leaving it at that, he insisted in continuing with the charade. "I don't have one," he said to the C.I.D. man, "I'm in the Special Branch at so and so town." The C.I.D. man pointed out that there was no Special Branch at so and so town, but 'Arnold' persisted with his story. "THIS IS A SPECIAL, SPECIAL BRANCH." The C.I.D. man wasn't impressed and 'Arnold' was hauled off to a local police station for interrogation and it was several hours before he cracked. His sacking from the Fire Service came soon afterwards.

A classic bundle which resulted in yet another 'departure' from LITTLE
SNOBSBURY, involved the treasurer of the Social Club. At a meeting,
the Chief personally recommended that this particular man be voted into
office, stating, "I have only ever interviewed this man once, but it is
amazing how much you can learn about a person in twenty minutes."
A show of hands and 'bingo' he had the job.

Several months passed by and one or two firemen informed us, "Go
to so and so pub, 'The Treasurer' buys all the drinks." Sure enough he
was. Along with many compatriots, I made frequent visits to 'The
Treasurer's' haunt, but he wouldn't let us buy him drinks in return. A
'jolly good time' was had by all, but what we didn't realise at the time
was that he was buying the drinks out of OUR MONEY.

Nearing the end of his twelve months stint in office, 'The Treasurer'
booked sick and was never seen in the station again — the day of
reckoning had arrived. In those days, the treasurer of the Social Club,
or as one fireman wrote on a cheque, 'The Socially Culb', was the master

of the cheque book, only being accountable for his actions at the Annual General Meeting. Two 'Heavies' from the Brewery arrived at the station and demanded to see him. Upon being informed that 'The Treasurer' was off sick, they went in to consult the Chief.

It later became common knowledge that 'The Treasurer' had 'diverted' the bulk of the Social Club funds for his own needs, one of which was a 'special' sports car, hoping to pay it back before the 'discrepancy' was discovered. When he realised he had 'borrowed' in excess of what he could possibly pay back, he then indulged in the 'conscience' binge of free drinks for the boys. He had managed to fob off the Brewery for weeks, if not months, until he received the 'seven day' letter informing him of the impending visit by the 'Heavies'. The 'sickness' and his 'disappearance' then followed and a little while later his resignation was received.

Many months went by and he then gave himself up. He was charged with theft/misappropriation of funds by the police. Before his court appearance, he even had the neck to stroll past the fire station whilst we were playing volleyball. 'Q.P.R.' spotted him and shouted, "What about our money?" but he never turned a hair. The missing money was repaid by a relative and he only received a suspended sentence, much to the disappointment of some of those involved.

Moving on to MAMMOTH COUNTY, 'The Messenger', whilst conducting drills at an out station, was ordered to standby there for the remainder of the night shift. He refused point blank, blew his top and caused all sorts of mayhem, before returning to his home station in a 'borrowed' van, prior to booking sick and going off duty.

He was later charged with half a dozen offences and ordered to attend a tribunal, overseen by the Chief Officer. Anyone remotely involved, including yours truly, were summoned to the 'Big House' as witnesses. Although we knew he was guilty of all charges, it was a case of doing ones best to help a comrade to fight 'The Establishment'.

The 'Prosecuting Officer', a Fire Service civilian 'top-dog', had unofficially interviewed many of us at our own station, prior to the 'trial'. One Leading Fireman, called to the dock, made a statement, but he was interrupted by the Prosecutor, who said, "Hold on Leading Fireman, you cannot say that," to which the witness rounded on him, retorting, "But last week you said I could." One very shell-shocked Prosecutor and raised eyebrows from the Chief.

It took most of the day to present all the evidence and after much deliberation, all of the charges bar one were proven not guilty, the guilty verdict being on technical grounds. A smiling 'Messenger' shook hands with his Defending Officer, a high powered representative of the Fire Brigades Union. As they turned to leave, the Chief said, "I know you are guilty, and you know you are guilty.........," but before he could finish the Union rep snapped, "But sir, you have just found him not guilty." He then instructed his 'client', "Come on, we are going," and they departed, leaving the Chief to reflect sadly on his 'own goal'. What a farce!!!

During a Union meeting at one of the stations I was based at, the bar had been opened, with the resulting sales of alcohol contributing to a more than rowdy session. An off duty fireman from the day Watch, Fm. 'Dunlop', normally a placid fellow, had possibly downed a few pints more than he should have, for he was particularly volatile in his remarks to the Union hierarchy. Like many such meetings it broke up in disorder and most members dispersed to the bar, continuing an 'unofficial' debate to which remarks were made like, "Why didn't you bring that up at the meeting?"

Fm. 'Dunlop' approached me, still in uniform, and asked if he could borrow the station van. Knowing he was off duty and been drinking, I jokingly remarked, "Of course you can, help yourself, take the Hydraulic Platform if you like," thinking that would be the end of the matter — I couldn't have been more wrong. A few minutes later, a more than breathless fireman ran into the room and shouted, "FM. 'DUNLOP' HAS DRIVEN OFF IN THE STATION VAN." My heart sank and I instantly regretted not adding a rider to my last statement, like, "Of course you bloody well can't."

There was an immediate conflab between ourselves (the junior officers) and the Station Officer. What on earth were we to do? It was around 9pm, dark, and Fm. 'Dunlop' was well over the limit. To make matters worse there was a 'Pea-Souper' of a fog, the first for many a year. At first it was kept quiet, hoping he would return within a short space of time, but he didn't. As time dragged by, the Station Officer decided to act and he contacted the duty officer, who happened to be the Divisional Commander, a good, decent man, one of the rarities. He in turn then contacted an Inspector whom he knew in the police and they both duly arrived at the station.

There were high level discussions and the D.C. wanted a low profile kept, unless Fm. 'Dunlop' was involved in an accident. Police officers were out scouring the streets for him, an all but impossible task in the fog. They had been instructed that under no circumstances were they

to breath test him unless he crashed. Into the early hours we went and there was still no sign of the wayward fireman. The D.C., Station Officer and Inspector were beginning to imagine all sorts of problems. Should the D.C. contact one of his superior officers and inform him of the situation — his mind ran riot as he pondered his predicament.

Eventually he decided to share the responsibility with a Principal Officer, an Assistant Chief Fire Officer. Once contacted, he insisted that when Fm. 'Dunlop' was found, he was to be charged by the police for taking away a vehicle without consent and brought to book in court. No mention was made of Fm. 'Dunlop' having been drinking.

He was eventually spotted by officers in a patrol car, heading towards his house in the van. They waited until he was inside his house before knocking on the door and arresting him. Upon enquiring as to whether or not he had to breathe in the bag after being detained, the Inspector said, "Once you have been arrested for another offence you are deemed to have lost your liberty, so therefore you cannot then be breath tested." A very good ploy, for if the newspapers had got hold of the fact that Fm. 'Dunlop' had been 'blotto', all hell would have broken loose.

The day of the court hearing of the suspended Fm. 'Dunlop' arrived and I was dreading it. Although I had mentioned my 'joke' statement to the D.C. on the night of the incident, he had dismissed it for the joke it was meant to be, but what if Fm. 'Dunlop' turned round in court and stated I had given him permission to use the van. I don't think the Chief would have shared the 'joke'.

We assembled outside the courtroom door. The Inspector — The Divisional Commander — The Station Officer — 'The Caped Crusader' — Leading Fireman 'Rainbow' — Myself — And one fireman, all potential

117

witnesses. The Inspector explained the 'batting order'. "I, as the officer responsible for the arrest will be called in first, followed by the D.C., Station Officer, Sub Officer, the two Leading Firemen, but you, Fireman Bloggs will not, in my opinion, be called in at all. It is an open and shut case of guilty."

First witness — the Divisional Commander — off he went. The Inspector remarked, "I cannot understand why I have not been called in first, there is some mistake. I must be next." In fact he was never called at all, along with 'Dave Rainbow' and myself, but Fm. Bloggs was. The police Inspector was flabbergasted. He was even more taken aback when the Divisional Commander emerged from the court, along with Fm. Bloggs, and stated, "Case dismissed — costs against the police."

Amongst the many questions asked by the 'Beak', was one directed at Fm. Bloggs. He was asked, "Was it possible that someone off another Watch could have given Fm. 'Dunlop' permission to use the van, earlier in the day?" not knowing the latter had been under the influence of drink whilst in charge of the van, "It was possible," answered Fm. Bloggs. — "CASE DISMISSED."

Despite being cleared by the court, the Fire Service hierarchy were not impressed, possibly because of the 'egg on many faces' amongst the senior officers. Fm. 'Dunlop' was duly summoned to the 'Big House' for an interview with the Chief and soon afterwards he handed his resignation in.

Shortly after this debacle, a senior officer was discussing the Discipline Code in our station office. He mentioned the need for a cast-iron case before proceeding with charges. He soon quietened down when I commented, "You mean like the 'open and shut' case concerning Fm. 'Dunlop'. They drove a bus through it."

As a finale to this chapter, there was a fireman who was reputed to have said to a senior officer, "If I *say* your are a w*nk*r you would put me on a charge?" — "Quite correct lad." — "However, if I were to *think* you are a w*nk*r, could you still do the same?" — "I wouldn't think so. I cannot stop what you are *thinking,*" replied the officer. "IN THAT CASE THEN, I *THINK* YOU ARE A W*NK*R SIR."

Drills and Training

Before becoming an operational fireman I had to attend a three month initial course at Training School. It was one hard slog from beginning to end, with a succession of ladder, pumping and other drills, complemented by sessions of boring lectures and each morning we had to march, in tin soldier fashion, around the yard.

The worst aspect of Training School was the almost daily dose of hook ladders. They had little practical use and were designed as a confidence booster. I hated them and far from boosting my confidence the higher I went up the tower with this suicide device the more of a potential 'brown trouser' job it became.

They were constructed of light alloy, were about 13' 6" long, with a dozen or more rounds (rungs) and towards the top, at right angles, was a large notched bill-hook. Commencing from the ground floor they were pitched to one side of the sill of the first floor of the tower, hanging vertically, with only the bill-hook for security.

We had to climb these ladders, with arms and legs in unison, leaning back as far as possible. Once at the top hands had to be placed on the horns of the ladder, with the body still leaning backwards for stability. Once in this position you stepped off the ladder and straddled the sill, side-saddle. Then, using your inside leg for support, you would lean out of the tower, pull the ladder up and pass it through your hands to the next floor.

Out of the window-less space you would climb, praying the ladder would remain stable or it would have been a quick 'Geronimo' and oblivion. These actions were continued until the top floor was reached and the whole process would then be reversed. The nearer you came to the ground, the less your heart pumped in fear.

One fellow recruit, using the ladder for the first time, pitched it to the first floor, climbed half-way up and froze with fear. Despite various threats he refused to budge an inch until the ladder was held secure, both at the top and the bottom. He then managed to conquer his fear and continued on alone, otherwise he would have been out of a job.

As if this method of climbing a tower vertically wasn't bad enough, to add to your terror there was an alternative far worse than the first described. Instead of mounting and dismounting side-saddle, you had to climb over the top of the ladder. Getting into each floor wasn't too bad, but climbing out again was terrifying. You had to mount the sill, turn round and crouch, holding the horns and slowly drop your legs onto the rounds. At times the ladder used to rock from side to side, partially caused by fear and partially due to instability. If you are not a lover of heights, like myself, when the rocking commenced at sixty foot high, with only the ground to stop your fall, it was no joke.

For the final test, three of us had to ascend using this method, all climbing in unison, with three sides of the tower being utilised. When I reached the top, shaking with fright at the thought of the lonely drop to meet my Maker, I turned to one of the other lads and in an effort to boost my morale I asked him how he was getting on. "I'M FFFF*!*!*G TERRIFIED," he replied. After this remark I was more scared going down than I was going up. It was another red-letter day, a few years later, when these loathsome devices at LITTLE SNOBSBURY were converted into roof ladders.

All of the ladder, pumping and rescue drills were divided between four and five man crews, each having a 'pretend' O.I.C. Each crew was numbered, as were the participants. The set drills were straight from the Fire Service Drill Book — "Numbers 1-5 come to attention and fall in, three paces to the rear and facing the fire appliance." On the order 'Get To Work', Nos. 1-3/5 would run and get the ladder, whilst No. 2 would engage the power take-off. Nos. 1 and 5 at the head of the ladder and Nos. 3 and 4 at the heel.

As you can imagine it was chaos at times, with men running round like headless chickens. Men would forget which numbers they were and often there would be a situation whereby there would only be one man at the head of the ladder and three at the heel, all arguing with one another. 'Bollocking' after 'bollocking' would follow, until the drill became like clockwork — in theory at least. One can train monkeys to respond to numbers!!!

All through the course each individual was assessed and given a set number of points per day, from which a point or points were deducted for the slightest misdemeanour. The Officer in Charge of Training School, a huge A.D.O., sported a massive 'Jimmy Edwards' moustache. He used to inspect us each morning and last thing every Friday afternoon. Up and down the motionless ranks of trainee firemen he went, with the tiniest speck of dust being noted and marks deducted for the same. This A.D.O. had a terrible dandruff problem and his shoulders were covered with flakes of the same — so much for smartness. I bet *he* never had any points deducted.

Sessions within the classroom covered the theoretical side of fireman-ship, which rarely, if ever, had any practical use on the fireground. What difference did it make that a hydrant had a 'Duck's Foot' or that the wheels etc., of a Wheeled Escape were made up from oak, ash and oregon pine. The most ridiculous course was First Aid. Instead of teaching the students the three most important basics, 'Breathing', 'Bleeding' and 'Bones', and leaving it at that, they tried to turn us into 'Brain Surgeons'. One fellow recruit from LITTLE SNOBSBURY, 'Dusty', constantly caused me to snigger during these sessions, for which I lost more points.

Also included in the curriculum (that's a big word) was Civil Defence, a throw-back to the days of the Second World War — 'Dad's Army' and 'Captain Mainwaring'. Contrary to the Government propaganda of the day about the 'Green Goddess' fire engines having been in 'moth-balls' from the 1950's until the fireman's strike in 1977, we trained with them on Civil Defence and had one based at LITTLE SNOBSBURY. Others were used during the dry summer of 1976. So much for 'propaganda'.

Our imagination used to run riot when informed of the effects of a nuclear explosion. The inner ring of the same would be completely obliterated, the second ring almost obliterated and the outer ring not quite obliterated. If enough notice was given, there were plans for long mobile columns of fire engines, crewed by the younger elements, to head for the safety of the countryside, whilst the older men would be sacrificed in the 'Epi-Centre', their only advice being — 'Hide behind a door and place a brown paper bag over your head to prevent you being blinded by the flash'. Presumably most of the senior officers would also scarper into the green belt, under the pretext of 'arranging things'.

Our first introduction to 'Dr. Death' was when we were ferried to the local mortuary, a former fire station, which was rather dilapidated and run-down. Once arriving there were no such niceties as, "If you have never seen a dead body before, then brace yourselves." We were ushered inside the building and without warning the mortuary attendant opened a freezer door and there, on three trays, were the occupants, all male and not pretty sights after post-mortem operations. Also present was the seemingly statutory 'Little Man' in a bottle. ('Animal' kept one in his locker.) For our part, none of us fainted. Good preparation for future tragedies to come.

We had trouble with all types of ladders. On one occasion a Wheeled Escape ended up in a position it should never have normally have been in, with a laughing 'Dusty' hanging by his finger-tips from the heel — more marks up the creek. Whilst at Training School, a new type of ladder was introduced, the aluminium 45', which ultimately replaced most of the wooden 50' Wheeled Escapes, being cheaper and lighter. The instructors trained us in the use of them, literally straight from the manufacturers manual. As a result, at least two were dropped from a great height, one missing the Chief's brand new car by inches. "If anybody laughs, he will be on a charge," remarked one instructor.

The finish of the initial course at Training School culminated in an 'extravaganza'. Parents of the recruits were invited along, as were members of the Fire Service hierarchy and various 'Big-Wigs' from the local Council. There were spectacular pumping drills, with different coloured jets for effect. Dummies were rescued from great heights within the tower, by 'brave firemen' haring up ladders. (It was amazing, but over the years I 'rescued' countless dummies and never once had a word of thanks off any of them. Ungrateful things!!!)

What the onlookers didn't realise was that there were lads placed at strategic places, out of sight, within the tower, to 'assist' each 'rescuer' to administer the 'Fireman's Lift', and to help ensure the dummy wasn't dropped half-way down the ladder its arms were 'pinned' to the 'rescuer's' fire tunic. Once the drills were completed we were all lined up and the 'pre-chosen' winner of the course, 'Fireman Golden Bollocks', was presented with his silver/chrome axe and a set of Fire Service manuals. A glittering career lay ahead of him, unlike the remainder of us.

Upon completing my initial training, I returned to LITTLE SNOBSBURY Fire Station and was allocated a regular place on one of the Watches —

'Glarer's'. Being a person who finds anything with more than one moving part rather complicated, I was more confused upon my return than I was when I first started and this was to apply throughout my career.

Towards the end of my Fire Service life, a probationary fireman arrived fresh from Training School and was immediately drafted to my Watch. He was one of those characters whom I classed as too tall and useless for most things. On his very first day shift, whilst on morning parade, a single rose was delivered to him from an old flame and he was immediately nicknamed 'Rosy'.

I once told him, after yet another hashed up drill, "Apart from myself, you are the most useless person I have ever come across and believe me I am an expert on useless people, having been one for so long. We ought to form a 'Useless Persons Society'. I would like to be the Chairman, but I am useless at that sort of thing." He was utterly dumbfounded and throughout the short period of time I knew this likeable lad, I'm sure he could never weigh me up properly.

Most ladder and pumping drills were still conducted using crew and individual firemen's numbers, even after Training School, and confusion often reigned supreme. Despite being numbered off, two or more men would still run for the same item of equipment and would collide with each other. On at least one occasion, all five members of a crew went and lifted a single length of suction hose, much to the fury of the O.I.C.

If the water pressure was too high, it was common for branch-men to be lifted bodily off the ground and 'The Gypsy' decided to 'test' a length of hose to its maximum. It swelled and swelled until the pressure ripped it in half close to its centre, whereupon thirty feet of hose, plus the branch, flew so high it cleared the Hydraulic Platform, which was parked some distance away.

This very same fireman, who made his departure from the job before MAMMOTH COUNTY arrived, was a most awkward and contrary fellow at times. On one particuar day shift, whenever he was asked a question by the 'Red-Cheeked' Station Officer, he would answer, 'Don't know sir.'' By the end of the shift, the Station Officer, in exasperation, said, "Why is it that all day long you have answered 'Don't know sir' to every question I have put to you?" The reply was superb. "I'm having a 'Don't know' day today sir," leaving the fuming officer speechless.

It was often quite amusing when a Sub Officer was roped into drills, usually probationary ones, caused by a shortage of men. These erstwhile fellows were splendid at planning difficult drills, ones they were to oversee, and would spend vast amounts of time in the office in harness with their Station Officers, who rarely took an active part in such drills. One could often hear these 'grown-up' men giggling together like schoolboys.

I was involved in a probationary drill in which Sub-O 'Tu-Tu' was taking part. It was one thing 'shouting and bawling' at firemen when they were doing something wrong, but it was totally different when personally involved. Hand and foot positioning were all over the place and much arguing took place within the crews involved. Upon Sub-O 'Tu-Tu's' order, we under-ran a 30' ladder in readiness for it to be re-housed on the roof of its appliance. I knew something wasn't quite right, but due to the general attitude of the Fire Service, 'act first and think afterwards', there was no time to halt and correct the ladder. Who was I to correct the Sub-O's order anyway!!! Whilst attempting to re-house the same, it became jammed in the runner. No wonder! It was upside-down! Off it had to come again to be turned over and housed correctly.

At LITTLE SNOBSBURY we had an Emergency Tender which carried on its roof three lengthy poles. Once these were removed from the appliance they were connected to each other at the top, and all three would be pushed into the air, forming a 'tripod' effect, to which heavy lifting gear would be suspended. This item of equipment was known as 'Sheer-Legs'. They were extremely heavy and cumbersome, needing some eight men to erect them. Prior to drills one day, Sub-O 'Squirrel' ordered the Watch to 'get the tripod to work', meaning of course the sheer-legs, indicating he would join the men a few minutes later.

The men trooped out into the yard, but instead of getting the sheer-legs off the E.T., one bright spark hit on an idea. Consulting his colleagues he said, "Sub-O 'Squirrel' told us to get the tripod to work, not the sheer-legs," although they all knew what 'Squirrel' meant. By the time 'Squirrel' came into the yard all he saw were the men in line in readiness for drill, whilst in front of them stood a solitary searchlight tripod. He went potty, "I ORDERED YOU TO GET THE SHEER-LEGS TO WORK." he screamed. "No you didn't," came the unanimous reply, "You ordered us to get the tripod to work, which is exactly what we have done," and as a man they all smirked at him, which did nothing for 'Squirrel's' health and temper.

One of the funniest drills which took place at LITTLE SNOBSBURY, was a 'rescue' from the tower of yet another dummy. (It's incredible how many 'fires' there were in metal or brick built towers, neither of which can burn, or how many dummies came to be trapped in the same.)

The particular drill entailed the use of a 45' extension ladder, being initially pitched to the third floor. A designated number of men would scale the same, taking a life-line (with two loops at one end) into the tower. The free end would then be thrown to the ground, with the looped end being fed through the third or fourth round from the top of the ladder. The idea was to use the ladder as a pivot to lower the 'casualty' to the ground on a stretcher, the speed of descent being governed on how quickly or slowly the man footing the ladder paid the line out from the base of it. Once the looped end had been fed into the tower the ladder would then be raised to the fourth floor.

As they were about to commence the drill, there was a shortage of junior officers to take command, so Station Officer 'Red-Cheeks' ordered the men to do the drill by themselves. Left to their own devices all went well, until it came to lowering the stretcher. Instead of utilising a lifeline, in their haste a 50′ line had been grabbed. In addition the men inside the tower had made themselves a chair-knot, further shortening the line.

The result of this was that as soon as they began lowering the stretcher the men on the ground soon ran out of line. Fm. 'Sealed Knot' (rather apt!!!) took responsibility and climbed the ladder whilst holding the other end of the line at the same time. A difficult task indeed. Gordon, observing this fiasco from the sanctuary of the kitchen, could hardy catch his breath for laughing as he watched Fm. 'Sealed Knot' struggle slowly up the ladder as the stretcher descended in fits and starts, swaying crazily before he finally completed his mission.

For many years, live carry downs, 'Fireman's Lift' style, were the norm, but when the 'Health & Safety' bods came into being, they were all but abolished with 'live' casualties being replaced by 'dummies'. Mind you, in some cases it was hard to tell the difference.

To combat this problem, the hierarchy at LITTLE SNOBSBURY contacted a 'super salesman' and purchased a 'safety' line. This device was anchored to the top of the tower and whenever a 'live' carry down took place, a harness from the safety line was attached round the 'casualty'. Should a fireman have fallen from the shoulder of the chap carrying him, the safety line would take over, preventing him from falling to the ground. However, nobody had calculated the amount of 'stretch' in the line, which was some six feet and when a six foot fireman was 'dropped' from this height he went 'wallop' on the deck and bounced up and down like a uncontrolled marionette. The safety device was withdrawn shortly after.

L.Fm. 'Messenger' asked me to set up a car fire in the middle of the yard. I selected one of the derelict vehicles and it was placed in the predescribed location and filled with newspapers and bits of wood. I then reported to him that it might take some time to ignite properly as it was extremely damp inside and suggested he kept the men talking for a while. I went back and lit the fire and couldn't believe my eyes. Despite the dampness it spread very rapidly, not so much in the way of flames, with huge volumes of black oily smoke pouring out of it, which headed straight for the H.Q. block where most of the windows were open.

Meanwhile the 'fire crews' who were in the engine house, had their backs to the incident and were unaware of the drama unfolding behind them. Even 'The Messenger' didn't notice at first, although I was frantically jumping up and down in the yard, waving my arms, trying to attract his attention.

Talking away, he suddenly stopped in mid-sentence, ''FOR F*!K'S SAKE, TURN OUT,'' he screamed. 'Foghorn-Leghorn' was driving the first machine and upon noticing the chaos in the yard he deliberately took his time starting the engine. By now 'The Messenger' was panicking

and his confidence wasn't enhanced when 'Foghorn' stopped at the traffic lights, politely waving motorists across, who had stopped to let him turn right.

By the time they reached the yard, the H.Q. block had all but disappeared in the smoke, its coughing inmates hastily closing windows. After the fire was extinguished several senior officers joined us, administering 'bollockings' all round and after this fiasco 'real' fire drills were banned.

Left alone by the hierarchy there was no limit to the number of interesting drill situations we could do. We set one up using the dormitory as a hospital ward, selecting the most awkward men as 'patients'. I too took part and by the time it was over I was all but helpless with laughter. The station was in darkness and we heard the B.A. crews searching the building until they arrived at the dormitory. All but two of us were reached and they were 'persuaded' to become 'walking wounded' upon being threatened with having their balls squeezed if they didn't co-operate. These lads were removed and the crews, consisting of four men, returned.

Apart from myself, the other 'patient' awaiting 'rescue' was 'Nestor'. He had been 'fixed up' as though he had a leg in traction (utilising a mobile coat hanger frame) and he was on a 'drip'. Normally the four B.A. men would have been able to remove the pair of us with ease. As has been mentioned before, 'Nestor' wasn't the sort of chap to be trifled with, so therefore he couldn't be 'threatened' to co-operate in the normal manner. The four B.A. men, once realising who they were dealing with, decided to ignore my presence and grabbed 'Nestor'.

They took no notice whatsoever of the 'drip' which was instantly ripped out and they cut the string (traction) holding his 'poorly' leg. Lifting him in unison they charged off with their patient who really acted the part. He screamed and screamed as they took him away, "MY LEG — MY F*!*!*G LEG — YOU HAVE PULLED THE F*!*!*G DRIP OUT — AAGH — I'M IN AGONY — YOU BASTARDS," etc., etc. Intermingled with his cries were comments from his 'rescuers', mostly swearing as they sweated with their struggling and screaming 'patient'. I was so taken over with mirth I fell off the bed with laughter and when I was eventually 'saved', I was still helpless from giggling.

LITTLE SNOBSBURY occasionally made its own films, one of which I took an active part in. It was a fake road traffic accident. I was suitably made-up, having supposedly gone through the windscreen of a car and I looked pretty gory as I crawled into position half-way through the screen and lay on the bonnet, at the side of a public highway.

To any passers-by it was really authentic and a number stopped to gawp, as they gazed upon the scene of this terrible 'fatal accident', which was being filmed. I overheard various mutterings, "Poor chap, gone through the screen, so young as well." They were even more shocked when the filming was over and the 'corpse' crawled off the bonnet and dusted itself down.

For a brief period we had on loan a brand new Hydraulic Platform which was destined for elsewhere in MAMMOTH COUNTY. 'Eli' decided to test its paces and arranged a drill at an empty, though not abandoned, large house out in the sticks. Upon arrival we were greeted by the caretaker, an obvious 'Hello Sandy' type 'Woofter'.

Apart from 'Eli' and myself, there was a third member of the crew, 'Buggy', whom 'Willy Woofter' took an instant liking to, much to 'Buggy's' obvious discomfort. Various pitches were tried round the outside of the house and our effeminate friend kept appearing from time to time at various windows, smiling somewhat affectionately at us and in particular at 'Buggy'.

'Eli' brought the second boom and cage down to ground level and said to 'Buggy' and I, "Next time 'Willy Woofter' appears, I will ask him if he wants a 'ride', sorry 'Buggy', a trip in the H.P. cage, I'll teach him a lesson." Sure enough, the next time he popped his head out he accepted the invitation (bait). The H.P. was positioned in front of the house, in front of which was a sunken garden, dropping to a depth of about twenty feet. Taking into account the height to which the H.P. could reach, it would have been in excess of 100 feet above the garden.

The excited caretaker arrived and climbed into the cage with 'Eli'. 'Buggy' was on the pulpit control and I stood watching. The first boom was already at its maximum height, leaving only the second and third booms to be raised. 'Eli' took 'Willy' up slowly so as not to frighten or forewarn him of what was about to happen. When the caretaker first got into the cage he was chattering away ten to the dozen, but the higher he went his chattering all but ceased. Upon gaining maximum height he was silent, and I could see his white knuckles protruding as he gripped the safety bar.

Without any prior warning 'Eli' dropped the second boom like a stone, so fast that 'Willy Woofter' didn't have time to scream. On reaching

128

ground level, the ashen-faced caretaker, trembling with fear, couldn't get out of the cage fast enough. He invited us in for a quick drink and after regaining his composure he carried on with his 'interest' in 'Buggy', especially after he discovered he was single. It was time for us to depart.

Not long after the first H.P. had been purchased by LITTLE SNOBSBURY, Station Officer 'Red-Cheeks' was totally dissatisfied with the performance of one of the operators, inferring he was incompetent, after a chunk of guttering had fallen due to a minor collision whilst manouvering with the cage. He took over the controls and proceeded with the same movement, with a look of 'I am the Station Officer, I will show you how it is done'. At that, the cage smacked into the same guttering and an even bigger section crashed to the ground. His health and temper wasn't improved when 'Pierre' appeared from the kitchen and shouted, "HA, HA, WHO IS THE STUPID PRAT WHO DID THAT? WAIT TILL THE STATION OFFICER GETS TO KNOW ABOUT IT."

One of the stations within our Division had specialist equipment and we used to pay frequent visits to the same to familiarize ourselves with the various items and in particular, new equipment.

The Brigade had, on trial, some new protective clothing suits, which we went to see in action. They were used in conjunction with compressed air sets and air was allowed to seep into them as an added safeguard. Whilst they were being demonstrated it soon became obvious that something was going amiss. The suits initially expanded, but instead of ceasing to do so at a pre-determined pressure, they continued expanding until the two wearers looked akin to moon-walkers — "Take me to your leader". Prior to them being deflated I fully expected the wearers to shoot off somewhere, as Norman Wisdom did in a diving suit in one of his comedy films.

As previously referred to, 'dummies' were often used during drills, but they had other uses too.

After an off station drill, I, as the transport man, was delegated to return a dummy to the station in the van. Instead of slinging it into the back of the van, it was placed in the passenger seat, dressed in my fire tunic and helmet. With the aid of the seat belt, the left arm was lodged, leaning on the open window frame.

On the way back to the station, after several peculiar looks from various pedestrians and motorists, I decided to call home for a cup of tea. I parked outside my house and knocked on the door. My wife opened it and I said, "Cup of tea please," as I brushed past her. She glanced at the van and commented, "Does your mate want some tea?" I replied, "I don't know. Go and ask him." She disappeared down the path, stopped, stared for a few seconds and returned, giving me a 'why don't you grow up' type of look.

One story quoted to me involved a station which was expecting a visit from a senior officer. Being winter time, it was dark during the training period of the early evening night shift and the occupants had all but blacked out their station with the exception of a dim portable light in the Station Officers' office. A dummy was dressed in reefers and a cap and placed in the 'gaffer's' seat, with feet on the desk. It had a pipe and was apparently reading a newspaper. When the officer arrived he was somewhat annoyed that there was no-one there to give him the normal salutation. He stormed into the office and upon seeing the recumbent 'fireman', who failed to stand up in his presence, proceeded to administer a right 'bollocking' before he realised he was shouting at a dummy. You might ask, which one was the dummy!!!

A further story related to me, concerned the disappearance of a brand new dummy, nicknamed 'Denzil', during a Divisional exercise. 'Denzil' had either been thrown into a canal or stolen. Either way, the Officer in Charge of the exercise was made responsible and took all the flack from the hierarchy.

Time passed by and out of the blue this O.I.C. received a barrage of postcards from all over the world. Whoever organised it deserves public recognition, it was so brilliant. 'Sunning myself on Bondi Beach' — 'Denzil'. 'Off to Blackpool today' — 'Denzil'. 'The Blue Danube looks glorious' — 'Denzil'. 'What a nice place Bermuda is, see you soon' — 'Denzil' and so on. How long the wretched officer had to tolerate this, I know not.

Apart from the normal run of the mill day to day drill sessions, there were a host of initial and refresher courses, covering all aspects of the Fire Service. The most important being Breathing Apparatus, Hydraulic Platform, Turntable Ladder, Cutting Gear and Heavy Goods Vehicle courses.

When I first joined LITTLE SNOBSBURY there were three types of B.A. sets, two being self-contained Oxygen types — Salvus and Proto and the third — Compressed Air. The oxygen sets supplied the wearer with a maximum of 2 and 2½ litres of oxygen respectively, whilst the compressed air supplied an unrestricted supply on demand.

Both oxygen sets were very basic. An oxygen cylinder, a detachable oxygen bag filled via a valve from the cylinder, a cooling canister, oxygen supply tube, nose-clip, goggles/full face-mask, warning whistle and other bits and pieces. Within the bag a quantity of granules (protosorb) were placed, prior to use. These granules absorbed the CO_2 when exhaling.

Once the bag was filled you could breathe the contents until they were exhausted, again refilling the bag from the cylinder and so on. Two large concertina tubes led from the mouthpiece/face-mask to the bag. One tube supplied the oxygen and the other returned the mixture to the bag. Inside both tubes was a simple valve. On breathing in, one valve lifted and the other closed and vice versa when exhaling. They made the most peculiar KER-PLOP-KER-PLOP-KER-PLOP sounds. One fireman, not quite being able to master the art of breathing through a mouth-piece took the same, plus the contertina tubes home with him, practising with them on the bus. He was all but thrown off after complaints from the other passengers, thinking him to be some kind of nutter.

During B.A. drills I had the advantage, along with a few others, of being slight of build. I could stand up in some of the tunnels in the B.A. complex and small entrances and exits within the same created no problems for myself, whereas the 'Too Tall', 'He-Man' types were always in some kind of trouble, stuck within the tunnels, requiring assistance from 'smaller' colleagues, whom they were normally taking the 'piss' out of with comments like 'Stumpy', 'Poisoned Dwarf' and 'That Gnome Like Creature'.

Two LITTLE SNOBSBURY colleagues were being tested by a 'Board of Examiners' to ascertain their knowledge of a C.A. set, in the recreation room. The 'Board' consisted of three officers including our 'Red-Cheeked' friend and the Deputy Chief. Apart from being asked various questions, the first man was ordered to put the set on and operate it. Once they had finished with him the second was summoned. The sets in those days didn't have a constant flow valve, which allowed a constant stream of air into the face-mask, even if you were not actually wearing it. The golden rule, hammered home to all wearers was, "You ensure the set is switched off by opening and closing the supply valve."

The second fireman was asked the same questions as the first. He too was ordered to don the set and operate it. The previous chap had fully opened the supply valve, but neglected to close it after he had finished. Fireman number two forgot 'Glarer's' golden rule and thinking he was opening the valve he closed it instead. Once closed the air was almost immediately exhausted and to his horror the mask went flat on his face, right in front of the impassive 'Board' who kept their thoughts to themselves, thus allowing him time to open the valve. He was given a 'bollocking' by the Station Officer later.

Shortly afterwards there was a fire involving a public house, in the early hours, and by this time the use of C.A sets as opposed to oxygen sets had become the norm. Up rolled Station Officer 'Red-Cheeks' who got his own set out of the boot of his radio car. He put the set on and felt for the valve down by his buttocks, but he couldn't find it, until someone pointed out that the valve was up by a shoulder. In his haste and panic he had put the set on upside-down, and *he* was the Training Officer!!!

All operational firemen have to have B.A. refresher courses. This should also apply to all operational senior officers, but in MAMMOTH COUNTY (at the time of writing) it was only discussed by the hierarchy and not put into practice. Mind you I am not suprised, most were not very fit and the thought of lugging a dummy round a B.A. chamber would have caused nightmares amongst most of them. Also, with the large 'girth' that some had I doubt if the straps on the sets would reach round their bodies.

During one such refresher course my regular partner was 'Baz', the former sailor, and we had many a good laugh together. Six of us were lined up and ordered to pair off in three's. Now the instructor meant us to pair off in three groups of two, but we formed two groups of three, a touch of the 'Forfar — 5' 'Fife — 4'. "NO, NO, NO," he shouted, "GET BACK INTO LINE AND LET'S TRY AGAIN." Back into line we went and once more the order came, "Pair off in three's." Two groups of three formed again, much to the exasperation of the instructor, so much that he muttered, "W*NK*RS," under his breath as he physically regrouped us in two's.

The situation had been so funny, with blokes milling round, unsure of themselves, oxygen bottles clanking together, that 'Baz' and I burst into laughter, a difficult thing to do in a self-contained oxygen set. Due to the uncontrolled giggling from within, this led to a build-up of back pressure, almost forcing the masks off our faces. A round of F*!K'S from the instructor eventually calmed us down.

"Right," he said, "Now face one another, we will now do the drill whereby No. 1 will use No. 2's oxygen supply, as No. 1's has failed." This entailed No. 1 disconnecting his valve group and holding his breath. No. 2 would then ensure his own bag was filled with oxygen before disconnecting his own. Once disconnected, No. 2 would then connect his supply into No. 1's set, whereby No. 1 could then have his oxygen bag filled. Sounds like a script from 'The Prisoner'.

Having gone through the previously described routine and given the order, "Turn your valves on," 'Baz' forgot his valve group was connected to my set and he groped around frantically, "I can't find my f*!*!*g valve group, " he said anxiously. "I'm not f*!*!*g surprised," I replied, "It's in my set." At that we collapsed once more, with our face-masks bursting at the straps. Another 'bollocking' off the instructor.

During the lunch break I chatted to an old time fireman, in the canteen, who was approaching retirement. Out of curiosity I asked, "How many firemen were killed during the last war?" "Not as f*!*!*g many as would have been if they had joined the army," came the acid reply. So much for conversation!!!

'Baz' didn't like small enclosed spaces, not for long anyway. One of the drills involved three of us in the rescue of (you've guessed it) a dummy, 'Baz', another fireman and myself. Having located the dummy we placed it on a wheeled stretcher. It was a damn great big thing (the dummy — not the stretcher) and it took the combined strength of all three of us to lug it through the narrow confines of the B.A. complex. We reached a 'tunnel' of open ended oil drums. I was leading with the other fireman with me, then the dummy, with 'Baz' bringing up the rear. As the two of us emerged from the tunnel we were stopped by the instructor, for several minutes. Meanwhile, poor old 'Baz' was left stranded in the tunnel with the stretcher and dummy.

Being aware that 'Baz' had 'problems' in confined spaces, I tried to speed the instructor up so that we could continue with the drill, but to no avail. Eventually there was a loud 'tapping' from the inside of the drums, accompanied by a muffled, "What the f*!k's going on out there?" "Ignore him," said the instructor and continued talking. Eventually 'Baz' could take no more and he, the dummy and the stretcher all shot out of the tunnel. Amazing what a combination of panic and temper can do!!!

At the end of the course we were assembled in the classroom and the instructor asked for a volunteer to sweep the floor and empty the ashtrays. Also present during this course, as an observer, was a visiting officer, dressed in civvies, from an Asian country. He was seated impassively at the back of the classroom when the instructor had asked for a volunteer to clean up. Trevor 'D', one of our blokes who rarely became ruffled, turned to 'Baz' and I and nodded nonchalantly towards the foreigner, saying "Get him to do the cleaning up, he has done f*!k all else this week." At that we burst out laughing once more, but this time we were not restricted by the face-masks.

Moving away from the practical side of the drills and training, other aspects of operational Fire Service life included lectures, topography and the like. In the early years of my career PROGRAMMED LEARNING came along. Read on:

To alleviate the boredom of the lengthy hours of duty and also in a vain attempt to improve the general education of the men, LITTLE SNOBSBURY Brigade introduced the concept of 'Programmed Learning'. One can imagine the hours of high level talks amongst the management prior to this monster being let loose. It was introduced and overseen with a certain amount of smugness by the officers, mainly because they didn't have to participate in it, thereby retaining their untested intelligence, superiority and credibility in the eyes of the men. This being the reverse of the normal officer to men relationship of 'What's good for us is not necessarily good for anyone else'.

'Programmed Learning' was very basic at first, for instance the inside front cover of each book would state: 'This is Programmed Learning, Book, Blah, Blah. Turn to Page One and commence reading.' An insult to our intelligence you might think!!! However, there were characters who had to read this simple instruction twice or more before proceeding. To aid the average fireman, the first page would pose an uncomplicated question such as: 'How long is a 50 foot line?' complete with a sketch to assist the pupil. The answer would be shown in three parts — a) 30', b) 50', c) 100'. Then it would state in bold lettering: 'THE ANSWER OF COURSE IS B. Now that you understand the theme of the 'Programmed Learning' courses we will progress to the subject proper'.

Page two would contain questions and explanations, ending with the usual selection of three choices of answers. Writing in these text books was forbidden and answers had to be written on separate pieces of paper, all of which would be collected at the end of each session. Page three would depict the correct answers. If the participant had any incorrect answers, he would be instructed to return to page two, until he understood (in theory) why the correct answers given appertained to the original questions.

At the beginning of each session, if anyone still had wrong answers from the previous shift, he had to go back through the programme once more, until he fully understood it (again in theory) before progress could be made. This created a dual headache for the hierarchy. Should *Fireman Clever* be allowed to advance away rapidly from *Fireman Dim*, thereby creating an inferiority complex for the latter, or should *Fireman Dim* be allowed to catch up with *Fireman Clever*, who, by the time *Fireman Dim* had caught up with him, was so frustrated and sneering in his attitude to *Fireman Dim*, that open hostility often occurred. As a com-

promise by the hierarchy, both methods were tried from time to time. This was never a satisfactory arrangement, which often ended in chaos, and in many instances more time was spent arguing than was spent on 'Programmed Learning'.

Subjects contained within these books varied from Maths, English and Science etc., to firemen being properly dressed and picking up objects correctly. For instance there would be two pictures of firemen, ready for out-duties, dressed in reefer jackets, trousers and caps — *Fireman Smart and Fireman Sloppy.* In case some of the men couldn't tell the difference, at the foot of the page would be two more drawings of *Fireman Smart and Fireman Sloppy* and, 'yes, you have guessed it', *Fireman Smart* was ready to meet the public.

Towards the end of one of these hour long periods, a bored 'Pierre' was caught by Station Officer 'Red-Cheeks', making paper planes out of his spare answer sheets. He was ordered by the S.O. to leave the room and climb the drill tower with his handywork. The unfortunate red-faced 'Pierre' proceeded to do so and once on the top of the drill tower he had to launch his squadron of aeronautical masterpieces into deep space, in full view of the duty personnel, who by now were reduced to tears of laughter.

One wonders what the thoughts may have been in the minds of any passing members of the public, as to the antics of a fully grown man who was throwing paper planes from the top of a sixty foot metal tower, in the middle of the day. Perhaps, as a ratepayer, he or she may well have thought that due to the long hours of duty of the men inside the fire station, that this was some sort of occupational therapy, to help keep the inmates sane.

It was stressed from the beginning that individual results of 'Programmed Learning' were not to be used for exam purposes, in the true sense of the word, it was simply designed as an aid. However, as the programmes became harder and more complicated, it became obvious to the powers that be, that more and more firemen were staring blankly at the questions, instead of putting pen to paper and it was decided at the top to call a halt, to enable the Deputy Chief to test one of the Watches at random, to assess how the men had progressed over the months.

Each person was set a selection of twenty or so simple questions, covering various themes from all books in the series. To his utter amazement, every man who took part in this exam failed miserably. This was due, in part, to genuinely not knowing some of the answers, but mostly the failure was deliberately engineered by the participants as they wished collectively to be rid of 'Programmed Learning'. In this they succeeded totally. The Deputy Chief stormed out of the room muttering under his breath and shortly afterwards 'Programmed Learning' was consigned to the dustbin or wherever, which was where it should have been in the first place.

One problem area was associated with forthcoming metrification. To me, even today, litres, centigrade and kilometres mean very little — about as useful as an ash-tray on a motor bike. When I left the former LITTLE SNOBSBURY fire station, the end of month returns for fuel in appliances were calculated in miles per litre. I wonder which bright person thought that one up. 'Miles per litre'.

One LITTLE SNOBSBURY Leading Hand was ordered to explain to the men on his Watch how to convert pounds into kilograms, yards into metres and fahrenheit into centigrade. Although he had the book with both the questions and answers, he too couldn't understand how the conversions were calculated. One fireman, an awkward person at the best of times, 'The Lancastrian', said, "Well, if you don't know how to convert those figures, how the f*!*!*g hell are we supposed to?"

Deeply insulted, the Leading Fireman simply informed them of the answer to each question, ordering the men to write them down. The answer sheets were handed in and the L.Fm. checked each one. He turned to 'The Lancastrian' after he came across his answer sheet and said, "Despite my giving you the correct answers, you have still got one wrong," to which the instant response was, "So what? If we all get the answers right, them next door will think it's a fix."

In the aftermath of the 1977/78 strike and in particular with the introduction of the forty-two hour week, the powers that be resented the time we now had off duty and the 'inflated' wages we were earning. One of the ways they could hit back at us was to lessen the stand-down periods. Set times were introduced for lengthier drill sessions. These were backed up by 'Hatchet Men' who ensured the rules were obeyed — to the letter.

To go hand in hand with the new drill schedule, the 'Drill Pigs' also invented a new style of drill sheet. This was divided into a host of practical and theoretical drills, over a period of twelve months. Advance plans for drills had to be drawn up on a tour by tour basis — two days and two nights. Copies of the same were handed to the senior officers section for them to scrutinize. Each man, including the Station Officer, had his own personal sheet of records.

These had to be filled in on a daily basis and were inspected frequently and signed by the duty officers on their rounds. Come hell or high water, the advance drill schedule had to be adhered to. "What are you doing tonight Station Officer?" an A.D.O. or D.O. would ask. "I thought we would do something different tonight sir." — "Such as?" — "Well sir, tonight's drill consists of a Jumbo jet crashing onto a busy railway marshalling yard, used for the transportation of dynamite and nuclear waste. As it is only a minor incident, I'm putting a Leading Fireman in charge."

The more than dry humour would be totally wasted as a stone-faced officer would say, "What does it say on the drill sheet?" — "It says that we are to stand in the yard and pour thousands of gallons of water into the third floor of the drill tower, for one hour." — "If that's what it says on the drill sheet, then get on with it."

We referred to the drill records as 'Dream Sheets' and many was the occasion we simply filled them in without actually doing the drills. As long as they were correctly filled in, that was all that mattered to the hierarchy. If a man dropped a ladder because he hadn't used one for six months, although the records 'proved' he had used it eight times, the blame would be shifted to the Officer in Charge of the Watch.

One 'Drill Pig', an A.D.O., 'Egg on Legs', came into the mess at tea break. The subject he instantly touched on was, surprise, surprise — drills, probably the only subject in life he knew anything about. He, 'Egg on Legs' said, "The trouble is, these days, you firemen, especially the older ones, are not interested in drills and don't treat them seriously." "But sir," I interjected, "I took charge of the drills this morning and I treated them very seriously." "Good man," he replied. "What did you do?" I thought for a moment and said, "Well sir, first of all we went through the square window . . . . . " and trailed off, leaving him to choke on his toast.

'Billy J' once turned round to us after a drill session one night and said, "This constant drilling is getting out of hand, especially off the station. You don't see the coppers practising arresting people in the High Street, or ambulancemen stopping and loading pedestrians into their ambulances." We all agreed. Today's officers are obsessed with drills and training.

Finally, in relation to drills and training, shortly before I left the Service, one of these 'new breed' of 'man-management' experts marched into the office and said to the 'Savage' Sub-O, "Why isn't the drill yard wet?" The 'Savage' one replied, "Because we have been doing First Aid sir." — "But that doesn't explain why the yard isn't wet." — "We don't wet the yard during First Aid."

I thought to myself, 'Why isn't the yard wet, indeed'. I then remembered a once famous saying of 'Nosy's', many years beforehand and it would have applied a treat to this particular smarmy person — "You jumped up, never come down, short-arsed, wizened up ghet." As a parting shot I commented, "What happens if it's raining? The yard will be wet, therefore you will have no way of knowing if we have been out there." There was an angry silence and he retreated out of the office, tail between his legs, like many before him.

Fiddles & Do-It-Yourself

'Fiddles' or part-time employment was once a way of life with firemen, between shifts, and nothing was too humble or large to be tackled. Anything from gardening, gang mowing (yes, mowing) heavy goods, light van and taxi driving, grave digging, pall bearing, coal humping, painting, decorating, building, plastering and window cleaning. All were attempted, not always successfully, often at low rates of pay.

One of my first 'fiddles' was a gardening job, for an elderly lady, who's husband passed away shortly after I commenced working for her. She gave me the impression she had never had to gain employment, in order to live, and that work was something other people did. She owned a large, modern bungalow, with extensive grounds, plus plenty of money to see her comfortably through the remainder of her life.

I was paid a pittance for the work I performed and when I summoned up the courage to request a shilling an hour rise, one would have thought her world had collapsed. "How on earth can I afford to give you a rise? I am only a poor pensioner," this being said having not long returned from a month long holiday at a top hotel in the Far East!!! She lived in the past in a world of the 'Upper Crust', with the 'Peasants' knowing their place in life. "Please use the tradesman's entrance — not my front door."

Her neighbour, a widow and another 'poor' pensioner, was even worse in her outlook towards working class folk. I once overheard her asking my 'employer', "That gardener chappy, is he alright? Does he work well?" Upon being informed that I was 'alright' and 'worked well', she further continued, "What do you give him for tea breaks?" — "Tea and biscuits in the kitchen," was the reply. "Oh, I cannot possibly entertain him in my kitchen. He will have to have his break in the garden, come rain or shine."

Both of these ladies were the epitome of the good old days of 'The Raj' and I could picture both of them sitting in the Governor's massive grounds, sipping tea from china cups and being fanned by man-servants. Eventually I could stand no more and moved on to 'better things'.

One of those 'better things' was a day spent shovelling swarf. The day began more than badly, when I was introduced to my mode of transport, an antiquated lorry, with a semi-crash gearbox. Both mirrors were broken, and the handbrake — well — that was something else. To release the same required all my strength and it had to be pumped several times before it came on again.

Each time I changed gear, it went in with a mighty crunch and whenever I stopped the engine stalled. Without exception I had nothing but trouble with the handbrake each time I used it and upon arriving at the job I misjudged the angle I was at and collided with a factory wall.

At the end of the day I was covered in oily metal fragments and swore I would never again be involved in that type of job.

Almost every lorry driving job I was employed on had an element of misfortune sometime during the day, like the time I stalled on a massive hill, foot firmly on the brake pedal, not knowing if the handbrake was on or off as it was faulty. (Fortunately it was on when I released the footbrake.)

I once drove a high-sided vehicle, equipped with a roller shutter door at the rear which was out of action. To help prevent goods falling off, a rope was tied in criss-cross fashion. It didn't succeed, as I discovered at my first port of call. Instead of having twelve casks of yeast on board for a Marmite factory, when I arrived there were only eleven!!!

One particularly catastrophic lorry driving 'fiddle' I had, was a multiple sweets delivery to a host of paper and grocery shops. The sweets etc., were encompassed within some fragile wire cages, with each individual delivery being separated by empty sacks. The first three or four drops were a piece of cake, but then disaster struck. Negotiating a traffic island, I forgot what was in the back of the lorry until I heard a mighty crash.

I immediately pulled up and upon opening the rear door I discovered that all of the cages had toppled over and the sweets and crisps etc., were all in one large heap. Instead of rolling up at each shop and simply picking out the pre-determined order, I now had to sort out each order from the delivery notes and wade through countless items. Until then I had no idea how many types of sweets and crisps there were. Well known brands were simple enough, but there were 'monster' brands of this, that and the other chocolate bars, bubble and chewing gum, about forty types of crisps and crunchy bars etc. By the last drop I was all but tearing my hair out and once more I was pleased to be heading homewards.

'Foghorn-Leghorn' was invited to take the place of 'The Guardsman', driving for an antiques firm, as the latter was unable to drive on one particular occasion. All went well during the course of the day and on his way home, fully laden, he pulled in at a service station, forgetting the roof of the truck was higher than the cab. It collided with an overhanging roof and 'Foghorn' winced as the contents of the truck fell over in the back. When he opened the doors the scene was exactly as he imagined it to be. Many valuable antiques lay broken, including a number of grandfather clocks, their springs hanging in all directions. Needless to say, he was never invited to fill in for 'The Guardsman' again.

During the course of a coal delivery 'fiddle', I was on a main road near to 'Foghorn's' home, when I espied his wife and two children waiting for a bus. I stopped and said, "Want a lift anywhere?" — "We were going to town," she replied, "But I have changed my mind, it is too cold. Come to our house and have a cup of tea."

I parked the coal wagon outside the house and after some refreshments I departed. When I next saw 'Foghorn' on duty, he said, in mock anger, "Thank you for parking your coal lorry outside my house when I was away. I wouldn't mind under most circumstances, but I live on an all electric estate — no coal fires. I don't know what the neighbours must have thought," and he walked away smirking, leaving me speechless.

His main hobby, when not on duty or 'fiddling', was military aircraft and he would visit as many air shows as possible along with trips near to bases. On one such occasion he was parked on a grass verge outside a top U.S.A.A.F. base when a local copper arrived. The 'Bobby' said, "You cannot stop here — double yellow lines." "But I am not on the yellow lines, I am off the road," 'Foghorn' replied. The 'Bobby' thought for a moment and said, "Well, I suppose it will be okay, but you might get into trouble with the American Military Police."

Sure enough, within minutes a jeep drew up with an M.P. on board. The occupant drawled, "You can't spot planes from here, this is a secret military establishment." 'Foghorn' replied, "Why can't I? — I am outside the security fence," and then proceeded to inform the astonished M.P. not only of the squadrons based at the 'top secret' airfield, but also the colours the planes carried and the types of planes employed. "How do you know all this?" asked the dumbfounded M.P. "Just a minute," 'Foghorn' replied and went to his car. He then pulled a book out and showed it to the stunned American serviceman. "It is all about current fighters and bombers and can be purchased from any branch of W.H. Smith." Exit one down-in-the-mouth M.P. and a laughing 'Bobby'.

I helped out at a garden centre for a while, for the princely sum of five shillings an hour. One job involved a trip to a private house to cut the lawns and trim the hedges. My 'employer', a large, red-faced Irishman, decided, once we had arrived and discovered it was an old lady we were doing the job for, to rip her off and he doubled his original price.

Judgement was soon at hand. Whilst trimming the hedge he disturbed a wasps nest, being stung several times. He went into a rage and poured petrol onto the hedge where the nest was and before I could stop him a match was struck and thrown. In an instant a sheet of flame leapt into the sky, causing him to back-pedal rather rapidly.

He screamed, "GET SOME F*!*!*G WATER, QUICK," I rushed to the house, but the only water supply she had was via a well pump, which was hand operated, delivering about three gallons a week. I thought to myself, as I saw him jumping up and down in the garden, 'If I hear sirens, I'm off,' for the lads from the fire station would have had a field day. Fortunately the fire went out before someone called the Brigade, much to my relief.

Most firemen used their own cars to go to and from their various 'fiddles', but on occasions some would roll up at the station in wagons of all shapes and sizes, complete with trade names. 'Nestor' worked for a time for a 'Skip Hire' firm and used to give demonstrations to all and sundry in the station yard. It really must have impressed the hierarchy next door, who, beavering away like rogue sloths in their offices, were distracted time after time with the crashing, banging, scraping and high pitched transmission noises associated with the off and on loading of the skip.

Many firemen once worked in their spare time at funeral parlours and acted as pall bearers. Some, like 'Glarer', were naturals, with their funereal style faces. Stories used to filter back of graves not being dug to the correct sizes, with fireman-bearers trying not to laugh as they were widened.

'Pierre', working as an assistant to a grave-digger, tried in vain to persuade his 'boss' to allow him to dig the graves, as it was more money. His 'boss' snarled, "I have the contract for digging them and I will continue to do so, even if it means me digging them at night. Your job is to fill them in."

Although his job wasn't as lucrative as his 'employer's', it was quite a cushy number and 'Pierre' used to pray for long, cold and damp winter's. "They pop off like flies in those conditions," he used to tell us. He had a problem at one particular graveyard where the ground was of clay. After filling in the grave of the departed, he still had a massive pile of clay left over and he had to keep jumping up and down on the grave until there was sufficient room created to accommodate the remaining clay.

'Baz', the former sailor, related a story of how he and his colleagues were struggling to carry a coffin which contained a man who weighed in excess of twenty stones. (A dead weight, so to speak.) On the way to the graveside, his distraught and blubbering widow, of equal proportions to her deceased husband, threw herself bodily onto the coffin. If the bearers legs weren't buckling before, they certainly were then and she literally had to be prised off the coffin before they could proceed any further.

I briefly worked for 'Jock', the 'Death Grip' Leading Fireman, who not only ran a Sub Post-Office, but also had a contract for a while maintaining a local churchyard.

One exceptionally sunny day at the churchyard, I had stripped to the waist, with my transistor radio churning out pop music from the top of a gravestone. I was merrily clipping away at the grass around a grave, when someone tapped my on the shoulder — it was the local vicar. Behind him was a weeping procession, complete with the coffin and bearers. The vicar solemnly whispered, "Would you be so kind as to turn your wireless down a shade, whilst I conduct the burial ceremony." I went scarlet, turned the radio off and retreated as far from the bereaved as I could."

One heavily mist laden morning, I saw 'Skin' working as I arrived, and, without being noticed by him, I crept up to a massive ancient gravestone a few yards away from him and hid behind it. 'Skin' was a jittery and nervous man at the best of times and at the appropriate moment I jumped out at him. Being in a churchyard it had more than the desired effect. I fled, as he waved his fists and shouted, "I'LL KILL YOU, YOU F*!*!*G BASTARD."

Finally, on the subject of funerals, firemen, due to their type of job, often appear to be callous to the outsider, as they have been hardened by many experiences of injury and death. Their sense of humour can be somewhat perverse from time to time. Recently I met up with a retired colleague who said, "So and so has died." "Has he?" I replied. "Well I hope so — we buried him last week."

Although the senior officers at LITTLE SNOBSBURY were far better off than the rank and file financially, they would still attempt to get various jobs 'done on the cheap', by employing firemen, rather than pay the proper rates of pay and get a decent job done in the first place.

'The Gypsy' was employed by the Chief Fire Officer to service and maintain his elderly car and as a result it was off the road more often than it was on it. The final humiliation came when it broke down completely not far from the station and the Chief and his family were towed into the yard by the 'Gypsy's' vehicle, whilst we were playing volleyball. Afterwards, his services as a 'grease-monkey' were dispensed with.

The Deputy Chief hired a chap called 'Lofty', who claimed to be a plumber, to modernise his central heating etc., and surprise, surprise, 'Lofty' turned out to be a 'cowboy', costing the Dep. a small fortune to put things right.

Despite being trained to work correctly and safely on ladders, men would purchase antiquated extension ladders for next to nothing and go to extraordinary lengths to reach virtually unreachable positions high up on buildings whilst painting and decorating for a 'fiddle'. They would also work at dangerous angles, with ladders tied together, mostly by 'granny' knots, and 'Pierre' was lucky not to be badly injured when he fell, spread-eagled, onto a glass verandah from a great height.

'Pierre', (who else?), once attended a lock-out where a window had been broken in order for he and his crew to gain entry. The occupier, an elderly lady, asked if someone on the crew could replace the glass. Before anyone else could get a word in, 'Pierre' was in like a shot. "I will do it for you madam, tomorrow morning." The grateful lady then gave him a pound note.

Thinking it was a tip, 'Pierre' shared the money between the crew members and himself — five shillings each. The following day he purchased the glass and replaced it. "That will be one pound and ten shillings please madam." She gave him just ten shillings. Upon enquiring about the outstanding pound, she said, "I gave you a pound last night," and closed the door on him. Try as he might, he was unable to retrieve the other fifteen shillings from his smirking colleagues.

'The Welshman', the fireman who had shouted abuse at his former colleagues during the carnival procession in LITTLE SNOBSBURY, drove a heavy goods wagon for a 'fiddle' when he was still in the Fire Service. Somewhere in the 'sticks' in remote countryside his lorry became jammed under a bridge. Cursing and swearing he studied the problem, but couldn't come up with any easy answers. A 'local' approached him on his cycle and suggested, "If you let the tyres down it will free your vehicle," and then cycled off. He thought to himself, 'Why didn't I think of that?' Sure enough it worked, but then he realised he had no means of inflating the tyres again and had to walk several miles to the nearest garage to summon assistance.

Gordon worked for a while as an assistant to a fellow fireman, a right 'Con Merchant', as he once described him. The 'Con-Man' had set himself up in business as a 'Jack of all Trades'. He once introduced an embarrassed Gordon to a potential client as a 'gas fitter'. (Gordon knew as much about gas fitting as most males know about the workings of the female mind.)

One of the 'jobs' they were contracted to do, was to repair and re-cement the 'U' bend in the toilet of a posh lady's house. After completing the job they returned to their respective homes. As soon as Gordon arrived home his phone rang. It was the lady of the house they had just been to. She informed him, "As soon as you and your colleage departed I pulled the toilet chain, but the water has remained at the top of the pan ever since." Gordon promised he would return and rang the 'Con-Man', arranging to meet back at the job.

He arrived at the house before his colleague and the lady showed him the pan, which was still filled to the brim. He stood shaking his head and said, "I'm only the assistant. I can't fathom out what is wrong." A few minutes later the 'Con-Man' arrived and after a quick inspection he turned to the lady of the house and said blatantly, "If madam wishes to dispose of her sanitary towels down the toilet, then she must expect it to be blocked." She flushed and indignantly replied, "I most certainly do not dispose of them in that fashion," storming off and leaving them to solve the problem. They soon found the cause. Being in such a rush to complete the task, the 'Con-Man' hadn't bothered to clean out the old cement, which was responsible for the blockage.

The 'Con-Man' owned a battered old van, which he utilised to carry his tools etc. He and Gordon were at a plumbers' merchants, where, amongst the items they were collecting was a large bath which they roped to the roof of the van. Whilst they were in the merchants, unknown to them, the police had closed the main road outside, prior to the Queen and her cortege passing along the highway in a cavalcade. Although a security move, it was only a token one, being in pre-terrorism days, unlike the blanket coverage of today.

Having conducted their business at the plumbers' merchants, they drove away and turned into the main road, not noticing it was empty. They then spotted some police motor-cyclists heading towards them, followed by a column of smart limousines. As the motor cycles passed by, the 'coppers' looked back in disbelief at the battered van with a bath strapped to the top.

Gordon said to the 'Con-Man', recognising the fluttering pennant coming towards them, "It's the Queen. What shall we do?" "Just smile and wave," came the reply. Whatever Her Majesty must have thought of this spectacle we will never know. They sped past the cavalcade and the startled occupants, dignitaries of all ranks, and disappeared into the distance, much to the relief of the 'Con-Man' as he didn't particularly desire having his van stopped and searched by the police, in case some of the materials he had acquired were recognised as having 'fallen off a lorry'.

A number of firemen were D.I.Y. merchants, 'experts', whom nine times out of ten did more harm than good. There were stories of home-made items of furniture, with legs of different sizes etc. One 'entrepreneur' decided to build a cot for his forthcoming infant. He constructed it with solid sides and it wasn't until the baby was tall and strong enough to haul itself up, that it could see over the side and view the outside world.

Another erstwhile carpenter/plumber decided to install a new toilet system. Once fitted he had great difficulty in getting out of the room. The toilet he had installed was larger than the previous one and the inwards opening door wouldn't go past it. Instead of removing and swopping the toilet for a smaller one, he cut slits in the door before realising his privacy wasn't all it should have been. He not only had to replace the toilet, but he also had to purchase another door.

Men Joining, Leaving and Promotion

LITTLE SNOBSBURY was one of the few Brigades that offered housing to its firefighters and their families, locally known as 'The Trap'. Once housed, many would have liked to have left the Brigade, but were reluctant to do so in case they lost their accommodation. Many transferred as soon as an opportunity came along within another Brigade which provided housing. Others left the job completely and moved to different areas of the country in their desire to escape from LITTLE SNOBSBURY. When one of the firemen called their bluff and resigned, but still remained in his council house without being evicted, the flood-gates opened.

Men came from as far afield as Inverness, Sussex and West Wales, lured by the 'carrot' of housing, some of which left something to be desired. Once based at LITTLE SNOBSBURY, most, if not all, couldn't believe what they had walked into, the attitude of the hierarchy was so childish.

Two men left the same day as they joined, one because he couldn't go home for his dinner and another resigned after being ordered to clean the kitchen, telling the Officer in Charge in no uncertain terms where to stick his mop. 'Foghorn' joined LITTLE SNOBSBURY from the local airport Fire Brigade, stayed for a number of years, rejoined the airport Fire Brigade again, and after a short stint, returned to LITTLE SNOBSBURY once more.

148

Another chap, 'Ollie', transferred to a Brigade in Wales and he and his wife were given a big Brigade send off party, with speeches and presents. When they went off to Wales there was something wrong with the legality of the accommodation they were living in, concluding in them becoming virtually homeless. Within days he was back in LITTLE SNOBSBURY Fire Brigade, but whether the farewell presents were returned, I know not.

Another 'regular' resigned but decided to rejoin a few months later. Having gone through the normal rigmarole associated with the same, he was again issued with his kit. Everything was duly marked with his personal number, 'painted' and 'stamped', but after completion he had a change of heart and resigned once more. I bet the hierarchy loved that one!!!

One immigrant, 'Frank', from London, having taken as much as he could, packed the job in and became a publican. After a few months passed by I decided to pay him a visit. When I arrived I couldn't find him so I enquired from a regular, "Excuse me, I am looking for the landlord, Frank," but before I could continue the regular said, "So is half the pub and the Brewery. He has been watering the beer down for months and pocketing the proceeds." I never saw 'Frank' again.

'The Apprentice' arrived from Scotland with his family, for an interview with the Chief and also to inspect his new accommodation. As he drove into the station yard they stopped to observe an unbelievable event. There in the yard was one of the old fashioned dustcarts, the ones where the sides slid up and over. Four firemen were swinging 'Pierre' to and fro and on the shout of three he was hurled protesting into the cart, where he disappeared into a mound of rubbish. 'Welcome to LITTLE SNOBSBURY'.

Moving on to promotion, this was extremely hard to come by at LITTLE SNOBSBURY, being a one station Brigade. Vacancies only occurred if officers retired, moved on to other Brigades or died. The hierarchy didn't have the foresight to promote men who had the necessary qualifications to move up the next rung of promotion, thereby creating a 'dead-mens' shoes situation.

If an additional appliance was purchased there was a mad scramble to obtain the jobs. "Yes Sir — No Sir — Three Bags Full." Much depended on being in the right place at the right time and having a face which 'fitted' the bill, promotion then being a cert. Being in the wrong place at the wrong time with the wrong face, then one could forget it. Quite often, 'trouble-makers', like union reps who had stirred things up, would be promoted, thus reducing a few thorns from the sides of the hierarchy.

Once promoted, many men completely changed their attitudes towards their former colleagues. The 'carrot' was in front of them. "Nothing will stop me reaching the top now, you know." (The working class can kiss my arse etc.) "I know it's a stupid order and you know it's a stupid order, but it came direct from the Chief, so get on with it. Everyone except him knows that coal is black and not white."

The wives of the newly promoted men would really go to town, especially at social gatherings. Looking down their noses at their former friends, whilst mixing with a clique more suited to their new stations in life, comments would be heard similar to, "Now that my husband is an officer ....." It mattered not if he was only a Leading Fireman — absolute snobbery, the epitome of LITTLE SNOBSBURY.

'Glarer' applied for a number of vacancies for Station Officer posts in other Brigades, but each time, much to our disappointment, he was turned down. We heard later, through the grapevine, that the main reason he failed was because he ended up quizzing the interviewers and shouting at them if they said anything he didn't like. One could imagine it: "Why do you wish to leave your present Brigade?" — "IT'S GOT F*!K ALL TO DO WITH YOU — sorry, sorry, I didn't mean that. I don't know what came over me."

After one such interview, 'Glarer' returned to the station at LITTLE SNOBSBURY and in a crowded recreation room 'Pierre' asked him how he had got on. "I've got the job," he announced. The room erupted in cheers which soon disappeared when he continued, "But I am not going to take it, the housing isn't good enough."

Eventually he gained the cherished position of the substansive Station Officer's job he had so longed for. He deserved it, or so he said, he had been denied what was rightfully his for so long. A number of men refused to attend his farewell function, but I went, for I was relishing in the fact that I would never see this hateful man again.

He moved to a City Brigade close to the sea (their loss being our gain) and within a matter of months news filtered back that he had been the Officer in Charge of two major 'cock-ups' in as many weeks — what a surprise!!! The last I ever heard of him was when we were leaving the same city after a sea fishing trip. We had stopped in the MAMMOTH COUNTY van at a newspaper shop when a Turntable Ladder pulled up and parked in front of us. Amongst the conversation that followed I asked one of the crew members how he got on with 'Glarer' and back came the immediate reply, "That w*nk*r, the sooner he f*!ks off the better, what an obnoxious prat." I cannot think of a more suitable epitaph to 'Glarer'.

I took the written section of the Leading Fireman's exam quite early in my career and passed first time. It was far easier in those days than it is now. Most of the questions were not even associated with the Fire Service, thank goodness. For instance, there would be a blank map of Great Britain, with dots all over the place, 'Pick out Carlisle, London, Liverpool and Glasgow' etc. Mind you there were a few who got these wrong. No wonder some firemen went from Liverpool to Devon via London and Southampton!!!

The second part of the exam, the practical side, consisted of a number of set drills and questions from members of the hierarchy, including the Chief. The drills were a piece of cake, but when it came to the questions and answers session, the officers hadn't the brains to vary the questions or keep the candidates apart. As a result, by the time I was summoned, I not only knew the questions, but all of the subsequent answers as well and I passed with 'flying colours' — what a farce.

As an individual I wasn't particularly interested in promotion, but by the mid-seventies MAMMOTH COUNTY was so short of qualified personnel, even I, at the bottom of the barrel, was asked to do a temporary stint to cover for a Leading Fireman who was attending the Fire Service College for a number of weeks.

A few months later three vacancies for Leading Firemen were created at another station in our Division and I was persuaded, reluctantly, to put my name forward for one of the posts. I heard nothing until a few days prior to the interviews. I was working in the bar one night shift when the Divisional Commander popped his head round the door and said, "About the vacancy you have applied for, you have got it." Just like that. I enquired about having an interview, but was told to forget it. 'What of the other candidates?' I thought to myself.

Now this was where some members of the hierarchy of the Fire Service really came into their own. Having already chosen the personnel for the jobs prior to the interviews, the latter would still go ahead, the remaining candidates being totally unaware that they stood no chance. They would then be torn to shreds, 'man-management' it was called, all in the so called name of confidence building — confidence destroying I called it. A cross-fire of difficult questions would be hurled at the victims, by officers who already knew the answers, having recently swotted them up, culminating in, "Give me a five minute lecture on a match," or something equally ridiculous.

Most men would depart from the interview like wet rag-dolls, but occasionally some stuck up for themselves, not only facing up to the flak, but also launching counter-attacks, regardless of the assortment of 'scrambled egg' on show. The 'Savage' Sub-O had been experiencing a torrid time during one particular interview and in his words he had given a good account of himself or so he had thought.

One of his tormentors, an Assistant Chief Fire Officer, had a stutter and towards the end of the interview he summed up, "I-I, I ddddd, don't th-th-th-th-th, think, you-you-you-you, you, gggggg, give us, th-th-th-th-th-th, the im-im-im-im, impression of bbbbbb, being co-co-co-co-co-co, confident, in-in-in-in-in, in your-your-your-your-your, your out-out-out-out, outlook."

The 'Savage' Sub-O looked at the other officers on the panel in disbelief and then returned to the question master, "I think you've a bleeding nerve saying I lack confidence. At least I can string more than two consecutive words together, which is more than you can apparently do." If the other officers were amused at their colleague's predicament, they didn't show it and needless to say the 'Savage' one didn't get the post he was after.

Being promoted, even on a temporary basis, opened the door to the inner sanctum, a world denied to lowly firemen. One could pass through previously closed doors and not be quizzed by senior officers as to why you were ogling at the typists in their offices, using this, that or the other trivial pretext for being there. Keys would be entrusted to your safe-keeping and you were allowed to dish out derv and petrol and sign for deliveries of the same. Also, once promoted, it was assumed you were a fully qualified typist, even if you had never used one before.

When it came to the issuing of fuel stocks, clangers were dropped from time to time. Junior officers in charge of the 'dip' checks for the fuel would often forget to re-order and many was the time that heating oil would run out in the middle of a cold snap, with 'bollockings' all round. One junior officer put heating oil in the derv tank — another 'bollock-ing' from upstairs. Yet another filled the tank of the H.P. with the wrong type of fuel and it clapped out on the main road in clouds of dense smoke.

Not long after MAMMOTH COUNTY was formed, three firemen from my Watch were summoned to the D.C.'s office. 'Chalky' the ex. marine, Clive 'G' and 'Foghorn-Leghorn'. There was speculation as to why 'Foghorn' had been called in as it was obvious the other two were in line for promotion.

They emerged one by one, with big smiles all round — promotion at last for 'Chalky' and Clive 'G'. We waited with bated breath for 'Foghorn'. When he returned he said, "I sat down and the D.C. con-gratulated me, offering me the post of substansive Leading Fireman, to which I replied, well that's very kind of you sir, but not only have I not got the exam under my belt, but I have never sat it." He then described the D.C.'s reaction. "Some stupid person in H.Q. has made a 'balls-up' to say the least." 'Foghorn' continued, "The D.C. seized the phone and once the recipient who had dropped the 'bollock' had been located, he was given a right going over. By the time the D.C. had finished the ears of the poor unfortunate on the other end of the line had been well and truly burnt. I was then dismissed from his room."

One man, who was well into his Fire Service career, once noted for stopping comrades from working by standing on their mops to talk to them, went from fireman to Station Officer in a relatively short space of time. With it went his humour, with everything being done by the book. He once rang me from his station and when I picked the receiver up he asked, "Is our petty cash in your safe?" I replied, "I don't know, I can't see through two walls and a metal box from where I am sitting." All that happened was a stony silence. So much for promotion.

'Arbut' was promoted to Leading Fireman and served on my Watch for a while and during one night shift 'Dave Rainbow' and I noticed him taping a second band on his helmet. I said, "What's this Arbut? Promo-tion to Sub-Officer already?" Replying in an 'up market' voice he said, "Only temporary at the moment, but the D.C. has assured me it will soon be permanent." Both 'Dave Rainbow' and I sneered at him. "Don't take too much notice of the D.C., he will say one thing and do another." "I trust him, I will show you," came the two fingered reply. A few weeks later, there was poor old 'Arbut' peeling off the additional tape. "Told you so," I said. "BOLLOCKS," was the snarled reply.

If there was some 'favouritism' shown in the promotion stakes, then it certainly came to light with reference to one 'officer' who had returned from a stint in a foreign Fire Service. Imagine him being interviewed by the Chief upon his return. "Well, old chap, we really need good officers like you, but I cannot promote you instantly to A.D.O. or D.O., those bastards in the union would probably object. You will have to start at the ground floor and work your way up. Know what I mean? Nudge, nudge, wink, wink." Sure enough, within a few years of starting at the ground floor he was a senior officer once more, appearing at various stations. "What are you doing for drill today?" as he tapped his hands with a pair of officers' gloves.

To sum up promotion, not only did you have to be an instant typist, but you also had to be an expert in dealing with the men, assessing fire situations, have full knowledge of all known chemicals, explosives, cylinders, radio messages and office work. Many men, who swiftly rose up through the ranks, became out of their depth. As 'Dave Rainbow' once said to me "You work at Divisional H.Q. and you *think* they don't know what they are doing. I work at Brigade H.Q. and I *know* they don't know what they are doing." So much for the wrong, sorry, right men getting the wrong, sorry, right jobs!!!

Open Days and Competition Drills

To the general public, open days at fire stations give them and their youngsters a chance to see the Fire Service at its 'dynamic' best, with spectacular fire and rescue drills, and mock traffic accidents. What the majority of the members of the public don't realise is that all of the drills are 'staged' and not spontaneous as in the 'real world'. Drills are practised and practised until every man involved knows exactly what equipment he is working with and where he should be at any given moment in time, hence it is seldom that major mistakes occur. One, a classic, will be described towards the end of the chapter.

I was involved in a four man pumping drill from open water in MAMMOTH COUNTY, and my partner in running out the hose was 'The Corporal'. He and I were always at loggerheads as to whom was the smallest or tallest with each of us having to suffer the indignity caused by others placing small step-ladders to enable us to reach into the cabs of fire engines and being tagged as 'The Jolly Green Giant' or a 'PORG' (Person of Restricted Growth).

As I was running my length of hose out, 'The Corporal' was some yards behind me with another length, running as fast as his little legs could carry him. Suddenly, I heard a loud gasp from the onlookers and a thud. I glanced round and saw the red-faced 'Corporal' picking himself up. He had tripped over right in front of the Chief and his entourage. I don't know what Chief Officer's think to themselves in such situations, but I would imagine it would be something similar to, 'Stupid prat, showing the Brigade up like that!' My wife, who was standing in the crowd, heard a woman behind her say, "What a shame for that poor *little* fireman, he has fallen over." This remark was repeated later to 'The Corporal' by myself, with gloating relish.

In LITTLE SNOBSBURY days, the jets used for open days were of different colours, helping to make the water-streams more spectacular than normal. Station Officer 'Red-Cheeks' delegated 'Pierre' to empty the contents of a plastic cup, containing a concentrated coloured substance, into the tank of a fire engine. He clamboured on to the top of the vehicle, opened the tank lid, but instead of pouring the contents into the tank he dropped the cup into the water.

The cup sank to the bottom, harmlessly at first, but whilst doing some pumping drills it became lodged in the outlet, blocking it. Eventually it was retrieved after the tank was all but dismantled at workshops. 'Red-Cheeks' went potty, "WHAT A BLOODY IDIOT. WHAT A STUPID PRAT. HE COULDN'T EVEN PERFORM A SIMPLE TASK LIKE EMPTYING A CUP PROPERLY."

During a practise session, two Pumps were utilised, creating eight jets with two different coloured water-streams. Joe 'The Boxer' attempted to organise things so that 'Pierre' got a soaking, but it backfired on him

155

and when he turned round after running his length of hose out, seven jets were trained on him and to make matters worse his own water supply had been isolated, making it more than one-sided, to say the least. Joe was absolutely soaked.

Watching this saga from an upstairs window, the Chief, in a rare show of humour, instantly ordered Joe, via another officer, to report to his office, once the water ran out. Fully expecting a 'bollocking', Joe shuffled and squelched his way to the Chief's office. In fact it was to the contrary. He gave Joe his full blessing to get even, which he succeeded in doing over the course of the day.

Competition drills in MAMMOTH COUNTY, although frowned upon by the union, were a blessing in disguise for the men, for it meant that the normal off-the-cuff drills could be set aside. Hours would be spent on set pumping and ladder drills, until the various crews were tuned to perfection.

There was much entertainment in the initial stages, with men falling over, ladders being dropped and hose-lines ending up as 'birds-nests'. Preliminary rounds were held at many individual stations until the winners of each category, from each of the different Divisions within the Brigade, were known. Then a 'Grand Final' would be staged, often at a neutral venue.

One lad, Fm. 'Night', from one of the Watches on my station, had fought his way through to the final of the 'one man' hydrant drill. Being 'one man' it involved no water. The starting pistol was triggered and he was off like a greyhound, attempting to break the Guinness Book of Records speed for the 'one man' hydrant drill. (As if they had ever heard of it in the first place!!!)

Upon reaching the hydrant he was unable to lift the lid off at the first attempt, thereby losing valuable seconds. Once off he then fumbled whilst shipping the standpipe, losing more time. After the standpipe, key and bar were in place he connected the hose, collected the branch, and set off on his run. Instead of running the hose out smoothly it kept dragging on his hands causing him much pain to go with his anguish for making a 'balls-up' of the whole run.

By the time he came to the end of the length of hose he was so 'pissed off' with the whole proceedings that he threw the lot into the air. Jumping up and down in a frenzied rage, he bawled, "F*!K IT," unaware that the Chief and his wife were seated a few feet away. The Chief must have been really impressed, I don't think.

A story recently related to me by the 'Savage' Sub-O, also concerned the Chief. This time the competition involved was First Aid. Some members of my old Watch had come second in the contest and had been awarded their trophy, not by the Chief in person, although he was in the near vicinity.

One excited participant, a young probationer, having never laid his eyes on the Chief, said in a loud voice, "What a pity we came second.

If we had won I would have kissed the Chief full on the lips." Upon hearing this remark, the Chief turned to him and replied, "If that is the case lad, I will have to ensure you never come first," leaving a scarlet-faced 'sprog' to reflect on the folly of his statement.

I was involved in the classic 'bungled' 'Open Day' drills at LITTLE SNOBSBURY where almost everything went wrong during the first run, from start to finish, despite weeks of intensive training.

One young fireman, a huge ungainly looking chap, 'Lofty', was to be a 'victim' in an open sewer 'rescue', but during a training session, he ran, or rather lumbered across the yard, forgetting the manhole was open and he fell down it, thereby making it a genuine 'rescue'. He was sick for a while with a bad back, but once he returned he continued to partici-pate in the same drill. (After all, he no longer needed to train for this particular part as he was already experienced!!!)

As he was a little on the dense side, the hierarchy didn't want him to perform too many complicated tasks, in case he made a hash of the main show. So another job they gave him was to act as a member of the public, running to a home-made telephone box and dialling '999', or rather pretending to.

He was a strange lad, our 'Lofty'. I could never quite make him out and I don't think he had all of his 'marbles'. He used to go up to the bar, or 'wet canteen' as it was referred to in those days and ask for chewing gum or chocolate. When given a packet of chewing gum or a Mars bar he would say, "No, not one, I want the whole box," and he would purchase the lot.

After resigning from the Fire Service he became a full-time ice-cream salesman and he appeared back at the station one hot summer's evening in his ice-cream van. He was so large he could hardly fit inside the van and he wore a white gown with a huge, black bowler hat. When he drove off something had been dripping from beneath the van, hopefully not ice-cream, for whatever it was it melted a section of the tarmac.

To return to the 'Open Day', on the day in question, one final 45′ ladder drill was performed prior to the doors of the station being opened to the members of the public. As a precaution, in case something went wrong during the drills, chalk marks were stencilled on the various ladders to denote the limits to which they needed to be extended.

Before long, the station, engine house and drill yard were swarming with visitors. Obviously the fire engines were the biggest crowd pullers and the cabs were jammed with folk, mostly children who played constantly with the bells, sirens and blue flashing lights. The little blighters even climbed on the tops of the machines.

The 'magic hour' arrived in which we were to commence with our first show and the crowd was ushered behind the safety barricades. Two men, Fm. 'Angry' and 'Skin' were to be rescued from the third floor of the drill tower. Whilst we were donning our fire kit and climbing into the fire engines 'Skin' and his partner set off up the tower. Apart from the hundreds of members of the public, the Chief, several officers and the hierarchy of LITTLE SNOBSBURY Council, the Mayor, Councillors and their wives etc., were also watching, from a privileged position.

Prior to turning out, 'Skin' and his crony set off some smoke bombs in the tower, the signal for 'Lofty' to rush to the telephone box and dial

'999'. Unknown to 'Lofty' some joker had nailed up the door of the box and he all but wrecked it in his efforts to gain access, much to the amusement of the audience, with the exception of the Chief and company.

Upon a given signal, all the paraphanalia associated with fire engines were switched on. Two Pump Ladders and a Hydraulic Platform responded to a fictitious fire call, 'Persons Trapped'. As we turned out I glanced round and observed an unsecured locker door on the H.P. open and flapping. I giggled to myself and thought, 'Someone will be in for the high jump', not realising the disaster I was shortly going to be involved in.

Meanwhile, back in the drill tower, things were not going as planned. The smoke bombs had been set off, but pieces of red hot material had jumped inside 'Skin's' fireboots and shirt and he was frantically attempting to strip off as we hurtled into the yard. As he was hopping up and down in the tower, men poured out of applicances to run out hose-lines. Ladders were snatched and the H.P. set up.

I was part of a four-man crew involved in the 'rescue' of 'Skin' and his mate. We ran to our base position in front of the tower, unaware of 'Skin's' predicament and under-ran our 45′ aluminium ladder into a vertical position. As it was being extended, I searched desperately for the pre-determined chalk line on the ladder, but it was gone. The horrid little urchins who had crawled on top of the fire engines had rubbed it out. By the time I realised it had disappeared, the ladder had been extended too high. Upon shouting the order 'Well', the ladder was dropped into the tower, but above the third floor.

To lower such a ladder, it has to be extended slightly first, but when we raised it the head became jammed under the sill of the fourth floor, embarrassing to say the least. Under normal circumstances we would have ceased working, thought about the problem, worked as a team, and lowered it to safety. With hundreds of people, plus the 'Big-Wigs' watching, we panicked and instead of working as a team the four of us tried different ideas to remedy the situation all at once.

The head of the ladder was eventually wrenched free from its trapped position at exactly the same time that someone lifted the heel. Another crew member attempted to steady the ladder from behind, but it commenced rocking violently from side to side as soon as the heel came into contact with terra firma once more.

It then became like a 'Mad, Mad World' situation, with the ladder swaying back and forth, the crowd going 'Ooh', 'Aah', each time the head reached its zenith. Other firemen, who could have helped, stood transfixed, like statues, mesmerized by what was happening. It was if time had stood still. Even 'Skin', by now over his own problems, who could have made a grab for the head of the ladder to steady it, did nothing, as if hypnotised by the swaying motion in front of him.

One man who hadn't noticed these events, was 'Jock', the 'Death Grip' Leading Fireman, who was in a world of his own at the end of a branch.

The ladder then decided to 'walk' sidewards and by now it was almost out of our control. Eventually it went beyond the point of no return and we had little choice but to drop it. It seemed an eternity before it crashed to the ground, rivets flying in all directions. Despite our shouting 'Jock' remained oblivious and it missed him by inches.

There it lay, twisted and broken, the crowd silenced, as if they felt for our predicament. I for one wished at the time the ground had opened and swallowed me up and when I glanced at the Chief and company, who were glaring at us, I felt even worse.

A quick witted Station Officer grabbed the microphone and stated to the crowd, "As you can see there has been a slight mishap, a very rare occurrence. That is why at least two fire engines are always sent to house fires, in case something goes wrong." (What a load of bull-shit.) At that we took the hint and fetched a similar ladder from the second appliance and completed the 'rescue' without any further hitches.

With the drills finished for the morning session, the crowd dispersed. The hierarchy disappeared next door and the crews repaired to the mess. Word came down from next door that the Chief wouldn't be pressing charges, providing all went well during the afternoon session. All did indeed go well, like clockwork, thank God.

I always hated being involved in 'Open Days', excellently summed up by 'Buggy' when he once said, "Why don't we have a 'Punch and Judy' show at the start of each drill? Here come the firemen, here they come, running round the yard. Watch them perform for you."

In the Fire Service there is nothing worse than being unable to find a particular location first time and the situation is compounded when it becomes obvious to members of the public. I always felt embarrassed when machines traversed roads in both directions, eventually grinding to a halt, with beacons flashing. Officers in Charge would confer with one another and crew members would run around in ever decreasing circles, mostly to no avail.

On our 'patch' most roads were clearly marked by the Council, one feature being that there were very few 'walk-through's'. We were most unfortunate, during the hours of darkness, to be called to a kitchen fire at a house in one of these latter locations.

Despite a swift arrival to the approximate area of the incident and also despite the usage of the A-Z and other aids, we were unable to pinpoint where this road was, even after traversing adjacent streets. It was obvious it wasn't a major incident as there were no flames to be seen, nor were there folk running towards the appliances as was normally the case if there was something seriously amiss.

As several minutes had passed by since our initial arrival Fire Control were going 'bananas', demanding to know why we hadn't booked in attendance. Then salvation arrived in the shape of a skinhead, who, dressed in an SS uniform, had cycled up to us from nowhere. At first he simply leered at us, but upon overhearing the name of the road we were by now desperately trying to find, he shouted, "I KNOW WHERE IT IS. FOLLOW ME."

A more than grateful O.I.C., Sub Officer 'Dave Rainbow', was immediately able to calm Fire Control down by booking in attendance, keeping his fingers crossed as we followed the SS attired skinhead on his bicycle, that he wasn't having us on. True to his word, he guided us to the road and the house we were searching for. No wonder we had been unable to locate the 'walk-through', the road nameboard had been stolen and the row of houses involved had all seemed part and parcel of the other roads on this modern estate.

'Dave Rainbow', myself and two B.A. wearers were greeted at the front door by a middle-aged woman, who at first denied there had been any kind of fire and she led us into the kitchen. As we passed the foot of the stairs I couldn't help but notice a bandy legged boxer dog looking down at us from the landing. I was always wary of dogs, but it seemed rather disinterested in our presence.

Despite there being a smoke-blackened cooker, which was always associated with burning fat, she still denied having a fire that day and tried to make out that she had experienced a fire several months beforehand and hadn't had the time to clear the mess up.

This conversation had only happened in seconds and in this brief timespan we noticed she had a black eye and was more than a little tipsy. We eventually were able to ascertain from her that she had overheated the chip pan (a fact we already knew as we could still smell the fumes). Her husband had quenched the flames, punched her in the face and disappeared to the nearest pub in disgust.

'Dave Rainbow' asked the woman if she wanted the police to intervene on her behalf, but she declined his offer. By this time the boxer dog had joined us and was seated by her side. As we were about to leave, she asked 'Dave Rainbow' if he liked dogs, to which he rather apprehensively said "yes." At that she said, "Seize him." In an instant this apparently placid creature leapt into the air and grabbed 'Dave's' fire tunic by the elbow, with two rows of rather ferocious teeth, gnashing and snarling for what appeared to be a lifetime before she called it to heel.

Why she had done this action, we never knew and we retreated from the house, back to the sanctuary of the fire engines, leaving her to the tender mercies of her husband upon his return from the pub. Fortunately for 'Dave Rainbow' it was only his ego which had been hurt, but this incident was to provide us with much entertainment for some time afterwards.

We were often despatched, with appliances, to the former 'Arsehole of the World' Fire Brigade's 'patch' to stand by and we always dreaded being turned out from the central station for it led us immediately onto their horrendous ring road. It was not so much a question of actually 'getting lost' on the way to an incident, for we were already 'lost' inside the station.

On one occasion that 'Pierre' was present on standby they were turned out, leaving just the H.P. and crew behind. They had been sent as a back-up to another machine from a different station. The H.P. crew watched their departure as they disappeared onto the ring road. A few minutes later they stared in amazement as 'Pierre's' fire engine whizzed by, with its crew waving at them, having gone full circle on the ring road.

Within minutes the same procedure was repeated as 'Pierre' tried in vain to locate the road to which they had been sent to. By the third circuit, with the fire crew still waving, the H.P. men had collapsed, helpless with laughter. There was no fourth circuit, for the 'Stop' message had been despatched by the O.I.C. of the other appliance and a more than grateful 'Pierre' was able to return to the station.

One of the first 'foul-ups' I attended, was in LITTLE SNOBSBURY, at a chimney fire. Normally it was a simple task — shove a few chimney rods up and with the aid of a stirrup pump, rubber hose and a bucket of water the fire could quickly be extinguished.

The property we visited was an old cottage, owned by an elderly lady, who was quite upset. "How much will I have to pay?" she sobbed. "Nothing madam," — "Please don't make a mess." — "You can rely on us," and the O.I.C. a Leading Fireman, took her into the kitchen, leaving a fireman to reassure her that all would be well. As there was a tight bend in the chimney we had to deal with the fire from the roof. We pitched a 35' ladder and ascended to the chimney using a roof ladder, hauling a hose-reel aloft at the same time.

The Leading Fireman gave instructions that he would remain in the living room, where the fire was, and as soon as any water reached the grate he would call up to us to knock the water off. Gallon after gallon disappeared down the chimney, but still no shout from below.

Water continued to flow, until eventually there was a loud scream from the Leading Hand, "KNOCK IT OFF." Somewhere along the downward route the water had been trapped and then, through its own weight, down the whole lot went, 'WHOOSH'. It soaked the L.Fm. and when

it ceased flowing the old lady's carpet floated on a black mass of H^2O. So much for the Leading Hand's assurance to the old dear. It took ages to sweep the water out and even longer to clear up the mess.

There were profuse apologies to the occupant and her carpet was slung over a washing line to dry. At least the fire was out — well and truly. We made up the gear and the tank was topped up via a short length from a nearby hydrant. Whilst the tank was being replenished we came to make the 35' ladder up, which we discovered was back to front. It was a good job we hadn't needed to extend it in sight of the public — another 'cock-up'. To complete the mayhem, the short length of hose then burst, soaking most of the fire crew and some passers-by.

A particular statement, usually issued by a senior officer, frequently crops up on our television screens after a major conflagration and it often gives me cause for amusement whenever I hear it. ''Fire Brigade *experts* are sifting through the damage,'' giving 'Joe Public' yet another reason to admire the professional qualities of the same.

In many instances this is 'bunkum', a 'smoke-screen' so to speak. Some Fire Service officers wouldn't know how most fires started even if they lit one themselves and the vast majority of the 'CAUSE OF IGNITION' comments on 'Fire Reports' comes under the metaphoric headings of 'Electrical', 'Children Playing With Matches', 'Discarded Cigarette Ends', and 'Sparks From Passing Locomotives', all of which covers a multitude of sins.

One such classic example of 'Fire Brigade Experts' sifting through the damage was related to myself by 'Dave Rainbow'. With the fire all but extinguished, 'Animal' shouted, ''I DON'T CARE HOW LONG IT TAKES, I WANT THE BODY FOUND.'' It turned out that he was standing on the charred remains of the deceased!!!

Generally speaking the average member of the community at large doesn't realise that the Fire Service has the right to despatch a fire engine for an inspection call, days after the event. The particular person involved in this next story, a 'late call' as it is described, had been a trifle hesitant in calling the Fire Brigade in the first place, but someone, a 'do-gooder', had advised him to do so.

A fire engine duly arrived and the O.I.C. was shown the slight damage by the occupier, who asked, again in a hesitant manner, if there was only one fire appliance coming to his property, as he didn't wish to be embarrassed by a large crowd gathering in front of it. He was given an 'assurance' that only one machine was sent to 'late fire calls'. Meanwhile, back in Fire Control, some sort of 'foul-up' was going on, with someone mistaking the 'late' call for a real one and in yet another 'cock-up', at least twice the normal number of appliances were despatched in error.

Returning to the affected property, soon after the O.I.C. had given the occupier his 'assurance', sirens and bells were heard in the distance, becoming ever louder, until, amidst a cacophony of noise, eight more pumping appliances and a Turntable Ladder arrived at this same address, blocking the road. Far from being able to maintain a 'low profile', the red-faced O.I.C. and occupier were faced by this melee, aggravated by the presence of a host of onlookers, fascinated to know why there were ten fire engines in their road.

Shortly after I departed from MAMMOTH COUNTY I met up with a former colleague at a social function, where he informed me of the latest fiasco he had been involved in, this being some time after he had transferred from the former station at LITTLE SNOBSBURY, to a station on a busier Division.

He had attended a fire at a large factory, where the flames had been all but subdued. From out of nowhere, further up one of the roads next to the factory, large volumes of smoke poured out of the windows of a residential property. The cause was later put down to arson. The house concerned, was allegedly occupied by two 'lesbians', one of whom had been jilted by her partner. In a jealous rage the jilted wench had deliberately set fire to it.

One fireman was so keen to be the first to be at the scene (so becoming a hero!!!) that he jumped into the cab of the first appliance he could find and without stopping to think (that was the way he was trained!!!) he then drove it to the affected house, but in his haste he hadn't bothered to check the rear of the fire engine before doing so. He screeched to a halt outside the house, engaged the power take-off (for pumping) and hurtled to the rear of the machine. The sight which greeted him left him motionless with shock.

Although the fire engine hadn't been actively engaged at the time he drove off, it had been, and it was connected to a hydrant, with two hose-lines leading into the factory. He discovered to his horror that one of the deliveries had been wrenched out of the pump casing by his actions and he had all but ripped the hydrant out of the ground. There was also a length of hose trailing behind the engine. The remaining hose-line had been dragged out of the factory as he had driven off and during its journey it had entwined itself round an A.D.O.'s legs, dumping him unceremoniously into several inches of water before he could free himself. Needless to say, the fire had to be put out by a different engine and crew. What ever happened to the 'hero' after this farce, I know not.

'Foghorn-Leghorn' was part of a crew mobilised to a Special Service Call — a young lad with his head trapped in railings. Upon arrival the Officer in Charge assured poor little 'Nigel's' (or whatever his name was) mother, that her son would soon be released. 'Foghorn' collected the railing expander, placed it between two railings and commenced expanding the same. "Don't worry sonny, you will be okay." As the implement began to bite and bend the railings, 'Foghorn' noticed that little 'Nigel' was going crimson. 'Cor Blimey', he thought to himself, 'I've placed the expander between the wrong rails.' Instead of releasing the boy he had been doing his best to 'throttle' him. The situation was rectified within seconds and the lad released. Good old 'Foghorn'.

'Animal' was in charge of an incident where the mains electric had shorted on the Electricity Board side of the system and it was sparking like the 'Fourth of July'. No matter how many Carbon Dioxide and Dry Powder extinguishers were used, the wretched thing refused to die down. Instead of waiting for the experts in this particular field to arrive and deal with the problem in a professional manner, 'Animal', in a fit of temper, belted the affected mains with his axe.

There was a tremendous explosion and a huge pall of smoke erupted. When the smoke cleared we all expected to find nothing but a pair of smouldering fireboots. However, 'Animal' survived unscathed, as usual. His action caused the mains to short all the way back to the sub-station, knocking out the power supplies to one in three houses, costing the local Electricity Board a fortune to restore.

During MAMMOTH COUNTY days we had a job way out in the sticks involving a pig farm which was severely damaged. Miles of hose was run out and so short were we of pumping appliances, with most being involved in a water relay which was being set up, an Ambulance and a Hydraulic Platform had to be commandeered to ferry hose, here, there, and everywhere.

Whilst in the latter stages of running the hose out, a 'yokel' type of fellow leaned over a hedge and commented, "Oh, arr. I don't know what thee lads are laying all that 'ose for, there be no point. The water only trickles around 'ere, oh, arr," and he laughed. We chose to ignore him, after all what would a 'Country Bumpkin' know about mains water supplies. Sure enough he was right. When the various hydrants were turned on, next to nothing happened. What a waste of time and effort and later in the day, as we were making the miles of hose-lines up, guess who peeped over the hedge once more. "I told thee it were a waste of time."

During the scorching summer of 1976, 'the year of the ladybird', we spent more time off the station than we did on, fighting fires in parks and woodlands for most of the time. At first, small fires were extinguished by the water contained within the tanks of fire engines, if no other supplies were available within the immediate vicinity. Where long term jobs were concerned we tapped into canals, rivers and ponds, with miles of hose being run out which remained there for weeks at a time.

The 'Savage' one, not long out of Training School, was sent by an O.I.C. to one of the branches deep in a wood. He followed the hose-line until he eventually came across the branch. At first he was fascinated by the flames which jumped out of rabbit holes without warning. (One used to point the branch down the affected hole and observe fire and smoke, deep underground, emerge from a dozen other holes — like 'Elmer Fud' searching for 'Bugs Bunny'.)

Bored with his 'waste-of-time' actions, the 'Savage' one decided he had done enough and sat on a log. Within minutes he had nodded off. He awoke later and thought he was dreaming. Amidst the smouldering peat and woods he saw half a dozen men in pin-striped suits, bowler hats and umbrellas heading towards him. He wasn't dreaming — more like a nightmare, for they turned out to be high ranking insurance officers from LITTLE SNOBSBURY Council who had got off their backsides in their offices and decided to assess the woodland damage. They really must have been impressed with the 'Savage' one's 'keen' attitude!!!

I attended these fires on countless occasions. During one incident where we had emptied the contents of a fire engine tank onto an affected area, I was sat on the trunk of a tree with two leading Firemen, whilst we awaited the return of the wagon which had gone to the nearest road for fresh water supplies.

Noticing a flicker of flame some distance away, I said to the junior officers, "I'll go and stamp those flames out." They looked at each other and one said, "Don't be such a prat — wait for the machine to return — one little flame won't hurt." I flushed with anger at his comment, but revenge was soon to be mine.

The fire engine returned and the hose-line connected once more. On the way back to the branch I stopped in my tracks and motioned for the two Leading Firemen to join me. A look of horror came across their faces as they observed what the 'one little flame' had done. It had burnt through the hoses on each side of a coupling, clearly leaving them open to a charge of negligence, as I smirkingly observed. The hoses were 'unofficially' repaired once back at the station. After all, who would notice the length of each had been reduced by some ten feet!!!

During this summer countless items of equipment went missing, along with many firemen, who, once out of radio contact used to find a local 'hostelry' to pass the time of day in. There were also a host of 'cock-ups', none funnier than the time when a water relay was being organised in a large park when the hose-lines being laid out from one particular appliance ended up back in the same machine!!!

The area around LITTLE SNOBSBURY consisted of several towns and villages within the Borough boundary and after MAMMOTH COUNTY Fire Brigade was formed the area was extended, giving us a larger 'patch'. During one night shift two Pump Ladders were turned out by Fire Control to a shop on fire and gave the address as the 'High Street' in one of the adjoining townships, some miles away from the station.

Out the machines went, negotiating a by-pass which followed a route away from LITTLE SNOBSBURY town centre, ploughing through dense clouds of smoke before racing off to their ultimate destination. Members of both crews must have thought to themselves, 'My word, there must be a lot of bonfires around to cause that amount of smoke'.

Both appliances were booked in attendance upon arrival, but there were no signs of fire. As the O.I.C. was about to query the call, Fire Control interjected and gave him a change of address, 'HIGH STREET — LITTLE SNOBSBURY'. No wonder there had been a lot of smoke!!! The fire engines raced back, but the shop had been all but destroyed when they arrived. A further twist of irony to this story was that this same premise had been the subject of a Fire Prevention visit a few days beforehand, with all being in satisfactory order. There was no need for any 'follow up' visits for quite some time.

The final two stories concerning 'Operational Foul-ups' were classic examples of 'own goals'. The first is applicable to MAMMOTH COUNTY.

The different Divisions, for the most part, had their own radio channels, where transmissions to and from Fire Control were restricted to fire engines and officers' radio cars from the same. Whilst in charge of the Pump one day, I hadn't long switched the radio on, prior to leaving on out-duties, when I heard one of the machines from our Division booking in attendance at a station in a different Division.

Now it wasn't uncommon for appliances to be sent on standby duty to 'foreign' Divisional stations, but it was most uncommon for them to be booked in via the radio. Standing orders stated that upon arrival at your home or other stations, the O.I.C. of each machine had to book into Fire Control using the direct telephone link installed at each station. It was quite common, however, for officers to disregard this instruction and call in using their radio cars as they were too idle to do otherwise.

Upon hearing the appliance being booked in, I thought, 'That's unusual,' but upon hearing no further transmissions I dismissed everything from my mind. However, it wasn't a case of them not using the radio again, it was simply because they had changed to the other Division's frequency.

It wasn't long before 'all was revealed' — 'through the grape-vine'. "Did you hear what happened at such and such station?" — "No." — "The kitchen was gutted." — "Get away." — "Chuckle, Chuckle — Ha, Ha, Ha." The station involved only had one fire engine based there and whilst the dinner was being cooked, they were turned out on a 'Shout'.

The cook, a fireman, forgot to turn the chip pan off and not long after they had left a deserted station behind, it over-heated and set the kitchen on fire. As the home crew were detained at the job they had been sent to, this meant that other crews had to deal with the emergency. What an embarrassment for the Officer in Charge and in particular for the cook. I wouldn't have liked to have been in their shoes for all the tea in China upon their return, with senior officers and reams of writing waiting for them.

What was to be their 'Hell', but to the attending crews their 'Heaven', would have been the 'Informative' message. "From Station Officer Blah, Blah, at such and such Fire Station, severe fire in ground floor kitchen caused by an overheated chip pan, two C.A. and a hose-reel in use." I would dearly have loved to have seen the expressions on the faces of the 'victims' as they too heard the same message, complemented with something similar to, "OH GOD — F*!*!*G HELL."

The most classical 'Foul-Up — Cum Fiasco' was the one I participated in and witnessed whilst in my early days at LITTLE SNOBSBURY. We had been called out to a Special Service call — 'Petrol Spillage on Roadway'. The crew consisted of L.Fm. 'Skin', Joe 'The Boxer', Fm. 'Meticulous', who always took great care in everything he did, and myself.

After rolling up at the said address, in the Pump, the perpetrator of the spillage, the occupier, a middle-aged man, informed 'Skin' he had accidentally knocked some petrol cans over, causing about two gallons to make their way into a nearby drain. We emptied the tank of the Pump into the drain, in an attempt to flush the petrol away. Just as a safeguard the tank was refilled from a hydrant, some distance away, its contents once again being discharged into the drain.

Satisfied, 'Skin' ordered us to make the gear up and as we were doing so the occupier, whom we had contacted, approached him and enquired if all was safe. 'Skin' said, "Aye sir, it's perfectly safe. We have flushed the petrol away with more than enough water." "But, how do you know it's safe? You may well have washed the petrol away, but what about the fumes?"

'Skin' said, "Look sir, I can assure you it's safe and to put your mind at rest I will prove it to you." At that he produced a box of matches. Without a word being spoken, all but 'Skin' took an involuntary step backwards. The first match he struck went out, but the second didn't. Making sure it was well alight he dropped it down the drain. For several seconds nothing happened — then there was a low rumbling noise.

'The Boxer' went to investigate (although he later denied it) and peered over the top of the drain. There was a 'Whoosh' and a large, oily black cloud of smoke puffed upwards out of the drain, enveloping him. He staggered backwards, fortunately not hurt, but rather surprised, his face covered in black splodges — like a member of the 'Black and White Minstrels'.

Within seconds the smoke cleared, being followed by a loud rumbling noise from beneath the ground, and I for one looked for somewhere to hide. All hell then broke loose, with flames shooting out of the open drains all the down the street. Four 'Yobs' passing by on the other side of the street laughed at our predicament, but their laughter was soon silenced when a solid drain cover took off in front of them, followed by a sheet of flame.

This was repeated further down the road, with drain cover after drain cover zipping into the air and crashing to the ground with resounding clangs, flames erupting from the ground. It was a good job it wasn't a sewer which had been involved, for anyone seated on the toilet would have had one hell of a shock!!!

We ran round like headless chickens, not really knowing quite what to do and by the time we had collected our wits, the flames died down as suddenly as they had started, with all of the petrol vapour now burnt away. I will give 'Skin' his due, for his comment of the year after the furore died down, when he turned to the man who had spilt the petrol and said, "Well, it's safe now sir."

How on earth the press never came to hear of this fiasco, I will never know, for armed with this knowledge they would have had a field day. For reasons best known to himself, probably because he didn't wish to let the 'Big-Wigs' on LITTLE SNOBSBURY Council get wind of one of his officers' gross incompetence, the Chief maintained a low profile and no charges were pressed against 'Skin'. The book should have been thrown at him for it is the motto of the Fire Service to 'Save Life and Protect Property', not the opposite as 'Skin' had attempted to do.

Out-duties covered a multitude of items e.g. Catering, Fire Prevention, Hydrant and During Performance Inspections. Visits to factories, fetes, gymkhanas, offices, old folks homes and schools. All of these were part of the daily lot of firemen and unless you were off the run in the station van, you were usually on call in a fire engine via the radio.

A large proportion of these duties were devoted to hydrant inspections. Two visits to each hydrant every year (in theory), though some were checked several times (by mistake) and others not at all (administrative errors).

The first check comprised of a quick look under the lid and if all was well underneath it was replaced and that was that. The second visit, six months later (again in theory) was a 'wet' test. This consisted of screwing a standpipe to the outlet, cracking the valve by utilising a key and bar and flushing the hydrant for several seconds. From time to time in LITTLE SNOBSBURY we also used to check the flow and gallons per minute with a flowmeter.

A variety of gear was carried on the fire engine or van for replacing hydrant lids and plates along with cans of yellow paint. In MAMMOTH COUNTY we had to paint any hydrant lids which were located in the road or paint arrows in the road to indicate where a far away hydrant was situated. On odd occasions, after completing one's handywork, a car or lorry would appear, driving over the fresh paint, leaving a trail of yellow oblong marks and several arrows behind it.

During hydrant inspections in the summer months, especially on hot days in the country, it wasn't uncommon to visit a pub, with the card being filled in on the way back to the station. Other popular venues on hydrants were ice-cream and cream cake shops.

One glorious summer's day found us actually working. We were conducting a 'wet' test outside a house in LITTLE SNOBSBURY when a Triumph Stag passed us and came to a stand in the drive. Out leapt a woman, with an extremely nice figure, but with a face like a 'Bag of Spanners'. She looked down her nose at us as if we had crawled out of the ground, before disappearing inside her house. Within seconds she flew out of the front door, her face contorted with rage.

In true LITTLE SNOBSBURY fashion she bellowed, in a snooty voice typical of one who had probably never done a decent day's work in her life, "WHAT HAVE YOU DONE TO MY WATER?" (pronounced 'WARTAH'). "I SHALL SUE. NO, I SHALL GET MY HUSBAND (HUS-BOND) TO SUE." Shocked by this unexpected tirade we meekly followed her into the house. The kitchen was about the average size of a fireman's house and we noted a small quantity of water on the floor. Whilst she continued ranting and raving we attempted to locate the cause. Thinking it may have been a burst pipe, I said, "Excuse me madam, do you know where your stop-cock is?" "Oh I don't know. How am I supposed to know these things?"

After a while we found the cause. Due to a change of water pressure one of the hoses from her washing machine had fallen off. Once reinstated, I then asked her where her mop was kept. Back came the pompous reply, "I don't know, the 'daily' keeps it somewhere." What an attitude! A mop was located and the mess cleared up. Once finished we were grateful to depart.

One tale about hydrants concerned one of the Chief Fire Officer's of MAMMOTH COUNTY. It had been brought to his attention that the hydrant outside his house hadn't been checked for several months and word was passed on to the station to which the onus for checking it belonged.

Thereafter the hydrant was 'checked' every Monday morning until the Chief put a stop to it. It was 'checked' by being cracked at the valve which induced dirty water into the domestic supply. As 'Chiefy's' wife normally did the washing on a Monday she wasn't too impressed and gave her husband some stick about it. What was he to do? He was in a dilemma. After having used his authority to get the wretched thing checked in the first place, he would have looked a total fool if he publicly issued an order to put the firemen in their place. He could hardly place men on any charges for they would have simply stated they were obeying his orders.

So therefore word was passed unofficially down through the grapevine to end the charade. It was the nearest the Chief would admit to acknowledging he had been had. He never again complained about his hydrant.

174

It was all well and good to despatch fire engines all over the place to do fire and hydrant inspections, but from time to time their absence from a fire station had devastating results. For some reason best known to themselves the average members of the public always expect a fire engine to be inside a station.

This happened to a licensee of a public house not situated more than half a mile from his nearest fire station. He couldn't understand, as his pub was gutted in front of his eyes, why it took more than ten minutes for a fire engine to turn up, and from the opposite direction to the station.

It later transpired that both of the fire engines based at the near at hand station were on out-duties miles away from the scene and the engine which eventually turned up was from a station in a different Division, again some miles away. It was months before the pub was back in action again — another 'great save' for the Brigade.

Being shut in an almost total male environment for many hours at a time, it was a relief to get out and about. Every time a pretty girl was sighted men used to leer at her out of the windows of the fire engines, often hurling themselves across the cab for a glimpse of 'skirt'. On one out-duty someone in the cab said, "Cor blimey, look at the tits on that," as we passed a rather more than 'well blessed' female. "Strewth, you don't get many of those to the pound." The driver, Trevor 'D', a newcomer to LITTLE SNOBSBURY, turned round to his crew and calmly stated, "Do you mind, that was my wife," to the temporary embarrassment of all those present.

175

Firemen always try to take advantage of any situations which come their way. One passing female was reduced to tears of laughter when she noticed a fire engine mount a deserted pavement on the opposite side of the road to her. Half a dozen arms reached out of the windows and in an instant a couple of dozen apples were seized from the overhanging branches of an apple tree in someone's private garden. This act of 'scrumping' was completed whilst still on the move and was over in seconds as the appliance roared off.

I could understand our visits to schools for the purposes of informing pupils and teachers alike of the various aspects of the Fire Service, but I could never understand why we attended fetes and gymkhanas. It was as if we were there to provide some kind of fairground side-show, with kids queuing up to use the hose-reels and play with anything that made a noise.

I only went to one gymkhana, thank goodness, an event which hosted the local gentry and their wives, all attempting to out-do one another in the various events. All spoke with 'plum in the mouth', 'La-Di-Da' tones. "I say old boy, make sure those firemen chappies receive some refreshments. Don't want them flaking out, it might reflect badly on our show," as if we were some kind of necessary nuisance.

Why do showjumpers all have Christian names like 'Cedric', 'Marmaduke', 'Henrietta' and 'Lucinda'? instead of Charlie, Joe, Pat and Sue, and say — "Mummy and Daddy" — breeding I suppose. When our relief fire engine arrived one of my crew stated, "Here comes so and so in the showjumping machine." Welcome relief during a boring morning.

Visits to factories and offices were meant to give the crews an insight into the premises in order to familiarize ourselves as to the layout, means of escape, firefighting equipment and knowledge of dangerous chemicals and other hazards. However, most of us spent more time ogling at the 'crumpet' than we did doing our home-work. 'Tut-Tut'.

One particular 'high risk' building within LITTLE SNOBSBURY was a 'friendly' mental home, where the inmates used to roam the streets quite freely. We came to know this 'home' very well over the years, with many false alarms and organised visits. On arriving the fire engines would be surrounded by inmates and it was often difficult to differentiate between them and the proper officials. You would sometimes be led up a corridor by an apparently sane person, until he stopped in his tracks and said, as one did to me, "Got a pen mate?" Before I had a chance to reply he opened his jacket and revealed a variety of fifty plus pens. I then had to return to the entrance in an effort to locate the 'right' person.

One fireman, who had joined the job at LITTLE SNOBSBURY shortly after myself, 'Kirby-Grip', was lured into a dormitory by one of these 'characters'. Once in the room, the inmate rushed to his locker and opened the door with a great clatter. Half-way into the room 'Kirby-Grip' was aghast when the inmate suddenly whipped round and pointed a gun at him. 'Kirby-Grip' backed away as the gun was waved at him in a menacing fashion. The 'gunman' then laughed and said, in 'Spike Milligan' fashion, "Look what I had as a Christmas present, a toy gun." One relieved 'Kirby-Grip', not that he had been frightened in the first place — not half he hadn't.

'The Old Recruit' shunned publicity for personal reasons and made sure he was never photographed at the station in case he appeared in the local press. That was until two volunteers, with the carrot of bags of overtime, were required to transport a spare Hydraulic Platform to a south coast town, in a show of mutual assistance to help a fellow Brigade in trouble. There he stood, or rather 'posed' for the press, from various positions on the H.P. for later headlines — 'Firemen on Mission of Mercy'. Didn't he take some stick from us later. "Anything to help the Brigade," he lied.

To sum up Out-duties there are two final quips about the attitude of some of the 'Good Citizens' of LITTLE SNOBSBURY in those far off days of yore.

'Pat' was stopped in the street one day, as he was walking along checking hydrants, by a local gent. The 'gent' hailed him, "I say chappy. Yes you. I understand you firemen types like to earn extra money by doing gardening and odd jobs. Is that correct?" 'Pat' replied in the affirmative. The 'gent' continued, "Let me show you round. Is 2/6d (12½ pence) an hour enough?" Without further ado 'Pat' departed without uttering a further word. (Firemen were a source of cheap labour to the rich, but not that cheap!!!)

'Pat' and I passed a well known private school and he commented, "Imagine sending your children there, with them asking other pupils" — "What does your daddy do for a living?" — "Bank Manager." — "Accountant." — "Solicitor."

"Why what does yours do?"

"He is a fireman."

"Oh, we are so sorry."

Fire Prevention for the men on the ground floor at LITTLE SNOBSBURY wasn't introduced until I had been in the Brigade for some time and this was only basic at first — re-inspections of small properties with the main work associated with the same remaining as a specialist subject for the F.P. Department.

Prior to being let loose on the public at large we had to undergo a short training course under the general auspices of the F.P. Assistant Divisional Officer. The theoretical side was extremely boring, but once completed we moved on to better things. As a final test of our new found abilities, several mock situations were set up within the confines of the station. The funniest involved Fm. 'Angry', the man who had hung 'Skin' out of the dormitory window.

A mock newsagents shop was set up in the recreation room, but before Fm. 'Angry' was allowed into the room, the A.D.O. briefed us that the 'proprieter', played by 'White Strength', was an awkward man, who would deliberately antagonise Fm. 'Angry' to test how he would react under pressure. One of our group informed the A.D.O. that although it was only a 'pretend' situation, Fm. 'Angry' might take it personally, a suggestion that was dismissed out of hand by the officer.

Fm. 'Angry' was invited in, dressed correctly, complete with his cap and a folder containing a mythical file on the mock premise.

Three or four of our group played the part of customers. Fm. 'Angry' approached the 'counter' and waited patiently for the first 'customer' to be served. After the 'customer' departed he said to the 'shopkeeper', "Excuse me sir, I am from the Fire......", but he was cut short by the 'owner', who replied, "Just a moment, I'm busy," and commenced serving the second 'customer'. Taken aback by this remark and our sniggers, Fm. 'Angry' flushed, his pride having been hurt.

When the second 'customer' had been dealt with, there was a similar approach, to which 'White Strength' totally ignored him. This time his 'redness' was caused by the anger building up inside, which we observed he was having trouble to contain.

The A.D.O. heard a whispered, "He will come to the boil shortly," but kept his thoughts to himself. Eventually Fm. 'Angry's' patience snapped and he snarled at the 'owner', "How much longer are you going to keep me waiting?" to which the rather abrupt reply was something similar to, "Look mate, I've already bloody well told you I am busy. Now why don't you clear off and come back another day." He then turned to another 'customer'.

At that Fm. 'Angry' went purple with rage having forgotten it was only a 'pretend' situation, and shouted, "DONT YOU F*!*!*G TALK TO ME LIKE THAT," and made a grab for him. Someone said, "Stop him A.D.O. he is going to hit him, we told you he could be violent." At that the A.D.O. intervened and calm was restored, with Fm. 'Angry' giving an assurance it wouldn't happen again.

With the mock final out of the way it was time for the real thing, under supervision of course. The A.D.O. stressed that from time to time we may be offered bribes from some owners of properties who would offer, this, that, and the other in exchange for turning a 'blind eye' to certain misdemeanours. Blow me if that didn't happen on the very first visit we went on.

It was a tyre centre for the storage and replacement of tyres on motor vehicles. All went well until we reached what was supposed to be a fire exit, but it was totally blocked by hundreds of tyres piled up to the roof. The A.D.O. stated that this was completely unsatisfactory and that the tyres would have to be removed.

Overhearing this remark, the 'guvnor' of the premise approached the A.D.O. and took him to one side, where we hear mutterings similar to, "These tyres will have to go" — "What kind of a car have you got?" — "What do you mean?" — "If you could see a way to forget what you have seen, I may be able to supply you with some ermmm..... errmmm..... tyres."

The A.D.O. gave us a wistful glance, but we were never certain as to whether or not he was disgusted with the offer or cursing his luck at missing a golden opportunity due to our presence. In either event he had little choice but to decline the offer and insisted the tyres be placed elsewhere.

In MAMMOTH COUNTY more and more initial and refresher courses to do with F.P. were introduced (invented) each as boring as the last. On one occasion, Fm. 'Angry', by now an F.P. officer (God knows how?) was in charge of an afternoon session. Upon noticing our 'Gaffer', 'Roger', had fallen asleep, he 'blew up', issued a stream of abuse, gathered up his belongings, dismissed the class and slammed the door on his way out.

During one course, when 'The Tasmanian Devil' was in charge of the Division, there were amongst the students a small contingent of men from the former 'Arsehole of the World' Brigade. One, a Leading Fireman, was summoned over the tannoy to go downstairs as the D.C. wished to see him. Upon his return he looked rather shaken and had been stripped of his rank markings. We had visions of 'The Tasmanian Devil' cutting them off with a sword, as in the days of the 7th Cavalry.

One instructor, a Sub Officer, smoked like a chimney and upon asking where his piece of chalk had gone, one wag made the suggestion he had smoked it. The same Sub-O asked if anyone in the room had any knowledge about the 'Arsehole of the World'. Before anyone else could reply I raised my arm and said, "The Luftwaffe," much to the amusement of the men from my side of the Division. The comment was ignored by the Sub-O, but I was subjected to glares of hatred from the others, especially the former Leading Fireman.

During a night shift standby duty at another station, I happened to mention to one of the lads, 'Stan', that my wife was constantly burning things when cooking and the final straw had come the previous day when she had ruined a steam pudding. The same, sealed in a plastic bowl, had been placed in a saucepan of water. As often happened, she forgot about it, with the water boiling away and subsequently the plastic melted into a solid mass. Both the pudding and the saucepan were ditched into the dustbin.

Having related this tale, upon 'Stan's' suggestion, we set about compiling a fake Fire Prevention letter to my wife on official notepaper. Once completed it was sealed in an envelope with a used stamp attached. Upon arriving home after the shift ended, I said to my beloved, who was in the kitchen, "Here is a letter for you." I gave it to her and disappeared into the living room, trying not to give the game away by laughing.

It read, 'Dear Madam, it has been brought to my attention that there is smoke constantly issuing from your kitchen and although, to date, there has not actually been a fire, one day someone will summon the Fire Service to your house, thereby wasting their valuable time and causing you great embarrassment. Therefore might I suggest that one of my officers will arrange to pay you a visit (about four hours) to teach you the basics of Fire Prevention and to perhaps advise you as to where you are going wrong with your cooking'.

An appropriate mythical name was typed at the foot of the page with a bogus signature.

I heard her stomping up and down in the kitchen, muttering to herself and then she came into the living room, eyes blazing and threw the letter at me. "Read that," she said. I managed to restrain myself from laughing as I read it. I said, "My dear, you have asked for it, you do burn a lot of things."

She snatched the letter back and snarled, "DON'T YOU CALL ME 'MY DEAR'.....IT'S HIM NEXT DOOR.....HE HAS REPORTED ME.....WHERE AM I GOING TO FIND FOUR SPARE HOURS FROM?.....WHAT HAS MY COOKING GOT TO DO WITH THE FIRE SERVICE?"

Before she did anything rash and rang up the F.P. Department, I let the 'cat out of the bag'. The reply was anything but ladylike. I then suggested a way of getting her own back on 'Stan'.

The distorted steam pudding was resurrected from the bin and I managed to find an old shoe box with Fire Service markings on it. My wife wrote a letter and it was sealed in the box along with the pudding and the original letter. The next day shift I managed to get the box to 'Stan' via the transport man and he had the shock of his life when he opened it. He had been expecting some 'goodies' from stores, but nothing like this. The letter was addressed to the 'Mythical' F.P. Officer.

'Dear Sir, thank you very much for your recent letter, the contents of which have been noted. As I am unable to find the time to spend four hours with one of your officers, I have taken steps to remedy the faults in my cooking by taking a crash course and I promise no more smoke will issue from my kitchen. As a token of my appreciation, please find enclosed a little something I have recently cooked, which I sincerely hope you will enjoy'. The letter was signed and finished off with, 'P.S. I have also written to your Chief Officer about your thoughtfulness and I hope you will get everything you deserve'.

'Stan' was so taken aback by all of this he still didn't realise he was on the end of a counter-strike. It wasn't until he undid the foil and discovered the steam pudding that it sunk in, much to the amusement of his watching colleagues.

During Performance Inspections (D.P.'s) were spot checks on premises to ensure means of escape were not blocked and that other things were not amiss during dances, disco's and other functions in public places.

One fire crew drew up at a night club and the O.I.C. asked for the manager. He duly arrived and the officer said, flashing his I.D. card, "We are from the Fire Service sir and would like to have a look round your premise to make sure all is in order." The rather bemused manager stated quizzically, "That's strange, you are the second lot tonight." It later transpired that a group of off duty firemen had earlier used their I.D. cards to obtain entry to the club, free of charge, under the pretext of an inspection.

One bright spark within MAMMOTH COUNTY invented a 'Rush Job Calendar', with the rider of 'Designed by the Brigade Think Tank', described as follows:

This calendar has been designed to deal with "RUSH JOBS". As every "RUSH JOB" is wanted 'Yesterday' we have run the dates backwards. Therefore, anything ordered on the 15th can be ready on the 9th. The 13th has been omitted to placate the superstitious. This space allows for sickness, day's leave and Christmas shopping etc. We have developed three Fridays in every week. This is to assist service to those who always demand delivery by Friday.

There are five completely new days at the end of the month in order to cater for 'end of the month' returns, late completion of which is discouraged by taking care to have no 1st of the month. Mondays have been obliterated because of the dislike of the same, Monday morning blues, slow starts and the tendency to take all day to get going again. There are no Saturdays or Sundays. This resolves the temptation to treat them as Bank Holidays. Each week has a special day called WONDAY. This is for the working of wonders and for 'it will happen'.

One Friday, a Fire Prevention A.D.O., with a face like a melted wax candle, rang our office and I answered the phone. "Hello Leading Fireman, I have a rush job for you, one that should have been done yesterday." I was able to stifle a laugh and was tempted to take him a copy of the "RUSH CALENDAR" to prove that a job required yesterday was no problem, but it would have fallen on stony ground.

He continued, "Could you possibly find a way of sending a man to Brigade H.Q. and get him to sweet-talk a typist into typing some F.P. figures for me as all of our own typists are off for one reason or another." He was flabbergasted when I informed him I could type. I went to his office and collected the information he required typing out. To this day I regret not altering the figures, for he would never have checked them prior to sending them off to the Assistant Chief Officer (Fire Prevention). The 'altered' statistics would have made interesting reading, with a bemused A.C.F.O. wondering why there had been 500 major chemical fires and only one caused by electrical faults, instead of the other way round.

Upon completion I took the figures back to his office. He was on the phone and waved me to sit down. He was discussing the result of the findings of a major chemical conflagration in a big city some months before. He put the phone down and said, "Sorry about that," in a posh voice, "It's those fellows from the Gas Board, trying to prise some information out of me". "You mean about the so and so incident?" I asked. "That's correct," he replied. I then commented, "That's the one where two gas clouds combined and caused a massive explosion." "How do you know that? Have you read the report?" "No," I said, "I read about it in a newspaper." He looked shocked, but commented no further.

I gave him the typed work and further goaded him by saying, "There you are sir, I hope it is okay and that you appreciate the Sub Officer took me off a very important task to enable me to do this for you." (Total bull-shit.) He said, not realising what a load of crap I had come out with, "This is very much appreciated and I would like to buy you a pint, but of course the bar isn't open during dinner time." "It is sir," I said, "And I am the barman," dangling the keys in front of him. His face dropped, but I will give him his due for he bought both the Sub-O and myself a pint each.

As a finale to this chapter, I was paired off with our 'Gaffer', Roger, on F.P. duties one afternoon. In the course of our inspections we passed a not long completed office block and Roger said to me, "Let's go and have a nose round.''

We went from one office to another, each one containing a different firm. At one, where they were still engaged in unpacking, Roger became involved in an animated conversation with one of the senior office girls. Amidst the conversation he happened to mention, ''This isn't an official visit, just a walk-about to familiarize ourselves with the building. Normally we have to show you our I.D. cards.'' The woman then commented, ''I suppose I ought to ask to see yours?''

The 'Gaffer' fumbled in his pockets and with his classic half-grin said, ''I..... Ermmm..... Errmmm..... Errmmm..... don't appear to have it on me..... Errmmm..... Errmmmm..... and anyway it's..... Errmmm..... Errmmm..... out of date.'' ''Then how do I know you are who you claim to be?'' she asked. ''You don't,'' Roger replied red-faced and we departed from the premise.

Radio Messages

My first 'real life' introduction to the transmission of radio messages was in the Control Room at LITTLE SNOBSBURY, although I had participated in 'pretend ones' at Training School. There I was taught that each vehicle in the Brigade, with the exception of the transport van, had its own radio and individual call sign.

I also learnt the Standard Messages employed by the Officers in Charge of each appliance and the senior officers. "Mobile to...." — "In attendance at...." — "Informative Message" — "Assistance Message" — "Stop for..." Most 'Stop' messages were straightforward, but as more and more Automatic Fire Alarms were installed in major premises, there were more and more calls to the same, mainly due to 'gremlins' getting into the systems and creating false alarms. Instead of employing a blanket 'Stop' for these wretched things, different reasons for the 'Stop' were invented and once again I have to thank 'Incognito Press' for the following.

'Have you ever considered the absolutely ridiculous classification of an Automatic Fire Alarm giving a 'False Alarm — Good Intent', when it is actuated in error by fumes from cooking, or an outside bonfire, insects, magic or gremlins, without any human being directly responsible. It gives visions of the indicator board apologising profusely to the Officer in Charge for being such a nuisance'.

'The dictionary definition of 'Intent' is:- purpose, a plan, mean to. Whoever heard of a mechanical and electrical appliance or device having an intent, or a plan to do something. Use of the term 'False Alarm — Good Intent' in these circumstances is a misnomer. Perhaps 'False Alarm (Facsimile)' or 'False Alarm (Accidental)' would be more appropiate, or, of course, it could be referred to the EMPIRE BUILDING DEPARTMENT for consideration'.

Returning to the chapter at hand, much importance was emphasised about the needs for Radio Procedure to be strictly adhered to at all times, which in the main it was. One exception was Sub-O 'Squirrel' who once called up an appliance on out-duties and ordered a bag of fish and chips. It was a good job for him that no senior officers were listening.

For a brief period of time 'Glarer' was made up to the rank of Temporary Station Officer. (Had the Chief gone off his rocker?) 'Punchy' was in the Control Room when we attended what ultimately turned out to be a 'False Alarm — Malicious' during the early hours. We had heard 'Glarer' book mobile, but for reasons best known to himself, he became totally lost and unable to find our location. He went absolutely berserk at 'Punchy' over the radio and later said to him, "If it wasn't for the fact that I know you don't drink, I would have accused you of being drunk." (It was his own incompetence which caused him to become lost, not 'Punchy's'.)

Personally speaking, once the Control Room operators took over, until

I was promoted in MAMMOTH COUNTY, I had little to do with radio messages, in an active manner, booking in an appliance now and again. On occasions we would hear odd 'clangers' such as the one committed by Station Officer 'Alf' who said to Fire Control, "Mobile to ....Roy (his driver), I think you've just hit a cat...."

He attended an emergency at the local airport when a Fokker Friendship was having a problem landing. As it happened it landed safely, allowing 'Alf' to transmit the 'Stop' message. His words were, quote, "From Station Officer 'Alf', 'Stop' for 'Fly By Night Airport', 'Friendly Fokker' now landed." Unquote!!

'Alf' used to be involved in the most bizarre situations, like the time he was doing press-ups on the floor of his office. In walked one of his firemen without knocking on the door. The result being that 'Alf' was trapped, screaming, with the bottom of the door jammed on his fingers. To release them, the door had to be swiftly closed, whilst other firemen held the trunk of his body. More screams.

He went to a car fire which was being watched by a large crowd. At the height of the blaze his lads had been struggling to open the bonnet, which had jammed, using a crowbar. The more they tried, the more it resisted their efforts.

Sensing a 'cock-up' in the offing, 'Alf' grabbed the crowbar and to his surprise the bonnet lifted at the first attempt. Caught on the hop, 'Alf' immediately fell over backwards into a water-filled gutter, much to the amusement of the host of onlookers, who gave him a round of applause. Instead of ignoring the saturated back of his fire tunic and getting on with the job, 'Alf' threw himself on a patch of grass and rolled back and forth, as a dog does when rolling in a cow-pat. Heaven knows what the watching members of the public must have thought?

Out walking one day he noticed a woman get out of a Rolls-Royce and take her poodle for 'walkies', the 'Roller' slowly following her. After the dog had relieved itself by doing a 'Number Two' on the pavement she returned to the car and her and her pet climbed in. Incensed by her action 'Alf' swooped on the 'doggy pile' and utilising his newspaper he quickly opened a door of the Rolls-Royce and deposited the 'pile' into the car, stating, "I believe this is yours madam," before walking off. Good for 'Alf'

As a Leading Fireman I was O.I.C. at scores of car fires, but very few were as spectacular as one involving a Scimitar sports car, an 'up market' 'plastic pig'. One rarely knew what type of car was involved until one arrived at the scene. Within a few streets of the incident we could see the smoke as we turned into the correct road and I commenced transmitting my 'In Attendance' message.

Being constructed of fibre-glass it had ignited readily and was 'going like the clappers'. Instead of simply stating, "In attendance at..." it came out as, "In attendance at — F*!*!*G HELL — LOOK AT THAT...." It was at that point I realised the transmitting switch was pressed in as I was shouting and I threw it away as if it was a hot potato, to the sniggers of my crew members. (As if my latter action made any difference — the damage had already been done.) The recipient at Fire Control couldn't have failed to have heard my 'blunder', but nothing was mentioned upon our return to the station.

The worst thing that could happen to you with regards to radio messages was if you had to transmit a lengthy message, but omitted to write it down first, a lesson I quickly learned. Quite often, after completing a lengthy message, Fire Control would ask, "What did you say after....?" To which a baffled O.I.C who had sent the message, would often look at his colleagues and enquire, "What did I say after.....?"

They would shrug their shoulders, leaving an embarrassed officer frantically searching his memory for what he had said. To make matters worse Fire Control would impatiently come back to the O.I.C. repeating, "Did you get my message? What did you say after.....?" I feel sure this was sometimes done deliberately, safe with the knowledge that they knew the recipient had been caught on the wrong leg. Eventually the second part of the message would be transmitted, but nine times out of ten it was nothing like the original.

One Control Room girl kept haranguing a particular O.I.C. by stating after each of his messages, "You are talking too fast, please ensure your messages are clear and concise." Eventually he could take no more and he evened the score by talking in a child-like manner, "From (pause) Sub Officer Bloggs..... at.....Mumbles premise.....Muttering Avenue....." It took him an age to complete and at the end there was a terse "Roger" from Fire Control — she had got the message!!!

During the baking summer of 1976, virtually every appliance within MAMMOTH COUNTY was out at jobs and the air waves were filled with transmissions keeping Fire Control busy twenty-four hours a day. Under normal circumstances most of the individual Divisions had their own radio frequencies and rostered Control Room staff to deal with them.

Occasionally, for technical reasons, all stations came under the control of a single master channel and on one occasion this created an absolute classic. As appliances could only transmit one at a time there

was usually a waiting period to transmit. During a very hot and dry spell there was an incredible quirk of coincidence when it appeared that every O.I.C. out on the road wanted to transmit messages at the same time and it created chaos back at Fire Control.

I was in the cab of my appliance awaiting an opportunity for a space to transmit and all I could hear was, "Charlie 8/1 are you at....." — "From Alpha 1/2 In attendance at....." — "Are you receiving me, Delta 5/1 over....." The air waves eventually became so congested that all I could hear was a stream of garbled words — "Bravo 6/2 — Help — ZWI*X!Y8*3/STATION***" etc., a complete mess. One girl at Fire Control in a frantic effort to restore some kind of order must have 'pulled the plugs' briefly, for all went quiet for a second or two, then she came over the air with, "WILL YOU PLEASE TAKE YOUR TURN TO TRANSMIT — THANK YOU." There was absolute silence for about thirty seconds and the whole charade commenced once more as each O.I.C. tried to get in first. What a farce.

One particularly amusing story concerning radio messages was when a fellow by the name of Fm. 'Salmon' was delegated by his O.I.C. to transmit an Informative Message to Fire Control requesting the attendance of the local Electricity Board at a domestic house. As he was transmitting he was unaware that the rear speaker of his appliance was switched on. After his request was received, Fire Control came back to him and said. "Are you aware that there is a £33.00 standing charge for the attendance of the Electricity Board?" Fm. 'Salmon's' immediate response was to shout, "F*!*!*G HELL," and the offending words reverberated up and down the street. The householders of the same must have been really impressed!!!

Our 'Gaffer', Roger, was a treat when it came to radio messages. The number of times he forgot to book mobile to jobs was nobody's business. Fire Control were forever calling him up to confirm he was on his way. Once, whilst paying a visit to a station in the 'Arsehole of the World', many miles away, he only realised his radio wasn't switched on when he went to switch it off!!!

On the way to an incident at the 'Friendly Mental Home', he and his crew were unaware that a locker was open on his machine, with gear being spilled out each time they turned a corner or rounded an island. With this situation becoming potentially more dangerous by the minute as we neared a more populated area, I, as O.I.C. of the Pump behind him, eventually had to send a message to Fire Control to inform him of the situation. Upon hearing such a message the embarrassment from within his appliance was somewhat acute to say the least.

During the lead-up to Bonfire Night one year, MAMMOTH COUNTY turned out scores of appliances to bonfires deliberately set afire prior to the event. Fire Control informed each station to use as little air time as possible, brevity being the yard-stick, thus enabling others to transmit messages without a long wait. Our 'Gaffer' appeared to be oblivious to

this instruction when he transmitted one of his messages.

"From..... Errmmm..... Station Officer 'Roger'.....Errmmm, at..... Errmmm..... Errmmm..... LITTLE SNOBSBURY playing fields..... 'Informative Message'.....Errmmm..... Errmmm..... Although we are..... Errmmm..... Errmmm..... dealing with the..... Errmmm..... incident..... Errmmm..... bonfire..... Errmmm..... due to the high winds..... Errmmm..... there are..... Errmmm..... many flying brands..... Errmmm..... heading towards a nearby clubhouse..... Errmmm..... so we will be de-tained..... Errmmm..... for quite some time..... Errmmm ..... Errmmm ....." End of message.

I was in charge of the Pump at another bonfire and we were in stitches. We thought the message was never going to end and how the person in Fire Control kept her cool I will never know.

Fire Control, for reasons best known to themselves, would often ignore routine messages for quite some time, although, in a reverse situation they expected Officers in Charge to respond immediately. On one occasion our 'Gaffer' tried several times to get in touch with Fire Control, but to no avail. On his final attempt, he turned to his crew, not realising he still had the transmitting switch pressed in and said, much to the

190

amusement of at least one fire crew which were out and about, "Nobody's f*!*!*g interested." At that Fire Control acknowledged him and he could hear muted sniggers in the background of the same.

As Gordon once stated, "Roger isn't like a real 'Gaffer' if you know what I mean." He certainly wasn't, he was a one-off. We once discussed what would happen in the unlikely event of him dying on the job, sorry, whilst on duty. Not wishing to have him replaced, as he was so popular, it was suggested we treated him like the dead 'El Cid' who was strapped to his horse, leading his men into battle, in Roger's case, strapped to his office chair or seat in the fire engine. Off duty we were going to put him in the station freezer!!!

Senior Officers

What is the definition of a senior officer and what is the prime force behind becoming one? Is it the lust for power, or the rich pickings and high social standing in society, which drives people to climb to the top of the ladder? Since time immemorial and the first armies were formed, there as been a structure of command from the humblest private to the highest general.

As mankind advanced, different intermediate ranks were introduced (invented) and little has changed over the centuries, with status and life-style being determined by the number of stripes or pips being worn by the owner. In bygone times, the highest ranks were mostly inherited by the recipients, many of whom did more harm than good in times of war, due to their lack of experience in such matters.

The First World War was a superb example of how dreadful the British system of the 'Old Pal's Act' style of promotion worked. Incompetent senior officers were directly responsible for thousands of deaths. Many of these officers were able to preserve their own skins by hiding behind their individual rank. "Over the top chaps. Sorry I cannot go with you, but someone has to stay behind and keep in command of the situation." (Fifty miles away!!!) When I departed from MAMMOTH COUNTY it had a 1980's vision, in up to date appliances and equipment, but in its rela-tionship with the men, many senior officers had a 1917 attitude.

The advent of the Second World War supposedly changed this attitude, with the break-down of most social barriers and people from all walks of life coming together to help fight a common enemy. Although most folk are better off today, both in economic and educational terms than their counterparts of many years ago, social standing and snobbery is still rife amongst the community at large. The Fire Service is no exception to these human failings.

The public at large, if in trouble, expect to see a fire engine or two, to attend to their particular needs. The men on these fire engines consist of firemen, with a Station Officer, Sub Officer or a Leading Fireman in charge. What the public don't generally realise is that behind the scenes are a legion of higher ranks. Many of these men rarely, if ever, attend incidents of a minor nature.

At large conflagrations (fires), major road and rail accidents, they usually turn up in large numbers after the initial life-saving and hard graft has been completed and are the first to be interviewed on radio and television. Some of these erstwhile officers who appear on our screens seem to be overawed by the occasion and become very cautious when closely questioned, as if frightened of dropping themselves in it. Others become arrogant towards the interviewer when asked searching questions. One senior officer, when asked if it was high speed which caused a fatal accident at traffic lights involving a fire engine, pompously replied, as if it was the public which served him and not the other way round, "We don't dash to incidents, we get there progressively." (Bull-shit!! I was once driven at high speed through red lights by a fireman who hadn't even noticed them.)

One of the standing jokes within the Fire Service was about a fireman who had been detailed as a runner at a major fire and was on his way to relay some messages, when he was stopped by a senior officer who had stepped from a darkened doorway and asked how the job was going. The fireman's instant reaction was to say, "Sorry A.D.O. you startled me," to which the reply was, "I'm a D.O. lad, not an A.D.O." The fireman then remarked, "Sorry sir, I didn't realise I had run so far from the job."

The senior officer posts consist generally of Assistant Divisional Officers (A.D.O.'s), Divisional Officers (D.O.'s) — three grades, including Deputy and Divisional Commanders, Assistant Chief Fire Officers (A.C.F.O.'s), a Deputy Chief Fire Officer and finally *the* Chief Fire Officer.

I am the first to admit that an emergency job like the Fire Service has to have a rank structure and appropriate measures have to be taken to maintain discipline throughout. However, it has always been a great source of mystery to myself as to why there are *so many* ranks within the Fire Service.

To distinguish the differences between the ranks uniforms are designed, with the best quality ones being allocated to the senior officers of course. The higher the rank, the more laurel leaves, pips and various embellishments are required, including 'Scrambled Egg' on caps.

The Fire Service, designed initially to help the public at large, has become something it shouldn't be — an elitist society, far removed from its humble beginnings. When I first joined there were small numbers of senior officers at LITTLE SNOBSBURY, well in proportion to the lower ranks employed. In the larger surrounding Brigades, there were obviously a lot more senior officers, but they were still well balanced, in ratio, as were the civilian staff. In most cases, the senior officers, including the Chief Officers, were termed as 'Firemens Officers', who had risen from the ground floor and called a spade a spade. (This, by the way, was not the way of the world in LITTLE SNOBSBURY.)

The amalgamations of 1974 were to transform all this and in today's Fire Service, the relationship of officers to men has all but deteriorated completely, with a few exceptions here and there, with an ever growing gap between 'Them and Us', which has left morale at rock bottom.

There are many, many examples I could relate of contempt by senior officers towards the men. I will quote two of them.

A newly appointed Chief Fire Officer of MAMMOTH COUNTY, crowing with self-importance, arrived at our station earlier than antici- pated for a pre-arranged visit. Upon spotting a fireman who had been caught off guard, 'Billy J', leaning against a wall chatting to a comrade, the Chief strutted arrogantly towards him, thus provoking the following:

"How dare you act so casually. Don't you realise you are in the presence of your Chief Officer. Stand to attention and click your heels together. How many years have you got in lad?" When the LAD replied, "Thirty-one sir," the Chief was somewhat taken aback and muttering under his breath he moved on to the next fireman (victim).

The second incident involved a senior Driving School instructor, the Sub-O who had once fallen off his tandem, and a freshly promoted Divi- sional Officer. Both had been on the same initial Training School course together and had served together in the 'Big City' Brigade as firemen for many years.

By his own admission, the Driving School instructor was deep in thought, in a world of his own, and hadn't noticed his former friend pass by, nor had he heard him say, "Good Morning." When he realised there had been no reply, the D.O. turned on his heels and stormed towards the by now alert instructor and said, "How dare you ignore me. In future, when I address you, you will reply, Yes D.O. — Yes Sir — or Yes Mr. Important." He then indignantly stomped off, leaving a bewildered, saddened, speechless and fuming instructor to reflect on how times had changed for the worse.

There is no such creature as a 'Bad Officer', because each appointment is endorsed by the Chief and he always has to be seen to be right. Also, the Discipline Code is worded as such that it is heavily loaded against the lower ranks. One could have a go at some of the 'Thicker' ones by using one's sense of humour against them.

'Desperate Dan', by now a D.O. and an even more arrogant and self-opinionated character than when he was a Sub-O, was in charge of some practise competition drills. He strutted round the yard with his chest puffed out, barking orders and laying down the law. To commence the individual drills he utilised a starting pistol, waving it about with great relish. To my mind he would have been just as happy in a German Officer's uniform, complete with Luger, or as a Commissar on the Russian Front.

Between drills, 'The Old Recruit' sidled up to him and whispered, "That gun is a bit noisy, isn't it? Why don't you use a silencer?" The immediate reply was, "But the Brigade doesn't have a silencer," and after some thought added, "Anyway, if I were to use a silencer, no-one would hear the gun go off." It never once occurred to him that he had been set up.

Like childrens fads, one month 'marbles', the next month 'conkers', the Fire Brigade too had its moments — called purges. Like most of the ridiculous ideas enforced upon us, these stemmed from the top, but after a short while commonsense would prevail, with a return to the status quo.

Yet another 'dictat', which came from the top, supposedly in the interests of 'Health and Safety', was the banning of the wearing of watches by the on duty personnel below the rank of Leading Fireman.

An understandable furore was caused by the men, who obviously felt insulted, until they saw the funny side of things and began to exploit this latest zany situation. At first, the men on my Watch wore 'Mickey Mouse' watches and a variety of home-made cardboard clocks. Then they turned up late for duty with excuses like, "I'm sorry I'm late boss, but

I have no way of knowing what the time is." Within a matter of days the hierarchy rescinded and modified this ridiculous order.

During a brief, but extremely cold winter snap, there was a purge by the senior officers, who commenced spot-checks to ensure that all appliances were having their batteries trickle-charged at all times. Like most stations in MAMMOTH COUNTY, our battery chargers were capable of delivering electricity via coils of suspended (spring-loaded) insulated wires in the engine house. Each bay had its own unit to supply each individual fire engine via the use of a socket in the cab.

For obvious reasons the lead had to be removed from the socket before the appliance left the station. I was in charge of the H.P. during one night shift, with 'Nestor', who was responsible for removing the lead, as my driver. When we arrived at the call, 'Nestor' leapt out of the cab and shouted, "F*!*!*G HELL, THERE'S FIFTY FEET OF CABLE TRAILING BEHIND US — I THINK I FORGOT TO DISCONNECT THE CHARGING CABLE." (Another 'bollocking' and more paperwork to fill in.)

The D.O. who called in at my station to perform the spot-check, was one of the more sensible ones, or so I thought. He was of Canadian origin, a character in his own right who had come up through the ranks, mostly on an operational basis. When he arrived he wasn't in the best of moods, having already visited two of the stations on the Division where he had discovered that some of the appliances wouldn't start, due to their not having been on charge.

We were all summoned into the general office and the D.O. walked in, accompanied by our 'Gaffer', Roger. The D.O. then proceeded to lecture us on the importance of appliances being on charge during the cold weather. The office we were in had a large window which overlooked the appliance bays. Half-way through his speech he suddenly ceased talking and strode towards the window. He had noticed that the nearest battery charging coil was housed in its metal container, instead of being plugged into the fire engine.

Sensing another 'victim' to render a 'bollocking' to, he turned on our 'Gaffer'. "Station Officer," he drawled, "There is a perfect example of negligence. That fire engine is NOT on charge. What do you have to say for yourself?". Roger said nothing at first, but simply smirked at him, a smirk that at the very least could have been interpreted as dumb insolence. Just as the D.O. was coming to the boil, our 'Gaffer' said, "Yes it is."

Filled with confidence that HE was in the right, the D.O. stated in a loud voice, "NO IT ISN'T," to which the reply once again was, "Yes it is." This brief exchange of words was repeated several times, before the senior officer, infuriated by the constant smirk on his opponent's face, grabbed Roger's arm and led him into the appliance bay, followed by the rest of us. Once inside, he pointed towards the ceiling and stated to all present, "THAT APPLIANCE IS *NOT* ON CHARGE — THERE IS THE PROOF, HANGING FROM THE CEILING." Satisfied he was correct, he then folded his arms in a gesture of triumph.

Our 'Gaffer' calmly said, "That particular charging outlet is out of order. The appliance is on charge from the unit in the second bay." In a final, desperate attempt to prove he was right, the D.O. marched briskly to the fire engine and wrenched the cab door open, but the gamble was lost. Without any mention of an apology, the defeated officer slunk off to the sanctuary of his office, his tail between his legs.

One absurd example of how ludicrous the chain of command could be, if taken to the n'th degree, occurred at LITTLE SNOBSBURY. Between the H.Q. block and the rest of the station was the boiler-house, hose tower and hose trough. Peering out of one of the upstairs windows on one occasion, the Chief espied a piece of paper in the hose trough. He summoned the A.D.O. who was passing by and asked him to send for the duty Station Officer.

The Station Officer duly arrived and from his window the Chief instructed him to arrange for one of the men to come and pick up the offending piece of paper. The Station Officer returned to the operational section of the station and told the Sub Officer of the Chief's instruction. The Sub-Officer then instructed a Leading Fireman to order a fireman to fulfil this task, which was duly done. A made-up story you might think!!! No. I had been able to witness and overhear most of this charade from the top of the hose tower.

After MAMMOTH COUNTY was formed, I was out in the yard taking drills one day, when a Divisional Officer with a surname identical to that of a well known specialist chocolate manufacturer, marched onto the scene. Without having the courtesy to ask if I didn't mind him taking over, he lined the men up and proceeded to carry out a 'question and answer' session.

In this particular field the senior officers were specialists. They would read up on certain subjects until they knew the answers parrot-fashion, and out they would come, fully genned up, knowing all the right answers and then proceed to ask ridiculous questions such as, "How many litres of water will flow out of a hose-reel at a given pressure?", knowing full well that all but a few could even attempt an answer and these would be the younger ones, fresh from Training School. No-one ever stood on the fireground calculating the same. The pump operators would simply look at the rubber ball in the water capacity gauge and when it reached the bottom it meant the tank was empty.

He then paraded up and down the line, humiliating each and every fireman. He was really enjoying himself at their expense. 'That will keep them in their place', he may well have thought to himself. Then the wheel of fate turned against him. He grilled one of the lads, 'Gupta', about hose. "What comes out of a hose when it is hung up in the tower?" (Meaning acids and chemicals which built up and damaged the internal lining of the hose.) Back came the reply, "Water sir." — "DON'T BE SO STUPID LAD. ARE YOU TRYING TO MAKE A FOOL OF ME?" — "But sir, it does, I've seen it. Look, I will show you." The Divisional Officer glared at

'Gupta' and said, "Carry on Leading Fireman," and stormed from the yard back to his office.

Most fire and accident situations were dealt with in an able and efficient manner by the crews on the initial attendance. It was only at larger jobs that the more senior ranks attended. In the case of LITTLE SNOBSBURY efficiency was rarely affected because of the small numbers of senior officers based there, but in MAMMOTH COUNTY things were rather different.

In the more potentially 'explosive' type of incidents, senior officers rarely arrived in large numbers, if at all, until the situation had calmed down. Indeed, I once witnessed an 'act' when we were called to a large tar boiler on an industrial premise. This boiler had been subjected to severe overheating and when we arrived it was 'throbbing', rather more than violently to say the least and Fire Control were informed of the precarious situation in which we found ourselves in.

Fire Control tried in vain to contact either or both of the duty senior officers, both of whom were known to be mobile in their radio cars and must have heard our initial radio messages. For a time they both appeared to be fortunate by later claiming they were in 'dead-spot' situations, where neither could transmit or receive messages (how convenient!!), each possibly hoping the other would 'crack' first.

The more than obvious reason for this was that neither wished to be in the same boat as us and were 'reluctant' to answer their radios. Fire Control eventually contacted both officers, who commenced arguing with Fire Control as to who should actually attend the incident, making excuses similar to, "The other officer is nearer to the job than I." After the arguments died down, the officer with the slightly lower rank was ordered to attend, much to his chagrin and dismay.

To complement the previous story I must include a further story from the observations of 'Incognito Press'.

'At a recent incident in Snootytown, involving a major gas leak, Gas Board officials and workmen could be excused for thinking that the Fire Service were planning to plug the gas leak with senior officers, since those with ranks above that of Station Officer, outnumbered at least one of the crews in attendance'.

'In view of their eagerness to attend, I have heard that members of the Division concerned are planning to hold a collection in order to buy them a fire engine of their own'.

'This incident was in total contrast to one at MAMMOTH COUNTY Chemicals Factory (the equivalent of Flixborough) when 10 B.A. men were used and the highest ranking officer attending was a Station Officer. Perhaps Snootytown is a nicer area than Industrialville?'.

For those readers who don't know, senior officers arrive in large numbers after five or more pumping appliances are called into action at any one particular job. The more Pumps, the more 'Top Brass'. They would normally report to the Control Unit and after being briefed take over command from the previous highest ranking officer.

If the incident expanded, even higher ranks would arrive, repeating the same old ritual until it reached a point where few firemen knew what was actually going on and even less knew who was in charge, unless the Chief himself had assumed command. As a result, firemen would be given an order by a Station Officer one minute, only to have it counter-manded by an A.D.O. the next minute. Then by a D.O. and so on, the 'Golden Rule' being 'Always obey the last order'.

We were called, as part of a large make-up, to the massive premises of a well known bottled sauce manufacturer, which was reportedly on fire and smoke-logged. At first all went well with the organisation of the fire and breathing apparatus crews, that was until the senior officers started arriving and ordering more and more appliances to the scene. Almost as soon as they arrived the communications situation deteriorated, with each officer jockeying with one another in an effort to make the correct decisions and so ultimately enhance their prestige with the Chief Officer.

Upon arriving, I couldn't help but notice some twelve or so fire engines which were parked nose to tail near to the main entrance to the building. I was always taught that appliances must have enough distance between them to enable crews to gain access to their ladders. Being positioned nose to tail meant that only the ladders from the fire engine at the rear could be used quickly in an emergency!!!

We were despatched to a section of the factory well away from the immediate fire situation and laid out hose-lines from the road-side to a basement via a sloping passage. Our initial instructions were to remain with the branch, to provide fire fighting cover should the fire break through. We were situated at a junction of several corridors, near to the foot of a large flight of stairs. The situation was somewhat confused with the presence of clouds of thin drifting smoke.

Within minutes I was ordered by an A.D.O. to find out who was in charge of the incident and was given an assurance by the same that he would keep an eye on my crew. Not long after setting off down one of the corridors, which was all but free of smoke, I was intercepted by a D.O. who ordered me to locate another senior officer. I informed him I was already under orders from an A.D.O. and he replied, "Never mind him. Do as you are told, Leading Fireman."

And so I set off once more, up this, that and the other corridor in search of the said officer, until, surprise, surprise, yet another D.O. appeared out of the mist. He said, in an urgent tone, "I don't care how you do it, get a 35', 45' or an Escape and get up on the roof with a crew to have a look round and then report back to me." How on earth I was supposed to find him again with all of the mayhem going on was in the lap of the gods.

As this was the most important order thus far, I once again criss-crossed the various passages until I came across the passage along which I had first entered the building from the outside world. I observed that my original crew had all been selected for different tasks by other officers and were probably as confused as I, as they searched in vain up and down the passages in an effort to fulfil their allotted tasks. By now, more fire personnel were being employed looking for someone else, than were actually engaged in looking for the heart of the fire.

I ran up the passage and into the daylight and looked up at the roof. So much for the idea of using a 35', 45' or a 50' Escape ladder. The roof was at least 60' above ground level. I hared off down the corridor once more, but was unable to ascertain the whereabouts of the D.O. who had issued the order for me to gain access to the roof, so I left a message for him via yet another officer.

By now I was completely fed up with this ridiculous situation and returned to open air, where I noticed some totally disinterested workmen sitting on a wall, eating their sandwiches.

They looked somewhat bemused at the antics of firemen running hither and thither, without achieving anything. I asked one of the workmen if he was employed at the factory, to which the answer was in the affirmative. I then asked him how I could get onto the roof. He replied, "You go down that corridor and up the stairs."

I mustered a couple of lads and we duly climbed the stairs, which were unaffected by smoke. Upon reaching the roof we were able to observe that the factory was divided into some three units of various sizes and height. What little smoke there was could be seen well away from our section of the premise. We returned to the basement and eventually I was able to locate the D.O. who had initially ordered me onto the roof.

He *had actually* received my message about the ladders being too short to reach the roof and had organised the availability of an H.P. on my behalf and it was waiting to be set up. I said, "But sir, I have already been on the roof." He stared at me, transfixed and speechless and after some thought snapped, "HOW?" When I stated I had gained some local knowledge off one of the workers, enabling me to gain access to the roof via the stairs, he was dumbstruck. Despite informing him that there was no sign of any fire coming from any part of the roof, he still insisted in my taking him up in the H.P.

We ran out of corridor and located the H.P., but it was devoid of any crew, the original occupants having been commandeered for other tasks. Their place had been taken by the crew of a Salvage Tender (a lot of use that was) who in turn had been delegated elsewhere.

I took the D.O. to the roof, where the situation hadn't altered, and upon returning to the ground he duly reported that all was well to the O.I.C. of the Control Unit, no doubt taking all of the credit for organising the H.P. to ascertain all was safe on the roof. ("Can't give any credit to a mere Leading Fireman, you know.")

As for the A.D.O. and D.O. who had first ordered me to do this, that and the other, I never saw them again during the course of the time spent at this job. They probably issued and countermanded so many orders they had forgotten whom they had spoken to in the first place.

A small fire was eventually located in one of the basements and duly dealt with after a couple of hours. Left to our own devices, without hindrance from the senior officers, it would have been dealt with much sooner.

One of the biggest 'cock-ups' caused by senior officers was at a large single storey, brick built warehouse, used for the storage of empty beer and pop bottles. It was during a night shift and I had been seconded to another station on the Division. The 'bells' went down and we were sent on standby to a station on a different Division.

This particular station had already despatched its appliances to the bottle store and it wasn't long before we too were on our way. The O.I.C. of our machine stated that 'Proto' wearers were required at this job and to my horror I realised I was the only member of the crew who was qualified to wear one.

Upon our arrival the usual chaos ensued, with firemen running all over the place and achieving very little. I was ordered to the Breathing Apparatus Tender (B.A.T.) where I was told to grab a set. I looked at the colour of the tally and noticed it was a two hour set. As I had only worn a one hour set beforehand, my heart sank, it was going to be a long and arduous job.

We were sent into the smoke and flames in pairs, my partner being 'The Messenger', with a jet each. After what seemed an eternity the water was turned off and we were told by another 'Proto' wearer to pull out of the premises. We stumbled towards the exit and passed colleagues, some wearing sets and others not. So much water had been poured into the building the floor and hose-lines had been submerged.

Due to the fact that the wooden and plastic pallets had been packed so closely together, our jets had done more harm than good by driving the flames further into the building, making access to the heart of the fire all but impossible.

We retreated outside for a cup of tea and a respite, awaiting our next orders. One of the officers had the bright idea of commandeering a 'stacker-truck' to remove the pallets of empty bottles. At first all went well, but the first stacks were not transported far enough away from the entrance of the building and before long the 'stacker-truck' was stranded in the centre, unable to move in any direction.

So far the Brigade had achieved nothing. In fact we had made matters worse. By now more 'Egg on Legs' were arriving, helping to confuse the situation even further. One suggested we block off the entrance with salvage sheets and fill the place with foam. All the fire crews were withdrawn and the idea put into practice.

This idea worked for a while, until the foam ran out. It appeared that none of the senior officers had bothered to calculate (they probably didn't know how to) how much foam would be required to fill the store and extinguish the flames and everyone present from the hierarchy blamed all and sundry for not ordering enough stocks. Rough estimates were worked out and transport drivers were despatched to various stations to collect fresh stocks of foam. They say that two heads are better than one, but if the one head doesn't know what the other head is doing, then problems occur!!!

The foam which had been pumped into the entrance was of the high expansion type, but somewhere along the line the order for further stocks went haywire. When the new stocks arrived, it wasn't high expansion foam, but the ordinary protein variety, as different as chalk and cheese. As it was all but useless to pump the protein foam through the ground floor entrance we were ordered to pitch ladders to the roof and pour foam in from on high, using foam branches. This too, worked well for a while, until, you've guessed it, we ran out again. Once more a round of 'bollockings' were administered.

The Officer in Charge, a Divisional Commander, then issued instructions for more ladders to be pitched and for the premises to be flooded by the use of jets. This was duly carried out, the first effect of which was the washing out of the mixtures of foam which had been pumped into the building at great expense.

Despite the use of water, then foam and more foam and yet more water, the heart of the fire refused to be subdued. One of the former Station Officers from LITTLE SNOBSBURY suggested the employment of an H.P. to bombard the fire from on high via the use of its monitor, but the suggestion was dismissed out of hand by the Divisional Commander.

Adjacent to the bottle store was a large hummock on waste ground, where dozens of men had gathered in the dark. Due to the darkness it was nigh on impossible to ascertain the different ranks from a distance. It became so crowded a Sub Officer was ordered to clear as many away as he could as it was becoming embarrassing in front of the public. He reported back to the officer who had issued the order and informed him that he hadn't been able to move anyone away because all of those gathered on the 'hummock' out-ranked him. Sure enough, upon closer inspection, there were more Chiefs than Indians. All were A.D.O.s and above, terminating with the Chief Officer himself.

This scene reminded me of the hill at the 'Alamo', where the 'Top Brass' of the Mexican army had assembled (in safety) to observe the progress of their troops. One senior officer, a D.O., who had been based at LITTLE SNOBSBURY, confessed later that he had been so disgusted at this mass meeting of senior officers, he had slunk off elsewhere in an effort to salvage his pride.

As dawn approached, the situation appeared to be under control and a confident Divisional Commander, who was still in charge of the incident despite being outranked several times, decided to relay the 'Stop' message to Fire Control.

It is a cardinal sin to request further appliances once such a message had been sent, but not long after the 'Stop' was despatched flames burst through the roof and the D.C. was forced to send for an H.P. to finish the job, something which must have pleased the Station Officer who had suggested the idea some hours beforehand. Was there a 'bollocking' for the D.C.? I know not, but he finished his career as an Assistant Chief Fire Officer!!!

Not too many weeks after this fiasco the offending building which had caused so many problems and hard work for the ordinary fire crews was demolished. Another 'Great Save' by the Fire Service and it became *yet another* 'car park' within the great metropolis of MAMMOTH COUNTY.

After the amalgamations of 1974, the new Brigade inherited the headache of what to do with the former Chief Officers and their cohorts, from the host of LITTLE SNOBSBURY'S which had been drawn into the MAMMOTH COUNTY net. Some retired, but most had to share the posts of A.C.F.O.'s, and senior posts in Fire Prevention and Training School etc. This must have really got up the noses of these once all powerful men, until things were evened out by natural wastage, years later.

Many of the lower ranking of the higher ranking senior officers, if you see what I mean, became Divisional Commanders. These men changed constantly as further promotions and retirements came along and some were better than others. A few communicated with the lower ranks, but others didn't. One particular D.C. wasn't seen by the men on the ground floor in the new Division in which LITTLE SNOBSBURY became a part of, for many months after his appointment. In the case of this fellow, his picture was posted on the notice board so that personnel could recognise him, should he set foot on our side of the fence.

One particular fireman, who hadn't made a mental note of the D.C.'s looks, was on relief Watchroom duty when the D.C. appeared in person at the Watchroom door, during a quiet weekend shift. He was clad in a civvy jacket and the fireman, who was on the phone, cupped one hand over the same and said to the D.C. "Hang on a minute 'shag', I'm trying to contact the Divisional Commander." One can imagine what happened after that remark!!!

Senior officers, upon visiting a fire station, expected, or rather demanded, that they be given a salutation by the duty Watchroom man. "Good morning sir — Blue Watch on duty — Station Officer Bloggs in charge." One day, when I was on standby duty, a senior officer, the one with facial features similar to a melted wax candle, stormed into the station office and all but exploded with rage when he blustered out, "WHEN I ARRIVE AT A STATION, I EXPECT TO RECEIVE THE CORRECT SALUTATION, NOT TO OVERHEAR — LOOK OUT LADS, HERE COMES ANOTHER OF THE F*!*!*G W*NK*RS." The fireman concerned was duly given a dressing down and the matter went no further. Mind you we all agreed with his remarks.

An example of how a former colleague from LITTLE SNOBSBURY could change, once promotion had gone to his head, was when he appeared at the station he had been based at for so many years, as a newly promoted Assistant Divisional Officer. In the days of LITTLE SNOBSBURY it was the norm to clean officers' cars (many were polished with wire wool and crevices filled with water) and he demanded of 'Pierre' and myself that we order a fireman to clean his car. He looked aghast when we informed him that the cleaning of officers' cars by firemen had ceased years before, so he had little alternative but to accept it.

After being promoted to A.D.O. he used to emulate one of the Divisional Commanders, even to the point where he wore a similar type of outer coat as the D.C. and used to walk around in exactly the same manner, with his arms tucked around his back. From time to time we used to wonder how on earth characters like him were promoted at all, let alone reach dizzier heights.

However many 'pips' or 'laurel leaves' one attains, it still doesn't alter the basic intelligence of the person involved. I remember a breathing apparatus lecture where he spoke so slowly it was a hard task to keep awake whilst it was going on. Instead of saying, "This is a B.A. line," in a straightforward and flowing manner, he would say, very slowly, "This.....is.....a.....B.....A.....line," the emphasis being on the letter/word 'a', as in hAt, rather than hAy, as one would expect a child to speak.

Bearing in mind that this 'superior' being now had three pips, it galled his former associates very much when he was posted to our Division for a while and it stuck in our throats each time we had to refer to him as 'sir'. As has been mentioned before, at every incident there has to be a cause. This A.D.O. was involved in a classic.

We attended an incident in late November one year, a bedroom fire. We duly arrived at a semi-detached house and two B.A. wearers were despatched upstairs with a hose-reel, where they discovered a small fire in part of a drawer in a divan bed, which had spread to part of the bedclothes, filling the room with smoke.

Once this small fire was extinguished and the bedroom vented, we set about finding the cause. We were informed, by the man of the house, that he had arrived home earlier than expected and within minutes of his arrival the fire had started, but he couldn't understand why. His wife was rather upset, which was understandable, but when further questions were asked it became obvious to us how it had started. Upon asking the husband if he or his wife smoked, he admitted his wife did, but she wasn't allowed to in the house.

After examing the evidence and the damage, even a village idiot could work out what had happened. The wife had been having a quick smoke in the bedroom and had panicked when her husband had arrived home early. In her panic, she had attempted to stub out the cigarette in the divan drawer, hoping her husband wouldn't notice, planning to clear the mess up later. Unfortunately for her some sparks had remained which resulted in the fire.

We were satisfied with the cause and were quite prepared to include it in the Fire Report, that is until the previously mentioned A.D.O. arrived to find out what was going on. We reported our findings to him and he then questioned both of the occupiers. Upon bringing up the subject of smoking the husband was adamant his wife never smoked in the house.

The A.D.O. dismissed our theory out of hand, preferring the husband's side of the story. We then trooped upstairs, with great interest, to find out what the A.D.O.'s theory was going to be. (After all, *he* was an *expert!!!*) After much investigation he came to the conclusion the fire had been started by the sun's rays, reflecting off, a by now overturned mirror, situated on the bed.

We were flabbergasted. I had only ever been to one such incident and this had been on a boiling hot summer's day, when the sun's rays had indeed started a fire in a chemists' shop, reflecting off a large glass bottle onto some toilet tissues, but I ask you, off a mirror in NOVEMBER? I will leave you to draw your own conclusions!!!

Due to his 'findings' we had little alternative but to put his 'cause' in the Fire Report. It was accepted — it had to be. After all, an A.D.O. couldn't be seen to be wrong in the eyes of his own kind. (Many of the same wouldn't have been able to hold down a 'Domino Dotter's' job outside the Fire Service!!!)

To bring this chapter to a conclusion, I would like to pose the question — what happens to senior officers when they retire from the Fire Service? Once out of the job their former power evaporates and they don't even have the comfort of retaining a title, as do retired army 'Majors' for instance. Do they approach members of the public they once served and state, "I say, old chap, I'm a retired Fire Officer!" If so, I'm sure they would get short shrift from the same. "So what? Do you want a medal or something!"

No, once they are gone they become another 'Joe Soap' on the street, except for a favoured few who instantly fall on their feet by becoming the Chief Fire/Security Officer of this, that or the other large conglomerate. As for the remainder, I suspect they disappear to some kind of 'Elephants Graveyard', never to be seen again. Such a shame!!!

Sickness

Sickness was rife in the days of LITTLE SNOBSBURY, with men booking sick at the drop of a hat. Most of the sick leave wasn't through sickness whatsoever, but to gain extra days off. It had a two-fold effect. Not only did sick day's enable men to be off duty, but it created overtime for those still 'able-bodied' enough to soldier on.

Men would ring the station an hour or two before their designated shifts and book sick in husky, weak voices (feigned of course) and after the two day or night shifts were over there would then be miraculous recoveries. Going sick over the two day shifts in effect created three days off as you were not back on duty until 6.00 pm on the third day. Two nights on 'the sick', plus two rota leave days, gave one four days off.

It was rare for men to exceed seven days casual sickness in any one year, though there were one or two notable exceptions, for to do so in great numbers would have attracted attention from above.

In MAMMOTH COUNTY casual sickness was monitored and if individuals exceeded more than a given total during the year, a letter would be issued to the miscreant from on high, forcing him to produce a doctor's note each time he went sick during the remainder of the year. Once such directive ordered the Station Officers in charge of each Watch to administer 'bollockings' to the men who had exceeded the limit. This placed our 'Gaffer', Roger, in a dilemma one year, for it was he who had abused the 'casual' system the most.

In LITTLE SNOBSBURY men would often come on duty, gain their 'mark' in the attendance register, then book sick, utilising a host of excuses, some more unusual and unique than others. 'The Gypsy' once went home after complaining that he had 'chilled blood'.

One fellow, who transferred to LITTLE SNOBSBURY from a town in the North-West, famed for its construction of submarines, 'used and abused' the casual sickness more than anyone else I knew in the Fire Service. Before joining his local Fire Brigade he had somewhat naturally served in the navy, in submarines, at least that was what he informed us and who were we to doubt his word!!!

He had a massive 'hooter', large manic eyes and a deep, booming voice. It must have been hell trapped for a tour with him for any length of time beneath the oceans of the world. As 'Q.P.R.' once said prior to a day shift commencing, "I have not seen 'The Sub-Mariner' yet, but I know he is here as I have heard his voice from forty yards away."

Once the 'Sub-Mariner' discovered the 'delights' of LITTLE SNOBSBURY he was forever booking sick for lengthy periods at a time, and he must have had his family doctor in the palm of his hand, for nine times out of ten he produced sick notes. He came up with some classics before he left the Brigade.

Twice he went sick whilst on duty. "Why are you booking sick?" asked the Officer in Charge. "It's my arm gaffer." "What's the matter with it?" "I can only lift it as far as my chest," he said, going through the agonised motions. "How far could you lift it before?" "Oh, up here," he replied, raising his arm above his head. It made no difference that he had made a fool of himself, he still went home sick.

On the second occasion he had been cheesed off with the drills and said to his colleagues, "That's it, I've had enough," and stomped into the engine house where he bumped into Station Officer 'Red-Cheeks'. He stripped his fire kit off and slung it to the floor in temper. "What do you think you are doing treating your kit like that?" asked 'Red-Cheeks'. "I'M BOOKING SICK AND GOING HOME," replied 'The Sub-Mariner'. "What are you booking sick with?" For the lack of any other logical reason he snapped at 'Red-Cheeks', "I'M SICK OF THIS F*!*!*G PLACE." He then strode past the incredulous Station Officer, who had been rendered speechless, and hurled his fire kit into the locker room before disappearing from the station.

He once came on duty, a night shift, after having had two day shifts off sick and was confronted by the O.I.C. who said, "What are you doing here? You are supposed to be off sick." "Ridiculous," was the instantaneous reply, "I gave my son sixpence to book me fit last night." "There's nothing in the book," said the O.I.C. and 'The Sub-Mariner' had to book fit there and then, in effect losing a day's casual sickness. He later discovered his son had spent the sixpence on sweets instead of ringing the station and booking him fit.

Within a few years of joining LITTLE SNOBSBURY it became necessary for me to go into hospital for a minor operation. I was off sick for weeks and felt like a dish-rag for most of the time. Eventually my doctor suspected I had contracted glandular fever and a neighbour transported me of to LITTLE SNOBSBURY hospital for tests. On the return journey I asked my neighbour to call in at the station as I thought it was only courteous to inform the duty Station Officer of my ailment.

I walked into the Station Officers' office where there were a gaggle of junior officers present, plus two Station Officers, one being the 'Red-Cheeked' one. He looked up in surprise and asked, "What are you doing here? Have you come to book fit?" "No sir," I replied, but before I could continue he interjected, "Then why are you here?" The more I tried to explain where I had been and my reason for calling in at the station, the more irritated he became, culminating in, "If you are fit enough to stand here, instead of being in your sick-bed, then you are fit enough to be on duty." At that I departed, more dejected with the Fire Service than ever before. 'Man management?'

'Punchy' was another casual sickness 'thoroughbred', but more by accident than design. More often than not he would oversleep prior to a day shift and due to him not being on the phone the duty transport man would be despatched to his house, whereupon, after being awakened by the banging on his front door and realising what he had done, 'Punchy' would mumble weakly, "Book me sick — stomach ache."

In between two night shifts, after consulting myself, he decided to take his 'fiddle wagon' to London. I advised him to forget it, stating there wasn't enough time for him to do so and be back on duty by 6.00 pm. Sure enough, he ran out of time and phoned in about ten minutes before his shift started. The receiver of the 'book me sick' call, once the pips had ceased, could hear the sounds of heavy traffic in the background. Although he later denied it, it was fairly obvious that not only hadn't he made it home, he was still stranded in London.

In MAMMOTH COUNTY firemen were not permitted to book sick immediately prior to, or after, annual leave, unless there was a personal appearance at a fire station or a sick note was produced. This was designed to prevent men from going away on holiday, particularly abroad, for more than their allocated leave. We once discussed the merits of ringing up from somewhere like Spain — "Ello, zis is Doctor Fernandez Gomez in Calella, Espana. Fireman *!*!*!*! is too seek to travel for annuzzer five days." This idea was never put into practice as we were too scared to give it a go.

Another dictat which came from the MAMMOTH COUNTY hierarchy stated, "When booking men sick it is not good enough to simply state in the 'Reason for Sickness' column — Stomach Trouble — One has to be more specific'. As most firemen used 'Stomach Trouble' as the ideal excuse for a day off, the vast majority of the persons receiving the call were baffled when it came to the correct spelling of DIARRHOEA, with all sorts of errors. Most would have loved to have simply stated — 'THE SHITS'.

As I approached my fortieth birthday the time came ever nearer for the statutory medical, the first since one for an H.G.V. licence many years before. This subject was often discussed amongst firemen with many ideas for inventive illnesses to enable one to be medically discharged with a pension being put forward, but none ever came to fruition. I suggested that 'amnesia' would have been as good a reason as any. "Why haven't you reported for duty today?" — "For duty. What do you mean?" — "At the fire station." — "What's a Fire Station?", but this was countered when someone suggested, "Lost your memory have you? In that case we will forget to pay you your wages."

'The Old Recruit' tried a stunt for a while, not dissimilar to one of the inmates of Colditz Castle, during the Second World War, who pretended he was a child in an attempt to be repatriated. He eventually succeeded, but by the time he was released he had forgotten he was only pretending and ended up insane. 'The Old Recruit' imagined he had a pet dog with him. "Come on Rover — Heel Rover — Sit Rover." It was shortly after I mentioned the 'Colditz Castle' fellow that he ceased his pretence.

The day of the aforementioned medical arrived and I rolled up at the door of the waiting room which was full of firemen waiting their turn to see the doctor and they were a right miserable looking bunch, with long bloodhound like faces. When my turn arrived I was greeted by the doctor's assistant, a female, who said in a patronising manner, as if talking to a scared schoolboy, "You have of course reached that *certain age,*" as if I was unaware of why I had been summoned to the 'Big House'.

Most of the other firemen were obviously trying their hardest to obtain a medical discharge, hence the long, miserable faces, which added to their problems, imagined or otherwise. Not I, I wanted to retire in good health. Some firemen who willed themselves to be ill ended up in a right state and lived a miserable 'retirement'.

During the routine of being weighed etc., I reached the section whereby I had to have my eyes tested. I read the card with my right eye and then she said, "Fine. Now the left one." I said, "I'm sorry I can't." "What do you mean?" she replied. "It's made of glass." I could almost hear her brain clanking as she thought to herself, 'If he has a glass eye, then how on earth did he get into the Fire Service in the first place?' She saw me smiling and it slowly dawned on her that she had been had and she laughed. I think it made her day.

'Incognito Press' referred to booking sick under the title of 'Writers Cramp'.

'To someone outside the Fire Service, the method of recording sickness on Fire Stations would be almost unbelievable. Let your imagination run riot for a few moments and try to imagine how members of a debating society would justify the administrative necessity of recording someone sick, so many times'.

'After all, they would argue, it is only recorded seven different times and the reason is very simple. A sponsored climb of the paper mountain at Brigade Headquarters is being organised. Any volunteers must bring their own climbing boots'.

Booking fit also had its hazards, as my wife would testify to. As she departed for work on the second morning of my enjoying a casual sickness, I mentioned that I would like her to book me fit later in the day, meaning after 6.00 pm.

She returned home at about 5.30, but before she set foot through the door she stated, "I've booked you fit." — "What do you mean?" I asked anxiously. Back came the reply, "I've booked you fit — like you asked me to." I was astounded. "How on earth could you book me fit when my Watch is still on duty?" She looked aghast. I then enquired, trying hard to contain my inner feelings, "What time did you book me fit?" fully expecting her to say, "Just before I left work," but it was far worse than that.

"About 10.30 this morning," she stated meekly. "ABOUT 10.30," I shouted. "WHO DID YOU SPEAK TO?" I demanded. "Someone in headquarters, I couldn't get through to the station side." "SPOKE TO SOMEONE IN HEADQUARTERS. WHY DIDN'T YOU SPEAK TO THE DIVISIONAL COMMANDER WHILST YOU WERE ABOUT IT?" I screamed. My poor wife looked abject and bewildered, until she realised I could be sacked for her blunder.

"GET BACK TO THE TELEPHONE BOX AND BOOK ME UNFIT. IF YOU DON'T GET THROUGH BEFORE 6.00 PM THEN DON'T COME BACK." As she disappeared into the darkness I couldn't believe what she had done. Luckily she managed to get through and right her misdemeanour and fortunately for myself, no-one else at the station had spotted this horrendous error, for, if you will excuse the pun, it would have been sickening to say the least.

Social Club and Entertainment

The Social Club played a big part in the lives of everyone at LITTLE SNOBSBURY Fire Station, more so than in MAMMOTH COUNTY days. Dances were frequent, almost at the drop of a hat, utilising the slightest excuse. "What shall we celebrate this weekend?" — "Ah. The drains are blocked — that will do."

The bulk of the participants were the station personnel along with wives and girlfriends, with few outsiders when I first joined. Folk would section themselves into cliques, according to rank and at most functions the knives would be sharpened, so much so that I thought, 'If there was a need to adopt any particular song to sum up the attitude of the same, a hit of the day, entitled 'The Back Stabbers' would have been perfectly apt!

LITTLE SNOBSBURY had a good track record of persons 'keeling over'. 'Skin' drank so much at one function he flaked out in the middle of a conversation, emptying his pint over a female party-goer as he collapsed backwards. 'Lofty', the ice-cream salesman, picked him up and threw him over his shoulder. He then marched upstairs, banging 'Skin's' head on a wall each time he turned a corner, before depositing him on a bed in the dormitory. Such were 'Skin's' powers of recovery that 'Lofty' couldn't believe his eyes when he returned to the party, for 'Skin' was back before him, another pint in his hand.

'Foghorn's' wife decided to have a go at guzzling brandy and babychams at one station dance and after a few of these she passed out beneath the dartboard. She was transported home unconscious by

'Foghorn' and when she awoke the following day she enquired as to what had happened to her. 'Foghorn' explained that his mate and he had brought her home after she had collapsed and to pile further humiliation upon her, after she had asked who had undressed her, 'Foghorn' jokingly replied, "We did."

Another female who ended up in the horizontal was the wife of a fireman who had transferred to LITTLE SNOBSBURY, Fm. 'McSnarl', an aggressive Glaswegian. 'Pat' the barman had been serving her Pernods and towards the end of the evening she slid off her stool by the bar, ending up in a crumpled heap at the feet of her husband. The latter rounded on 'Pat' and growled, "WHAT THE F*!*!*G HELL HAVE YOU BEEN GIVING MY WIFE?" "Only what you ordered," Pat replied. Later 'Pat' realised he had been dishing the Pernod out in the wrong measuring container, the larger one. No wonder she had passed out.

Two disco's were so loud that in one instance we received a complaint about the noise from a resident who lived over a quarter of a mile from the station and in the second there was a massive explosion in the centre of LITTLE SNOBSBURY and we must have been the only people within a mile radius who never heard the sound of the blast.

For a brief period of time some of the wives of firemen participated in and organised station fund raising sessions for the Benevolent Fund, having regular sales stands in the recreation room. Their presence was resented by the men, particularly the married ones, who didn't wish them to witness what they used to get up to when they were away from their spouses during the night shift — drinking, gambling and dirty joke sessions.

The fund raising episodes were a flop and soon disbanded, with one wife making the comment, "I think it's disgraceful that they won't purchase our goods, after all, the proceeds are for our ultimate benefit (their benefit) should our husbands be killed on a fire call. To the observant onlooker, the 'fund raising sessions' were simply an excuse for a gossip 'get-together', so that the bulk of the wives attending could stab other wives of firemen in the back, when they were not present.

As a finale to their meetings coming to an end, one wife discovered the Chief Officer was soon to retire and she found a tin in the station office, used for voluntary donations towards a farewell present. She gained access to the contents of the tin and was disgusted to find the bulk of the 'donations' were washers, farthings and foreign coins, which came as no surprise to us. She then commenced a campaign to force personnel to donate a fixed amount each. It was a non-starter — surprise, surprise. In the end the senior officers had to dig very deep in their pockets in order to get the Chief a decent present, for the majority of the firemen weren't interested in donating anything of value.

With the fire station open twenty-four hours a day throughout the year, crews were on duty over the Christmas period. During my first duty shifts over the festive season there was an unprecedented act of generosity from the hierarchy. One of the senior officers sent down word that the Chief, Deputy Chief and Admin. Officer had clubbed together to buy the duty personnel a drink. Talk about 'Dad's Army' — "Halves of mild. If the men want bitter, they will have to pay the difference."

The following Christmas the offer was repeated, but the senior officers omitted to stipulate 'halves of mild'. When the Deputy Chief discovered the men had consumed pints of the most expensive beers, thereby doubling the bill of the previous Xmas, he was outraged. "PINTS! — PINTS! WHAT DO YOU MEAN THE MEN HAVE HAD PINTS?"

This same man, a northerner, tried stoically to rid himself of his regional accent by adopting a 'plum in the mouth' LITTLE SNOBSBURY style of speech, which he tried hard to maintain at civic entertainment functions, even more so when in the company of the Mayor etc. On at least one occasion he was let down by his wife, who rushed into the room shouting, "EH DUCKS, WHERE'S THE SARNIES?"

Amidst the plethora of Social Club and other station meetings, in which the Chief presided over, was one known as an 'Etiquette Meeting'. The Chief and his officers had become disturbed at the lowering standards of dress during the stand-down periods and a new code of ethics was agreed upon, including the wearing of caps at all times.

Joe, 'The Boxer', raised an arm and posed the question, "Does this mean we have to wear our caps when we are playing table-tennis sir?" The Chief had a habit of removing his half-spectacles and rubbing his eyes when baffled by questions or thinking. (It appeared to all the world on this occasion that he was thinking — 'What a prat'.)

He went through this routine for quite some time before conferring with his colleagues. They all agreed it was quite impossible to partake in a game of table-tennis whilst wearing a cap and a waiver was introduced. Within a matter of weeks the whole ridiculous idea was quietly scotched and life returned to normal, if there is such a thing as normality in the Fire Service.

Many meetings of the Social Club were presided over by the Dep., when he wasn't playing second fiddle to the Chief. For a while, at each meeting he would introduce a new word into his speeches e.g. 'Scenario'. This must have boosted his ego when he observed perplexed firemen looking at one another and whispering, "What the f*!k does that mean?" — "F*!*!d if I know." The Dep. may have thought to himself, 'That will show them why the officer class is superior'.

With the advent of MAMMOTH COUNTY the Social Club scene changed little at first, but there was a gradual change and dances eventually became a rarity, with there having to be official reasons as to why one could be held, like a retirement.

Three dances still pervade my memory. The first around Christmas of one year was in full swing, with the off duty personnel and their wives well on their way, when the Divisional Commander and his family arrived. A table and chairs were provided for them in a secluded corner of the recreation room. Being non-drinkers and non-dancers, his family and he proceeded to play chess, whilst many around them swayed to the music in a more than drunken fashion.

The second was fabulous — a Caribbean night, complete with a genuine steel band. During the interval a brother of one of the lads on my Watch, a policeman, who was a D.J. in his spare time, played a host of records. A girlfriend of one of the younger firemen asked the D.J. (demanded) if he would play some 'Punk' music for her. He totally ignored her at first, due to her rudeness.

After a while her patience snapped and she confronted him, her face contorted with rage. "WHY WON'T YOU PLAY SOME 'PUNK' MUSIC?" she screeched. "Because I don't want to," he replied. "WELL, I THINK THAT YOU AND YOUR MUSIC ARE CRAP," she shouted. He then calmly said to her, as he set another record up, "Well, if that's the case why don't you f*!k off?" She went potty and had to be dragged from the room, screaming and swearing. 'Chalky', the marine, intervened and when she swore at him, both the girl and her boyfriend were also told to f*!k off in no uncertain terms by a clench-fisted 'Chalky'.

The third dance was a New Year's Eve shindig, a fancy dress effort. Despite the fact there were few visitors, it turned out to be a great night. Blokes were dressed as bears, schoolboys, SS men, and even the 'Devil' paid a visit. I was kitted out as a 'garden gnome', complete with a beard, tights, large stomach, wellies with cotton balls attached, a pointed hat, large false ears, fishing rod and a toadstool. The only incident which marred the proceedings was when 'Nestor' lost his rag and kicked my toadstool across the room.

I attended a number of retirement functions, one of which the Master of Ceremonies was none other than the redoubtable Station Officer 'Alf', of 'Friendly Fokker' fame etc. He made a right 'balls-up' of his speech. "We are gathered here tonight to bid farewell to Fm. ******. I have known him since we joined the job together many years ago. Now just because I am a Station Officer and he is still only a fireman doesn't mean he has been a failure."

He then paused and realising he had dropped a clanger tried desperately to remedy the situation. "Well.....Errmmm.....Errmmm.....What I meant to say was........" The more he tried, the more he dug himself in deeper and to compound this farcical situation he kept fingering his 'Dicky-Bow', which I fully expected to commence twirling, with water spurting out. What a man!!!

Other retirements which bordered on the ridiculous were when Trevor 'D' (who's wife had the big knockers) went out on medical grounds and the Divisional Commander who was giving the farewell speech forgot Trevor's name, and when 'Billy J' departed, with our 'Gaffer', Roger, being in charge of the proceedings, there were that many "Errmmms," Gordon turned to me and said,"When I retire, for Christ's sake keep that prat away from the speech."

When one of the Administrative Officers from Divisional H.Q., an attractive female, moved on to pastures new, there was a farewell party amongst the civilian staff and the officers. For many months there had been strong rumours that the Divisional Commander had been 'knocking her off'. The only person at the get-together who was apparently unaware of this rumour was Station Officer 'Red-Cheeks'.

During his farewell speech the D.C. said to the departing girl, "Well, it's nice to have had you." Station Officer 'Red-Cheeks' managed to stifle a snigger and later in the proceedings he drew the D.C. to one side and whispered to him, "It's nice to have had you — might be interpreted in the wrong fashion, as if you had been having an affair with her." I know not of the D.C.'s reply.

During MAMMOTH COUNTY days, a local 'Do-Gooder's Society' obtained permission to park their 'Father Christmas/cum Christmas Carols' charity van in the yard of LITTLE SNOBSBURY Fire Station. 'The Old Recruit' took an instant dislike to them and would dearly loved to have spliced a filthy, lavatorial rendition by two famous comedians, from what can only be described as a more than disgusting L.P., into the middle of one of the Christmas tapes, but he never had the opportunity. "Hello children, this is Father Christmas.....F*!K OFF THE LOT OF YOU — BOLLOCKS ETC." Imagine the surprise on the childrens faces. "What's he saying mummy?"

During my days in the Fire Service, many house parties were organised and no-one was more keen to host them than 'Foghorn-Leghorn'. During one such party at his house he couldn't be bothered to trek upstairs to the toilet and decided to relieve himself out of a downstairs window. Too late, he realised he had forgotten he had double glazing and had only opened the inner window as the water splashed back over him from the unopened section.

My wife and I, along with 'The Bush Baby' (a fireman with large marsupial-like eyes, a real life 'look-alike', both in words and deeds, of Frank Spencer, out of 'Some Mothers do 'Ave 'Em') and his beloved were out having a drink one evening, when by chance we bumped into 'Foghorn' in one of the pubs in his locality, where he was entertaining his next door neighbour, who hadn't long moved in. After some more ale was consumed we were invited to 'Foghorn's' house. There were some protestations from 'The Bush Baby's' wife, as he was slightly sloshed, but she reluctantly agreed to the invitation.

When we arrived, apart from 'Foghorn', Mrs. 'Foghorn' and ourselves, the neighbour had fetched his wife round and a small party commenced. The initial topic of conversation was that of 'Foghorn' attempting to convince his neighbour to join the Fire Service, with the 'Bush Baby' and I backing up the merits of the case.

As the drinks flowed the standard of conversation gradually deteriorated, as became more and more obvious from the glares of the neighbour's wife. The 'Bush Baby' commenced relating some slurred tale and in the middle of his story came out with, "And this f*!*!*g bloke said....." 'Foghorn' and I sniggered, but neither of our wives had absorbed his foul language. The 'Bush Baby' hadn't either, for he continued with his tale as if nothing was amiss. The neighbour and his wife said nothing, but the 'Bush Baby's' wife went potty.

She shouted to her husband, "THAT'S ENOUGH — YOU ARE DRUNK — WE ARE GOING HOME." Much to her utter astonishment, as she was used to having her orders obeyed, he turned on her and snarled, "DON'T YOU TELL ME WHAT TO DO WOMAN. WE WILL GO HOME WHEN I SAY SO, NOT WHEN YOU SAY SO, now where was I ......" He was cut short when the neighbour's wife, a woman not to be trifled with, grabbed her happily drunken husband and before she departed with him, she shouted, "WE ARE GOING. AND *THEY* WANT *YOU* TO JOIN THE FIRE SERVICE. THEY ARE ALL DRUNK — FORGET IT." Off they went and that was the end of the party.

Clive 'G', once held an all night shindig at his house. Most of the firemen on our Watch attended, accompanied by wives and girlfriends and during the course of the proceedings 'Nestor' turned round to the occupants of one of the downstairs rooms and said, with menace in his voice, "Anyone want a fight?" Within seconds, apart from himself, the room was empty.

Also present was a character who up to now hasn't been mentioned, 'Mel D'. At first, second or even third glance he could only be described as a 'potential thug'. He had one of those smiles associated with someone who took great delight in pulling the wings off flies — slowly. To add to this outward appearance was a large scar on his face. It was rumoured that he drew up seasonal 'mugging' lists. (I know, because I started the rumour!!) How he ever came to be a fireman I will never know.

Having said all this I will now contradict myself by saying he was a 'softy' and a 'romantic' at heart. The day I first met him I was on relief duty in the Watchroom when a call came in for him from his girlfriend. He was duly summoned and as I handed the receiver to him, the first words he said to her were, "What do you f*!*!*g want?" I couldn't believe my ears.

By the time of the party he and his girl were engaged. After a couple of hours had passed they had a fearsome row in the front garden, which culminated in her slinging her engagement ring at him in the gathering gloom. "F*!K OFF," she bawled. "RIGHT", he shouted and stormed off to his 'hot-rod Mini' and after several high pitched revs he roared off into the twilight.

Once he had departed she put her hands to her face and started crying. She was comforted by some of the girls and between sobs she said, "He's gone. I'll never see him again." Within minutes we heard the unmistakable sound of his car coming ever nearer. He screeched to a halt and shouted out of the window, "WELL, ARE YOU F*!*!*G COMING, OR AREN'T YOU?" — "NO, I'M F*!*!*G NOT," she screamed and off he roared again, accompanied by her wailing once more — "He's gone again." (Sob.)

This act was repeated once more and after another round of "F*!K'S" he disappeared for a third and final time. It had no lasting detrimental effects. The ring was located and a short while afterwards they were wed. A good job they didn't have to write the wedding vows themselves, for they would have read something similar to — "Do you take this f*!*!*g woman to be your lawful wedded f*!*!*g wife," etc.

As dawn broke the survivors of the all night party decided they were famished and a sumptous feast of beans and chips was prepared and wolfed down. After the meal the hostess asked, "Has anyone seen the pan in which I cook the dog's dinner?" After a few moments silence my wife confessed meekly, "That's the one I warmed the beans up in." The party ended shortly afterwards.

A number of us attended 'Mel D's' stag party. It commenced at LITTLE SNOBSBURY Fire Station where 'Mel' forced down a dozen or so Pernods before we set off for a night club. Within minutes of arriving the bridegroom didn't feel too well and spent the remainder of the time we were in the club pattering round in the urinals on his hands and knees. He *really* enjoyed his last night of freedom.

I was at one house party when I heard a squeal of brakes, followed by a rumpus outside the front window. I peeped through the curtains and could hardly contain myself. 'The Gypsy', worse the wear through drink, had arrived at the party with his mistress in his Land-Rover. He had parked on a grass verge which was angled very steeply. He was on the side nearest to the ground, with the door jammed on the same as he had hurled it open. Being tall, he had great difficulty climbing out, whereas his girlfriend, who was five feet nothing, had fallen several feet out of the other door. Most amusing.

Finally, in this section, a number of us went to another fellow firefighter's stag night, again ending up in a night club. Well after midnight, myself and my colleague, Mick 'The Goalkeeper', noticed two very attractive girls seated on their own, chewing gum. We approached them and 'The Goalkeeper' asked if they wanted to dance. "We don't dance," one of them replied. "You come to a disco and you don't dance?" he further enquired. "That's right," came the reply. "Why not?" he persisted. "Because we don't." Finally, in exasperation, he turned to them and said, "WHAT THE F*!*!*G HELL DO YOU COME TO A DISCO FOR?" — "Charming," came the gum chewing reply.

Special Services cover everything, and I mean everything, with the exception of fires, as the title suggests and apart from 'R.T.A.'s' (Road Traffic Accidents) there were a multitude of across the board incidents which we were called upon to attend.

We tended to be called out to very few R.T.A.'s in LITTLE SNOBSBURY compared to MAMMOTH COUNTY simply because the 'Station Ground' was smaller at the former. One crew was called to an R.T.A. at night, which involved a man and a woman. The man was neither injured nor trapped, but the crew had to free the woman who's foot was trapped in the pedals. She had received an injection to sedate her by a doctor who was at the scene.

As the firemen beavered away to free her from her predicament, the men involved observed her skirt riding up her legs until it reached the top of her thighs. They then observed she had no panties on, thus possibly lengthening the time it took to free her!!! (As if firemen would allow such a minor distraction to devalue their professional instincts of public duty which had been hammered into them!!!)

Meanwhile, in the background, the doctor informed the shaken driver that he was suffering from the effects of shock (the driver — not the doctor). Although his wife was trapped she wasn't badly injured and he had given her an injection to calm her down. (By now the firemen needed calming down as well!!!) At that the driver turned to the astonished doctor and said, "She's not my wife, just some old slag I picked up down the road."

At another R.T.A., during an ambulance drivers dispute, where the police had been instructed to ferry the casualties to hospital, we were ordered to attend as the police were unable to gain access inside the car. It had crashed into a tree and upon impact the anti-burst device on the doors had come into action trapping the injured occupants.

Two fire crews were in attendance, but try as they might the lads couldn't budge the doors. Without stopping to think, the duty senior officer, Station and Sub Officers issued a stream of instructions to the men. Out of the lockers of the appliances came a variety of hydraulic equipment and a host of other devices, all of which were to prove useless for the job at hand.

During this chaos I thought to myself that it was a good job this incident was on a quiet by-way rather than a busy major road, for it wouldn't have gone down too well with a large crowd observing the 'headless chicken' syndrome that was going on. Whilst the hammering and banging was going on I examined the structure of the car and noticed large rusty patches near to the hinges of the driver's door. With no more ado I fetched a 'tuppeny-halfpenny' hacksaw and worked methodically on the weakened area.

Within minutes the door fell off, much to the amazement of all present, as none of them had noticed what I had been doing. I motioned to them with the hacksaw, as if to say, "You can put the fancy gear away now, the job has been done, thanks to this little item." It had been the old, old story of 'Act Before You Think'.

A LITTLE SNOBSBURY crew, with a Leading Fireman in charge, were called by police after being alerted by a woman who hadn't seen her neighbours for days, two elderly sisters. A forced entrance was gained into the bungalow where they found one of the sisters in a state of shock at the bedside of her kith and kin who was obviously deceased. The surviving sister was hastily despatched to hospital for a check-up. Her sister had been dead for several days, but the other lady hadn't realised she had died. Feeling that she was cold she attempted to warm her sister up by piling hot water bottles and masses of blankets on top of her and by the time the emergency services arrived the blankets were almost as high as the ceiling. One of the firemen was a rookie, a 'sprog', who had never laid eyes on a dead body before. As the weight of the blankets was all but removed the body 'sat up and gasped'. The 'sprog' was so terrified by this spectacle he left the premises via the french windows, but without opening them first, a shattering experience all round.

Although I never personally experienced any small boys arriving at fire stations with saucepans stuck on their heads, as is often depicted in comics, there were plenty of lads and housewives with rings which had to be removed from swollen fingers and many was the time that chaps would walk in, to have 'balls and chains' removed after stag nights which went wrong.

One morning, as the breakfast was being cooked, the normal exchange telephone line rang and it was picked up by the fireman/cook, who discovered the call was from the local hospital in LITTLE SNOBSBURY. They had a patient who had walked around the streets during the night, before he had summoned up the courage, or had been driven there by the pain. He had a piece of conduit piping rammed over his swollen 'chopper'. "Do you mind," said the cook, "That's put me off the sausages I was cooking."

The Emergency Tender was despatched to the hospital and after all but losing his 'night fighter' the piece of conduit was sawn off. This being after a section of flat metal had been forced between 'his pride and glory' and the conduit, before the sawing could commence. (Makes one cringe — the very thought of it.) How it came to be there in the first place always remained a mystery, for the poor unfortunate never revealed the truth.

Many Special Service calls were to persons locked out of domestic premises. This was a chargeable call at the discretion of the Chief Fire Officer. Prior to gaining entry a form had be signed by the member of the public who was locked out, thereby placing the onus on them should a bill arrive from the Fire Service.

Apart from signing the Special Service form it was always wise to have a police officer present when entry was gained, in case of any skull-duggery. 'Pierre' once forgot this 'golden rule' and on the say-so of a neighbour — "Yes, that's Mrs. Bloggs," he forced the lock on the front door thus allowing 'Mrs. Bloggs' into the flat.

What happened next must have caused poor 'Pierre's' heart to sink to the bottom of his Leading Fireman's fireboots. Sure, 'Mrs. Bloggs' had lived at the flat, but what the neighbour and 'Pierre' didn't know was that she was now the 'estranged' 'Mrs. Bloggs'. She rushed into the flat and proceeded to wreck it in front of his very eyes. I'm not too sure, but I think he came in for a 'bollocking' on his return to the station.

A prime example of LITTLE SNOBSBURY snobbery happened to myself after I was turned out to a lock-out in a small block of private flats. After parking the appliance and establishing the identity of the person involved, a retired woman, she informed me she was locked out of her second floor flat. As access could easily be gained through a window on her balcony, I instructed my lads to fetch a ladder off the fire engine.

With a policeman in attendance, all that was left to do before pitching the ladder was to have the form signed. She had a female companion with her and after I had explained the possibility of her being charged for our services and pointing out I had to have her signature, she retorted in a loud, haughty voice, possibly in an effort to impress her friend, "WHAT IF I REFUSE TO SIGN YOUR LITTLE FORM ?" Her haughtiness was somewhat deflated when I replied, "If you refuse to sign, I will have to order my men to replace the ladder on the fire engine and we will return to the station and you madam will have to remain locked out." The form was signed in an instant.

This snooty attitude was on a par with another female citizen of LITTLE SNOBSBURY who rang the station up and informed a Sub Officer that there was an owl in her tree in the back garden. "What do you expect us to do about it?" he enquired. "It should be removed," came the lofty reply. "Where to?" — "I don't know." — "I'm sorry madam, we cannot help you." At that she slammed the receiver down in disgust. The Sub-O then remarked to all present, "I ask you, an owl in a tree. Where else do you expect to find an owl?"

One of the funniest Special Service episodes was when the lads at LITTLE SNOBSBURY, including 'Pat', were called out by a member of the public, in the early hours, who had discovered a length of railing missing from a bridge over a canal and he or she had feared a car had crashed through the railings and had ended up submerged in the canal, trapping its occupants. Although they weren't to know at the time, a 'yob' or 'yobs' had ripped the railing out and slung it in the canal.

When the crews arrived all was quiet. They gathered round the darkened canal and a line was thrown across. Once secured, the O.I.C., a Sub-O, suggested someone was going to have to plunge into the icy water to search for the vehicle. At this suggestion all of his men backed away from the canal, making it rather obvious to the Sub-O that none of them were going to 'volunteer' for this task.

As he was about to order one of them into the canal, a saviour arrived on the scene. The 'Saviour' turned out to be a local man who had been listening to the various messages which had been going back and forth to Fire Control on his short-wave radio and had decided he was qualified to help the firemen as he was a member of a sub-aqua club and owned

the relevant gear.

The lads couldn't believe their eyes, when from out of the darkness along the towpath came a 'frogman' who flip-flopped towards them fully kitted out. Upon reaching them he immediately threw himself into the canal, where to his horror and to the amusement of the firemen, he discovered the water was only three feet deep. Even the car owned by 'Noddy' would have stood out proud at that depth. He was thanked for his 'public spirited' attitude and the incident was closed after the railing was found.

On the subject of water there was a certain Sub Officer in MAMMOTH COUNTY who once owned a 'Beetle' motor car and whilst cautiously negotiating a flooded ford his car stalled, stranding him. As it started to float away he was forced to abandon it, recovering it at a later date. Somehow this story became common knowledge and 'The Old Recruit' really got one over on him when he came out with the classic line, "It's not often you see a 'Sub' this far upstream."

During one of the winter thaws, with MAMMOTH COUNTY in bedlam due to the overwhelming numbers of calls for help, I found myself deep in the heart of another Division. We were sent to a house which had a burst pipe. The occupier was away and the call had come from a next door neighbour who had heard the sound of running water in the kitchen.

Whilst I was scanning the front of the house for the easiest point of access, 'The Corporal' was despatched on a reconnaissance mission round the back, where ill fortune befell him. Many of the rooftops, including the house we were at, still had large amounts of snow on them, despite the thaw. At exactly the same time as 'The Corporal' disappeared round the side of the house most of the snow decided to descend on him as his snow covered shroud paid testimony to.

After brushing himself off he informed his smirking comrades and myself, plus a smiling P.C. and W.P.C. who were also present, that there was a partially open bedroom window at the back. A ladder was obtained off the appliance and I gained access to the bedroom via the ladder. The W.P.C., not thinking, decided to follow. Normally it takes only one man to foot such a short ladder, but as she ascended at least three firemen and her male colleague gathered round the base of the same, giving all those present a nice 'view' of her.

After this incident was closed we were sent by Fire Control to standby at the nearest station, which normally housed two fire engines. Naturally, we expected to find it empty. On the contrary, both machines were stabled inside and we had to park on the road outside. Using the internal phone to book into Fire Control, I posed the question, "Why are we standing by here?" "Because the station is empty," came the impatient reply. "But there are two machines here, apart from ourselves." "Don't talk rubbish," came the sardonic answer, "They are both out on jobs." I then retorted, "No they aren't and here is the Officer in Charge," and handed the phone over to him.

I would dearly have loved to have been a fly on the wall at Fire Control, but I never had the opportunity to ascertain where the other crews should have been, for whether or not out of spite, we were almost instantaneously despatched on a standby duty to a station in the 'Arsehole of the World', many, many miles away.

Roger, our 'Gaffer', was in charge of two crews which were called out to an overturned vehicle. Just as they arrived the Divisional Commander happened to be passing by and he stopped to observe the proceedings. Roger appeared to be in two minds as to what he was going to do with the vehicle, a flat-backed transit van which had a large piece of wood behind the cab to support ladders. Due to the apparent lack of progress the D.C. asked Roger what he intended to do to clear the vehicle which was obstructing the road. At that Roger ordered the men to combine their strength and right the van. They heaved and strained until at last they were in a position to right it.

While this was going on Roger continued talking to the D.C. right next to the van and he didn't notice a projection off the same snagging his tunic. As the van was righted Roger disappeared upwards, much to the amusement of the fire crews and watching members of the public. All of a sudden the tunic ripped under Roger's weight and he flew downwards, fortunately managing to land on his feet. Then, despite the sniggers, he continued chatting to the D.C. as if nothing had happened. The D.C. said nothing about what had been going on, but he must have thought to himself when Roger was airborne, 'Come down Roger, you look a right idiot up there'. He confessed later he had indeed felt a right prat.

We once had to rescue two cows stranded in a slime-filled pit and the main participants in the rescue were our 'Gaffer', 'Pierre', 'The Gambler' and yours truly. Talk about, "We are all in the shit lad, it depends on the depth," we were up to our necks in it. It was like being at the swimming baths, once you were in it didn't matter after that.

Whilst we struggled, slithered and cursed as we attempted to dislodge the cows, the farmer who owned them was located, clean, dry and warm, attempting to drink his local dry and wasn't in any fit state to assist us. It was very gratifying to save the cows, which took several hours, but I did wish on the return to the station, with us 'honking' to high heaven, that we had received a call to a 'posh person's' house in LITTLE SNOBSBURY. I would have loved to have seen the occupants' faces when they noticed the state we were in and the smell exuding from us.

From time to time we were called upon to rescue cats from trees and it was always 'Pierre's' ambition to tie two tomcats together by their tails and sling them over a washing line in revenge for being pissed on by one he was trying to rescue. He could never understand the futility of risking his neck, when, after retrieving a spitting, claws outstretched, ungrateful 'pussy', it would then run straight up another tree. His attitude to cats was, "They will come down when they are hungry enough." If he could have had his way he would have sawed off the branch the cat was perched on or knocked it off the same with a jet of water.

230

One of the last Special Service calls I attended involved a cat stranded on the roof of a house. We had been summoned by the R.S.P.C.A. and the job bordered on the boundary of a neighbouring County Brigade. I was supposed to acquire a signature on the form from an R.S.P.C.A. official before rescuing the cat. After arriving at the incident Fire Control informed me it would be quite some time before such an official would arrive. I therefore decided to go ahead with the rescue without a signature which was duly carried out by 'Rosy', who had been involved with a few 'pussy's' in his time, but never from the apex of a detached house roof.

Upon our return to the station an unsigned Special Service form was forwarded to Divisional H.Q., but it was instantly returned by an A.D.O. with the rather terse comment, "Where's the signature ?" I was so incensed I suggested to our 'Gaffer', "What does the prat want under the circumstances? A paw print off the cat?" I was sorely tempted to go out and find the nearest cat and obtain a print, but the situation was diffused by Roger. A great pity, for I would loved to have seen the look on the A.D.O.'s face as I presented him with the S.S.C. form with a paw print.

To prove how wide-ranging the endless numbers of stories I could obtain by harnessing the experience of men from other Brigades, I will relate a final Special Service tale as told to me in recent times.

I was at a printers discussing various problems when a fellow publisher happened to overhear my comments about 'Programmed Learning'. After being introduced we chatted for a while and it transpired that for many years he had been a fireman before leaving to become a publisher. Being of around the same age we had experienced similar life-styles even though our respective Brigades had been many miles apart.

He informed me of the time when he and three colleagues, which included a Sub-O as the the O.I.C., had attended a more than unusual S.S.C. to a swarm of bees. The 'Queen' had settled into the lower branches of a tree near to a public highway and she was attended by thousands of worker bees. A local beekeeper had been summoned, but he couldn't reach the swarm, hence the attendance of a fire crew.

A large step-ladder was constructed and placed in a position so the keeper could climb up and secure the 'Queen'. Two firemen, one of them our friend, had to foot each side of the ladder. The beekeeper had the 'Queen' in his safekeeping, but at the last moment he dropped her and she landed on the unfortunate said fireman's helmet, followed by the swarm.

All went black round the vicinity of his face and head. "DON'T MOVE," shouted the beekeeper, which was something of an understatement. "I'M COMING DOWN." What else could the fireman do, as he froze in fear. Whilst this was happening the other fireman opposite him footing the ladder looked on in amazement. The fire engine driver shut himself in the cab, with the windows firmly closed and the Sub-O, seated on a wall on the other side of the road, doubled up with laughter. The keeper descended and the 'Queen' was safely removed as was the swarm, much to the relief of our friend. As a final irony the only person to be stung at the end of the day was the Sub-O. A perfect case of, "He who laughs last ...."

Not being an all round sportsman nor of any great height I often dipped out on official sports contests like cricket and volleyball, having to settle in the main to participating in friendly matches, with the exception of some football games.

At LITTLE SNOBSBURY we had access to a local municipal sports club and most Sunday mornings during the soccer season we played friendly matches against anyone who was willing to take us on. As three or four members of our team were often on duty the Chief allowed us to take a fire engine to the match provided someone remained on the radio in case a call came in. The looks on our opponents faces were something else when a third of our team rushed off the pitch and disappeared into the distance on the engine.

As most teams of any note were committed to Sunday League games, the opposition we encountered was rather inferior to say the least and as a consequence we invariably won our games by a handsome margin.

During the course of one 'friendly', 'Nosy', not the most sportsman-like of centre halves was given his marching orders by the referee. The fact that he had hacked someone to the ground from behind or elbowed the same in the face for the umpteenth time was irrelevant to 'Nosy' who loudly protested his innocence that he had been the perpetrator of such violence.

For a while the ref stuck to his guns, insisting that 'Nosy' should go. Another footballing fireman, 'Kirby-Grip', a close pal of 'Nosy', stated at the top of his voice, "IF 'NOSY' GOES, THEN SO DO I," creating a scene of mayhem with half of the side in support of 'Nosy' and the remainder on the side of the referee.

In an effort to steady things, yet another fireman intervened, stating in a voice louder than the rest, "COME ON YOU LOT. ALL OF THEM THAT WANT TO GO, GO. ALL OF THEM THAT WANT TO STAY, STAY." The opposition and the ref were astonished by these goings on and in the confusion the referee either forgot the identity of who he had sent off or chose to 'let sleeping dogs lie'. In any event 'Nosy' stayed on the pitch and the match was completed.

By far the most entertaining match in LITTLE SNOBSBURY was when we installed a new goalkeeper, Mick, who hadn't long moved to the area from a Brigade in Humberside. There he was, proudly prowling around his goal line, dressed in black, like a panther, no doubt hoping he would give a good account of himself on his debut. If he had known prior to the match what he was in for he probably wouldn't have turned up.

The score at the end of the game was 4-4, quite a creditable score you may think, until I inform you that we were responsible for all eight goals!!! For the opposition we scored three own goals (two were mine), and gave away a penalty. At the end of the game we apologised to 'The Goalkeeper' who commented, "I didn't like to say too much in case you played the game differently here."

On odd occasions we played at other grounds within our 'patch', one match being at the 'Friendly Mental Home', though not in opposition to the inmates. They would crowd round the touchline in groups and each time the ball went out of play the whole group would run helter-skelter after it, arguing and colliding with each other in an attempt to reach the ball first.

There were two inmates who stood by a remote corner of the pitch dressed in the type of clothing associated with escaped P.O.W.'s awaiting their train or a couple of spies from the 'Thirty-Nine Steps'. Not only did they have the clothing and hats, but each had a 'war-time' type of suitcase and they somberly whispered to one another throughout the entire game, not taking an iota of notice as footballers and the football constantly rushed by them.

Another pitch we played on was in the grounds of the monastery where the roof had been gutted and where I had run into the mirror. For the most part we were left to our own devices, but there were times a few monks would stand and watch, but what they must have thought of the fouls and obscene language that was forthcoming only they and the omnipotent one knew!!!

After several years, of 'friendly' matches it was decided that our team should join a league. It took only a few matches for us to realise how 'over the hill' we all were. Teams of youngsters ran rings round us and after several double figure thrashings we were forced to throw in the towel, especially after we noticed that 'Nosy' was so slow he couldn't even judge his fouls correctly. After we dropped out of the league most players hung up their boots.

Once MAMMOTH COUNTY was formed I was all but left out of anything competitive and it wasn't until I was transferred to our 'Gaffer's' Watch that I was able to compete again, this time in friendly cricket games.

I arranged a trip to 'Chigley' to play a team representing the Benevolent Home, which included 'Bruno', Clive and Steve 'The Gardener'. We made arrangements to meet at LITTLE SNOBSBURY Fire Station taking two vehicles with us to Devon.

By the time we had assembled 'The Team' was down to nine participants — our 'Gaffer', the 'Savage' Sub-O, 'Buggy', 'The Corporal', 'The Warder', Andy, an 'Alfred E. Newman' look-alike from the 'Mad' magazine, 'Tommo' (Captain), 'Jimbo' and myself. Comments similar to, "What did your wife say about the trip?" were passed amongst ourselves with the general reply of, "Best of luck, hope you win, enjoy yourselves." One exception was 'Jimbo's' reply. "She told me to F*!K OFF and not to bother about returning home."

'Jimbo' was normally a quiet and placid man who rarely drank alcohol, but once free of his wife's shackles he let rip. Throughout the motorway journey can after can of lager disappeared down his throat. By the time we arrived at our overnight venue, 'The Ship', in 'Chigley', he was well on his way. An obvious ploy by the opposition was to detain as many of us as possible in 'The Ship' so as to limit our capabilities on the field of play. All but a couple of lads, one being 'Jimbo', refused to fall for the bait.

We commenced play in the late afternoon of a sun-soaked Spring day. The opposition were at full strength, but our numbers had grown to ten, as we had enlisted the services of 'Buggy's' dad, who by chance happened to be staying at the Benevolent Home. There they all were, all dressed to look like cricketers and there were we, a ragged looking band to say the least, clad in jeans and T-shirts etc., with the lone exception of 'Tommo', our captain and wicket-keeper, who was a 'proper cricketer' in his own right.

We batted first and made a respectable eighty odd runs. During our innings we fell about laughing from the pavilion when two members of the 'Chigley' team collided whilst attempting a simple catch and the ball dropped to the ground. Hoots of derision towards the two unfortunates were halted when 'Tommo' said sternly, "It's not good cricket to take the piss out of the other side if a mistake occurs."

When 'The Corporal' went in to bat it immediately became obvious that something was wrong with his stance, confusing his opponents, and at first no-one could work out what was amiss. It then occurred to one of the brighter cricketers that although 'The Corporal' was standing in a right hander's position, he was holding his bat in a left hander's grip. (More hoots of derision.)

Our opponents then batted and off the very first ball from 'Alfred E. Newman', 'Bruno' belted a mighty six. However, the cheers from the pavilion were soon silenced when 'Alfred' extracted his revenge by clean bowling him off the next ball. With their ace player dismissed the home side were soon on their way to a collapse and an ignominious defeat, thanks to our lads taking some exceptional catches.

'Buggy's' dad bought a new dimension to the game of cricket by constantly halting the progress of the ball by utilising his chest and a 'drink-sodden' 'Jimbo' introduced a new example of non-etiquette after being harangued for a mis-field by screaming across the pitch to his tormentor at the top of his voice, "IF YOU CAN DO ANY F*!*!*G BETTER, THEN TAKE MY F*!*!*G PLACE."

Under normal conditions 'Jimbo' was one of our ablest bowlers and although still quite fast, due to his swaying motion we had to place two fielders either side of our keeper as 'Jimbo' bowled, for his line and length were rather erratic. This ploy saved several byes.

When it became evident the home side were going to lose, whether by accident or design, one of the supporters let his dog, a small terrier, loose onto the pitch where it instantly bit our 'Gaffer' on his ankle and was only deterred from causing further damage to him by a kick from the 'Savage' Sub-O's boot.

With victory secured we adjourned to the clubhouse bar, we in celebration and the opposition to drown their sorrows. From there we travelled to 'The Ship' to continue the festivities well into the early hours. Our team was berthed in an upstairs room with each player being allocated a large sponge mattress. At around 9.00 in the evening the 'Savage' Sub-O and I discovered 'Jimbo' staggering round the 'dormitory' clutching his head after being afflicted with a dreadful headache from a hangover, desperately searching for some aspirins. He was provided with the same and took no further part in the proceedings that evening.

'Alfred', like 'Jimbo', hadn't been in the job very long and up until the time we were celebrating in 'The Ship', he too had been very quiet. Once the drink took over any vestige of decorum wilted, with a constant stream of swear words bursting forth and he all but filled the swear-box on his own.

During the course of the evening the 'Savage' Sub-O brought up the subject of the terrier which had bitten our 'Gaffer'. Although within earshot, Roger wasn't actively involved in the conversation, that was until the 'Savage' one said out loud, "It had a stupid name similar to Trudy." Roger instantly retorted, "Do you mind, that's my daughter's name," to which the 'Savage' one tried to back out of the corner of his own making by stating, "What I meant was, Trudy is a stupid name for a dog." (It was a good job the owner wasn't at hand.)

Another highlight of the night was when Clive's legs buckled beneath him after his umpteenth gin and tonic and he had to be half-dragged, half-carried out of 'The Ship' before being driven home by Heather. "Shorry about thish, only my legs have gone, sheerio."

'The Warder', the worse for wear from drinking, was captured by the camera wrapping his six foot plus body around a five feet nothing Sharon, no doubt promising her the earth in return for certain favours, when all too late he realised he had been photographed. At a later date when the story was repeated round the bar at LITTLE SNOBSBURY he denied all knowledge of the incident whilst in the company of his betrothed, until the evidence was produced. "Let me explain my dear ......"

Within minutes of us collapsing on our makeshift beds the room was filled with snores, belches and farts and by morning it was filled with 'methane' fumes and the odour of sweaty armpits and stale socks — an awful combination. After a hearty breakfast we set off for home in triumph.

'Buggy' had a habit of drinking a pint of milk during his breakfast and 'The Warder' tried to emulate him by doing the same, but in this instance he drank it in one go which was to produce dire consequences. We had only been on the motorway for a few miles when he complained of feeling sick and I informed him that I would pull off at the next junction.

He went green and cupped his hands over his mouth, spluttering, "I can't wait that long." This latter act and statement forced me to pull up rather rapidly on the hard shoulder. The door was flung open and in his haste during his exit he banged his head on the roof structure. He fled from the vehicle with one hand nursing his head and the other over his mouth. He then hung like a collapsed marionette over a crash barrier as he spoke several times to 'Hewi'. So much for the milk steadying his stomach down! Again, this world shattering event was recorded on film.

At a later date another match was arranged at the same venue, but unfortunately the weather became so bad the game was abandoned as a 'disputed' draw. Again there was a massive booze-up at 'The Ship', followed once more by bed and breakfast, the latter after the same fume filled 'dormitory' had been ventilated. On the previous visit I had kipped down next to the 'Savage' Sub-O and quite by accident had dumped my 'humming' socks next to his head, something he hadn't appreciated when he awoke.

The second time round he refused point-blank to kip anywhere near to me, choosing a spot by our 'Gaffer'. The latter wasn't too chuffed, when, in the early hours he was trodden on twice by the 'Savage' one after going to and from the toilet.

Prior to breakfast a number of us adjourned to a tea shop in the High Street, owned by two old ladies, for cups of tea and toast. One lad who was with us this time round who hadn't been on the first trip was 'The Gambler', one of those people who always looked like a sack of spuds no matter how smart his attire was. He paid for his tea and toast and along with the rest of his companions he departed from the shop.

'The Gambler' resides in a world famous town, famous amongst other things for ripping tourists off, especially Americans, so he had little excuse when he stopped in his tracks half-way down the street after calculating he had been overcharged. "I'VE BEEN RIPPED OFF," he shouted, but he was too ashamed to return to the shop and confront the old ladies. He took stick for this incident for several weeks. "Fancy you of all people being ripped off by two, sweet old dears."

The other main sport I participated in, many times, was sea fishing, sometimes within sight of land and other times fishing over sunken vessels miles out to sea. Amongst the venues visited were Aberdovey, Blackpool, Bridlington, Plymouth, Rhyl and Teignmouth.

One fireman, a fanatic from the 'Sealed Knot', went on a trip organised from LITTLE SNOBSBURY. It was his very first outing and also his last. He was poorly right from the moment he left the station, at the thought of being ill on the boat. Sure enough he was and he spent much of the day lying in the bottom of the boat, moaning and groaning, between bouts of sea-sickness. Even on the journey home he was bad — he certainly had a fun-filled day.

The first time we went to Bridlington, to fish for cod, one of the participants said, "I know a good cafe a few miles from the coast. It's run by two smashing birds." Who were we to argue with him and we duly stopped at the said cafe. However, there had been a change of management, as we were soon to discover.

Inside we trooped, eagerly scanning the room for the 'crumpet': Not one female was to be seen. Instead, when we filed to the counter, a tall, thin man, with an enormous head appeared. Scarcely being able to conceal our mirth, eight teas and a single coffee were ordered, along with several breakfasts. After taking the order one of our crew noticed that the cafe owner had 'odd' eyes. One was normal, but the other one faced outwards — the perfect 'EGOR'.

This must have impaired his vision somewhat for he actually served the second man in the queue before he noticed the first. Every man in the queue commenced giggling, but all pretence at self-control went out of the window when 'EGOR' was being paid for the food and drink.

He said to the first customer his independent eyes came to, "What did you have to drink?" "Coffee", was the reply and it was paid for. 'EGOR' then said to the next in line, "And what did you have?" He must have been as thick as two short planks (pieces of wood?) considering we had ordered one coffee and eight teas. That did it, each man-jack collapsed sniggering as he repeated his ritual and in the end we were glad to depart before we broke some ribs through laughing. 'The Messenger' said, between bouts of laughter, "If the captain of the boat looks anything like 'EGOR' I won't be able to get aboard for laughing."

The next occasion we called at 'EGOR'S' cafe, 'The Messenger' and I were reduced to giggling idiots even before we reached the entrance. Having gained some measure of composure I went in, before 'The Messenger' had recovered any vestige of self-control, but I was only half-way into the room when I spotted 'EGOR' and I about-turned, helpless with mirth, tears streaming from my eyes, grabbing the top of the juke box for support.

Thinking he was in firm control of himself 'The Messenger' came through the door, but at the sight of my being slumped, 'crying', over the juke box, he too immediately turned about and disappeared outside again. Eventually we both managed to control ourselves, so long as we didn't look at 'EGOR'. This was the last time we were to see him as the next time we called in, 'EGOR' had moved on — home to Transylvania perhaps?

After completing a fishing trip it was customary to go for a 'few jars'. This was all very well, but it meant we had to have frequent stops on the journey home in order to relieve ourselves. On one occasion by the time the driver, who hadn't been drinking, was persuaded to stop, we were bursting. A score of firemen hurtled out of the van, including myself, and made for some nearby undergrowth at the side of the road. About twenty pints of water cascaded onto stinging nettles and bracken much to our relief and the relief of our swollen bladders. For some reason our organiser, Clive 'G', arrived on the scene as we were doing our flies up. In his haste he tripped over a tree stump and floundered amidst the urine soaked stingers, much to our enjoyment.

On another occasion when we were at bursting point, our driver pulled in at a lay-by on a single carriageway on top of a hill. The night was extremely black and we were unaware that the lay-by was on the opposite side of the road on which we had been travelling. As a consequence we lined up against a crash barrier, thinking we were facing away from the oncoming traffic. It wasn't until a Jaguar swept past us, headlights blazing, that we realised our error. The sight of several firemen lined up with active personal hoses in use must have made an everlasting impression on the driver of the Jaguar.

One of the funniest fishing episodes occurred during a national Fire Service contest which was held at Blackpool over a weekend. All of our lads were participating in the sea fishing section, not being interested in the beach-casting duels. Our event should have taken place on the Saturday, but due to rough weather it was postponed until the following day. This meant that bed and breakfast had to arranged for the bulk of our team. Being in a Caravanette meant that another fireman and myself were in a position to kip in the same and it was duly parked in the yard of one of Blackpool's Fire Stations.

Having nothing better to do with ourselves we went out on the town, where more than a few drinks were consumed. Our organiser Clive 'G', ended up with a tray of shorts and boasted he could drink until it came out of his ears. Later that day it came out of everywhere with the exception of his ears. During the evening most of us spent the night around the station bar. Not long before closing time, four Scottish firemen, all the worse for wear, staggered into the station and weaved their way, eyes rolling, to the counter.

The first to reach the bar was in a terrible state and after attracting the attention of a barman, he said, in a slurred Scots accent, "I'll have ...." but before he could say anthing else he passed out and slowly slithered down the facia of the bar until he slumped prone on the floor. His colleagues, instead of coming to his assistance, their instincts telling them it was almost closing time, stood on him and continued with the order. "We will have ......"

My partner for the night, 'Bernie' and I were just settling down for the night in the Caravanette, when we heard them departing. The chap who had passed out was still unconscious, for as we heard them pass by it was obvious his mates were assisting him home, for we heard his heels clicking on the pavement joints as they dragged him away.

Despite his 'experience' it didn't put him off fishing, for I spotted him the following morning boarding a fishing vessel. It was bobbing up and down, but his natural 'swaying' motion soon overcame the problem, though his eyes were rolling like two marbles in a cup. I don't think he won any prizes though!!!

Station Life

The very first day I joined LITTLE SNOBSBURY Fire Brigade was to create an impression that was to last for over twenty years — 'I have got to get out of this place'. There was constant bickering between the men and as previously stated Sub-Os like 'Squirrel' and 'Glarer' ran the Watches. One Sub-O, as yet unmentioned, 'Harry', ran a Watch of lively characters, all of whom liked a few 'tots' at night, resulting in lengthy binges until all hours. As a result of their frivolities they were more than quiet the following morning, ideally summed up by 'Harry' when he used to say to them, "Not so lively now, are we?"

I started off on the wrong foot by calling Leading Firemen F.L.'s instead of L.F.'s and was rewarded with the onerous task of scrubbing two flights of concrete stairs with yellow soap and wire wool. Every mark and blemish had to be removed — or else. 'Pierre' had the habit of admiring the finished work and then took great pleasure in creating more black marks with the polish from the toecaps of his shoes. "Tut — Tut. 'Glarer' won't like that. Get it cleaned." As I was on my hands and knees I reflected on the folly of my having left the comfort of my signalbox some twelve months before.

For many years firemen performed the station chores until civilian cleaners and cooks were employed, releasing us for 'better' things. Unless there were a number of 'shouts' to break up the day shifts, life was one of almost total boredom. Life in the Fire Service in the sixties at LITTLE SNOBSBURY was summed up by 'Q.P.R.'. "I don't give two F*!K'S. I come here at the start of each shift and I go home at the end. What they (the officers) do and say in between, matters not."

Day shifts from Monday to Friday consisted of checking machines, drills, station cleaning, lectures, hydrants and of course the infamous 'Programmed Learning'. Men on duty would be rostered for various tasks, cleaning and polishing fire engines, scrubbing cars, windows, stairs and polishing floors. With the latter, polish was applied by hand and buffed up when dry with an antiquated 'bumper', again in a manual fashion. One fireman had a 'bollocking' for not polishing a floor in lines, as one would do when cutting a lawn.

At a later date in time, after a visit from a 'salesman', our lives were transformed with the advent of a latest piece of advance technological equipment — a swivel duster/mop which saved the user from having to move around when dusting round corners. Eventually we arrived in the 20th century by being supplied with an electronic floor polisher. Despite having attended a 'course' on how to operate it, 'The Apprentice' almost disappeared through an upstairs window after he lost control of it.

Saturday mornings were set aside to clean and tidy the station (which had been tidied countless times during the week) polishing polished fire engines and painting the walls of the tyres black (until it was discovered the paint was rotting the rubber).

One Saturday afternoon the television broke down. Gordon, along with two or three others, were going crackers at the thought of missing the horse racing. 'Pat' mentioned he had a portable T.V. at home, so Gordon asked the O.I.C. if he could go and get it in the station van. Permission was given and Gordon duly rolled up outside 'Pat's' house. As he walked up the drive 'Pat's' wife threw open the front door and with tear-filled eyes said, "Oh, no — not my Pat?" (As if a lowly fireman would be despatched to inform a loved one of her husband's accident or death!!!)

Gordon said, trying hard to contain himself, "No, I've come for the portable T.V." After returning he mentioned what had happened to everyone except 'Pat', who could be touchy from time to time. It was suggested to Gordon that when next on duty on a Saturday afternoon, he made a return trip to 'Pat's' house. "Have you come for the portable television?" — "No. 'Pat's' dead."

As soon as a wheel was turned, if a fire engine or engines returned to the station dirty, they had to be washed and leathered, regardless of the hour of day or night. 'Pierre' often posed the question, "Why do we have to constantly wash and leather fire engines? Won't they be able to move if they are dirty? Dustcarts are dirty, but they still operate."

The introduction of physical training prior to drills was the brainchild of one of the senior officers and like many an idea from the 'Think Tank', it was eventually doomed to failure. To ensure all of the men participated it was made compulsory. There were the usual arms flapping up and down routines, along with other basic exercises, all supervised by an 'unfit' Station Officer, a non-participant of course.

From goodness knows where some covered telegraph poles appeared on the station. The exercise consisted of rows of men lifting the poles above their heads. This was all very well providing the groups of men were of similar height. Five feet five 'Taffy' once found himself with a crew of six footers and each time they lifted the pole he was either lifted clear of the ground or left stranded.

As all sensible folk know, volunteers are better than 'pressed men' and it was due to one of the latter that physical training was abandoned. The man in question had often voiced his unwillingness to take part, pointing out he was only doing so because he was compelled to. When Station Officer 'Red-Cheeks' ordered the men to throw medicine balls to one another, he flatly refused, stating it was dangerous due to the weight of them.

'Red-Cheeks' said, "Nonsense." He then stood in front of the rebel fireman and threw the ball at him, expecting him to catch it. The fireman did nothing. He never even raised his arms and the ball hit him fully on the chest, to which he immediately booked off sick. Another great idea up the creek.

As soon as the men were stood down during the night shifts they would rush off to the dormitory (providing there was nothing of great interest on the T.V.) to make their beds. Despite the regulation gear many would have a variety of sleeping bags, with multi-coloured blankets and pillows. A section of the dormitory only housed a few beds, reserved for the older serving men and was known affectionately as 'Rose Cottage'.

Morning routines commenced after parade at 7.00 am. All of the dormitories had to be cleaned and floors buffed up. A favourite trick of 'Glarer's' was to hide a match beneath the small carpet in his dormitory. Woe betide the rostered 'cleaner', if, after his room had been cleaned, the match was still in place. From time to time massive house spiders would be placed beneath 'Squirrel's' or 'Glarer's' blankets. They were so big we could see them moving, but neither of these hated Sub-Os ever commented about them. They probably frightened them away by looking or breathing on them, especially in 'Glarer's' case.

Despite the lengthy hours of boredom many firemen grabbed at the opportunity of making extra money from overtime. It wasn't uncommon for men to be on duty for 33 or 39 hours at a time. The O.I.C.s used to keep a list of volunteers and each fellow at the top of the list would be given the opportunity to accept or refuse overtime in rotation, when it became available.

Once accepted, the participants' names would then drop to the bottom of the list. Some firemen were so greedy that if they managed to gain access to the list they would erase a rival's name from the top of the roll and substitute their own. 'The Guardsman' accumulated so much money during one month he picked up more than the Station Officers, much to their jealous dismay.

Some firemen used to walk in their sleep and it wasn't unknown for them to climb into personal lockers, thinking they were opening a toilet door, sometimes relieving themselves in the same. A number of us were having a late night drink by the bar when we heard the sound of running water. At first we thought it was caused by a leak from the main water tank at the top of the stairs and moved off to investigate. It was a leak alright, but not from the tank. It came via 'Nosy' who had sleep-walked into a first floor pole-drop for a 'slash'.

Without doubt, the most popular pastime during night shifts was cards — brag, bridge, cribbage, poker and shoot, interspersed with liar (poker) dice sessions. Of these games, shoot was the real killer. If for instance there was £5.00 in the kitty and one was dealt three aces — hearts, diamonds and clubs, one would have to 'shoot' — go for the kitty. If the dealer turned up any card from those three suits he would lose the £5.00. If, however, he turned up a card from the missing suit, spades, the punter had to match the kitty, making it £10.00. Small fortunes could be won and lost within minutes.

One night 'Pat' was winning handsomely. In a moment of generosity (weakness and guilt) he went to the bar to buy his opponents a drink, leaving his cards with a 'trusted' colleague. By the time he returned with the drinks his 'pot' had evaporated and he had to borrow some money to continue in the game.

The fireman who has been referred to as Fm. 'Sealed Knot', gained his nickname after becoming a fanatical member of the SEALED KNOT SOCIETY. He would dearly have loved to have been a cavalryman, but he couldn't afford a horse, so he had to settle for the infantry. One of the reasons he left the Fire Service was due to the fact that he was a cavalier (he may well have been a roundhead!!) and therefore needed to grow his hair long, with a flowing beard, something the Brigade wouldn't tolerate.

Shortly after becoming a member he acquired a musket of some description. He brought this 'blunderbuss' into the station one night to show it off to his colleagues. They suspected (rightly) that he had been too frightened to use it, despite his denials. Eventually he was goaded enough to load it. Out into the yard they trooped and when he pulled the trigger there was a loud explosion and a sheet of flame erupted from the barrel, followed by the sound of hundreds of tiny pellets peppering the wooden fence forty yards away. He never brought it onto the station again.

'Arnold', who later made his exit after attempting to impersonate a policeman, tried to bolster his unpopular reputation by bringing a brand new 2.2 air rifle into the Control Room. He pointed out the various parts, giving the impression he knew everything about his weapon. When asked if it was loaded, he snarled, "Of course it bloody well isn't. Do you think I am f*!*!*g stupid or something? Look I will show you." At that he pressed the trigger and a hole appeared in the Control Room ceiling!!!

With the advent of MAMMOTH COUNTY it enabled men to transfer

to and from different stations within the Brigade. It also meant that we had to perform standby duties within our Division and for a long time LITTLE SNOBSBURY Fire Station became somewhat of a transit camp.

Men sent on standby duties were paid travelling expenses, but they had to fork out of their own pockets initially, not being reimbursed until pay day. Fm. 'Sealed Knot' was ordered by Station Officer 'Red-Cheeks' to go on a standby duty, but prior to going he asked the S.O. for his travelling expenses.

'Red-Cheeks' snapped, "You will get your expenses on pay day. You know the regulations." Fm. 'Sealed Knot', a stubborn man, replied, "But I don't have any money on me to buy the petrol to enable me to get to my destination." (A bluff of course, as he didn't want to go on standby.) A furious argument developed which culminated in the 'Red-Cheeked' officer dipping in his pocket and offering his opponent the appropriate amount of money. He was quite taken aback when Fm. 'Sealed Knot' took it off him. To add insult to injury he informed 'Red-Cheeks' that HE would have to wait until pay day to get his money back.

With the banning of overtime in November 1974 our employers were forced to recruit more personnel to enable us to switch from a 56 to a 48 hour week. We basically remained on a 56 hour structure with extra rota leave days thrown in on a seven week cycle.

Some of the characters who were employed had to seen to be believed. One was 'Frankenstein', featured in the fake transfer in Deliberate Set-ups. Now 'Frankenstein' was a good worker, if ordered to dig, he would dig. The trouble was he had to be told when to stop. To say he became easily confused is something of an understatement. He arrived at the station one Sunday morning in a taxi, thus ensuring he wasn't late for duty, which had happened several times in the past. He had the right Watch alright, but no-one bothered to inform him until the taxi had disappeared that he was on extra rota leave.

I don't think he ever recovered from this humiliation and so as not to be caught out again at going to the unnecessary expense of hiring a taxi on his 'day off', should he make the same mistake again, he bought himself a moped. After many weeks of use one fireman asked him if he could have a ride round the yard on it. Off the fireman went and as he speeded up he went through the gears. Upon hearing the engine notes changing 'Frankenstein' asked a watching colleague, "What's those noises?" Up until then he hadn't realised his moped had gears!!!

He was on his own in the television room watching a 'Dracula' film when 'Nestor' poked his head round the door, but 'Frankenstein' didn't notice him as he was too absorbed in the film. The plot had reached a point where 'Dracula' was about to emerge from his coffin. The hero of the film was poised over him with a stake in his hand, but he was undecided whether or not to kill him. As 'Dracula' rose 'Frankenstein' screamed at the hero, "KILL HIM — FOR GOD'S SAKE — KILL HIM — LOOK — HE IS GETTING AWAY." He then wrung his hands in despair and jumping up and down he shouted, "HE HAS GOT AWAY — I TOLD YOU HE WOULD GET AWAY." 'Nestor' couldn't believe it.

He went out on the town with a mate and his mate's girlfriend. On the return journey he managed to wangle himself into the back of the car with the girlfriend, as he didn't have one of his own. As she straightened out whilst she was getting in she banged her head on a roof support. Falling over himself to be sympathetic towards the girl's obvious discomfort, he patted her on the head and without thinking said, "I bet that f*!*!*g hurt."

When he eventually got himself a girlfriend he hadn't the slightest idea how to conduct himself with her and he was about as romantic as a rogue sloth. He would be on the outside line telephone for hours 'serenading' her, but each time I went past him all I ever heard was, "Because I f*!*!*g say so — for f*!k's sake — why do we always f*!*!*g argue?"

'Frankenstein' wasn't the only fireman to suffer the ignominity of going on duty when he should have been off. 'Buggy' went one better, not only did he go on duty at the start of his annual leave, but he also went on standby. It wasn't until 'Pierre' and I were doing the manning board for the following day that we realised he shouldn't have been at work. I had the great pleasure of relaying the news to 'Buggy', who, despite putting on a brave face, must have felt a right prat.

There was hardly a day which passed by without some sort of 'cock-up' happening. Many such 'cock-ups' have been included within other chapters, but there a couple remaining worthy of a mention, one being after one of the stations within our Division had a freshly laid tarmac yard. It looked very nice and professionally completed. It was only when a crew went out to drill that they discovered the internal hydrant had 'disappeared'. It took weeks to locate it.

Another concerned an instruction which had been issued to all stations from the 'Big House'. Some bright 'Herbert', upon discovering he or she had a choice of three options within the instructions, must have thought, 'Hang on a minute. A choice of three!!! Now two is either, so therefore, three must be eithers'. There it was in black and white for all to see. "When operating blah, blah — one of the eithers must be obeyed."

There was a challenge from one of the stations to all-comers and went something like — 'We would like to chall*a*nge anyone to any sport or quiz comp*i*tition'. When I contacted the station concerned I challenged them to a spelling contest, pointing out the errors in their notice. The recipient obviously took the huff and slammed the receiver down. No doubt the mistakes would have been rectified by the use of 'Tipp-Ex', commonly referred as 'Idiot Ink' within the Fire Service. There were certainly enough idiots qualified to use it!!!

As you will have gathered throughout this book swearing was and still is rife within the Fire Service. Unlike most other firemen our 'Gaffer', Roger, rarely swore, but when he did it was extremely funny. During a night shift the internal phone rang in the early hours, being answered by Roger. During the time we having our early morning cup of tea someone asked Roger, "Who was that on the phone last night gaffer?"

The 'Gaffer' thought for a while and replied, "It was Errmmm ..... Errmmm ..... it was ..... never mind who, he was ringing up about .....

Errmmm..... Errmmm ....." He then trailed off and as a sheepish grin came over his face he said, "Come to think of it I haven't the faintest idea who it f*!*!*g was or what he was f*!*!*g ringing up about."

We were playing crib during an evening stand-down and seated behind our 'Gaffer' were two guests, the local station milkman and his wife. It was very quiet in the room and the card game had been a staid affair until out of the blue Roger threw down his hand in digust and said in a loud voice, "I'VE GOT F*!K ALL IN MY HAND," forgetting the presence of the visitors. Our laughter did little to ease his embarrassment.

On another occasion we were seated in his office and one of the cleaners was fussing round by his desk. Roger and I were on the subject of holidays and I asked him if he was going away during his next leave. "Not this time, but we are f*!*!*g (choke, choke, mumble) hoping to ....." trailing off as he saw me depart from the room in a fit of helpless mirth.

As a finale to our 'Gaffer's' language 'blunders', we were on parade in the muster bay with the men being allocated various tasks by him. Included in the line-up was a new recruit on his first day of duty after leaving Training School. The same female cleaner was within earshot of Roger, when he turned to the youngster and said, "You can f*!k off with the transport man," once again turning brilliant red when he realised the cleaner had heard his latest 'clanger'.

Romances were part of the station life at LITTLE SNOBSBURY Fire Station and as mentioned in an earlier chapter there was only one female member of staff for many years, until cleaners and cooks were employed. Therefore, unlike later times in MAMMOTH COUNTY when firemen used to run away with cooks and cleaners, most romances (affairs) took place between the girlfriends and wives of the firemen.

When I first joined, the premises behind LITTLE SNOBSBURY Fire Station used to be occupied by Post Office sorters and postmen. One misty autumn night one of the lads was having it away with his girlfriend in the back of his car near to the G.P.O. premises. It wasn't until they had completed their romantic duet that they noticed eight or more postmen peering from all angles into the vehicle, after having watched their performance. It isn't known how many marks out of ten were awarded to them!!!

As the men had no young females to ogle at whilst on duty in the station, it was hardly surprising there were numerous affairs, especially during station dances where girls and firemen were discovered in dormitories and cupboards. At least one couple performed on top of the snooker table where more than the 'black' was being potted. One would officially describe them as 'heavy petting sessions'.

Alongside the station were a row of houses, the nearest of which contained a married couple with two children. The husband couldn't exactly be described as the most honest of persons due to the fact he was in and out of prison like a 'yo-yo' for various shady dealings. "Honest copper, it fell off a lorry."

Whilst the 'cat was away' the 'mouse would play', or rather 'mice', for the wife of the 'jailbird' had a female friend, who was also, shall we say 'interested' in sex and most of the participants with this duet were on and off duty firemen. Lads used to observe the comings and goings of their colleagues during the hours of darkness. "Can't quite make out who he is, it could be ....." — "And he is married with kids" — "I knew he was interested in bird watching, but not women," and so on.

Eventually these romantic interludes came to the attention of the senior officers and the Chief issued an anti-sex dictat. "You are all banned from entering the house next to the station," and to enforce his rigid order a yellow line was painted between the two premises with a further order of, "Anyone crossing the yellow line, with the exception of men arriving or departing from the station, will be for the high jump."

Most firemen adhered to this order, but the more determined (sex mad) used to carry on, but luckily for them they were never caught by the senior officers. It was eventually left to the husband of the wayward wife to put a stop to the cavorting, in a rather bizarre fashion.

It was during a day shift, whilst the duty Watch were in the recreation room participating in a 'Programmed Learning' session, that the recently released husband returned home. During his time in prison, he had learned, 'through the grapevine', that his wife had been having numerous affairs (sex romps). As soon as he walked into his house he commenced beating 'seven bells' out of her and when he had finished he drove off with the children.

This particular incident made local television headlines. 'Police are looking for' etc. The men on duty had heard her being beaten to a pulp, but assumed, despite her screams, she was enjoying one of her 'sexploits'.

It wasn't until the police arrived that they realised how serious the situation had been. The husband was eventually tracked down and he was returned to his 'second home', with the children rejoining their mother. The sexual 'liaisons' immediately ceased with all parties involved 'getting the message'.

Returning to the station yard and yellow line at LITTLE SNOBSBURY, whenever it was fine roll call for the oncoming Watch and for the dismissal of the off going men used to be performed out in the open in the yard, with military precision. One of the younger elements of the oncoming Watch was snogging with his girlfriend on the pillion of his motorbike, which he had deliberately parked on the yellow line so as to antagonise the senior officers into thinking, 'Any moment now he is going to cross the line and we can nail him'.

Such was his involvement with his girlfriend he missed the time for roll call and failed to see the men being assembled in readiness for parade. Once they were lined up and all was quiet, the O.I.C., a Sub-O, glanced across at the couple on the bike and bawled, "HAVE YOU QUITE FINISHED ? YOU DON'T MIND IF YOU COME AND JOIN US DO YOU?" Within seconds the red-faced fireman shot off his bike and fell into the ranks smiling, until the Sub-O shouted, "GET THAT STUPID SMILE OFF YOUR FACE."

It's a small world, as the saying goes, but none was smaller than what happened to a MAMMOTH COUNTY Fire Brigade union official, who, in a great effort to abide by the maxim 'Never Shit on Your Own Doorstep', retreated to Scotland for a dirty weekend with his mistress. 'I'll be okay up here miles away from anyone who is likely to know me', he may well have thought to himself.

He and his 'Lady Chatterley' hadn't long settled down for a cup of tea in the cafeteria on the M6 in the early hours, when in walked into the all but deserted room the entire Executive of the Fire Brigades Union, most of whom he knew, on their way to or from an important meeting. There are no prizes for guessing some of the comments he came out with, but I bet one of them was, "Oh, f*!*!*g hell," as he choked on his tea.

As previously mentioned, cleaners, especially the younger ones, were the targets of amorous firemen, some of whom were successful, others not. One of the MAMMOTH COUNTY Sub-Os took a fancy to a more than large and buxom cleaner, who continuously rejected his advances. On a par with most cleaners she worked part-time, but in her case it was during the evenings. The Sub-O awaited his moment and cornered her in a small room used for the storage of station cleaning materials on the top floor of the station, where he approached her with his 'chopper' hanging out. Instead of going red, agog with curiosity, excited or angry, she calmly commented, "That looks like a 'cock', but smaller," and brushed past him, more than deflating his ego.

One lady, who ruled the roost in the cleaning world, became involved with one of the Station Officers at an out station for a time. She was an attractive, self-motivated girl, who knew exactly who and what she required in life, with a large pair of 'knockers' — a real man-hunter. She also enjoyed her booze and on her way out of the station one night, she tripped and fell down a flight of stairs. When she landed at the bottom, on her head, she was all but senseless and wasn't in a position to notice that her breasts had popped out of her dress. The chaps who rushed to her assistance were mesmerized by the sight of them and were most put out when one of the officers put her 'tits' away.

'Pierre's' attitude to 'loose women' was one of, "You can't beat a bit of Hairy Annie." He is hardly likely to ever appear in 'Love Story' or great romances of our time on the big screen with an attitude like that. He once courted a large, robust woman, whom we instantly dubbed 'Widow Twankey'. After several visitations he ditched her after she stated, "I like to have my man three times a night." No wonder her husband had done a runner or snuffed it.

To sum up the 'Romances' side of station life I would like to conclude with two statements, one from 'Pat' who once said, "You spend half of your life looking for the right woman and in between you get married." The other was issued by the 'Red-Cheeked' Station Officer who commented about one of the LITTLE SNOBSBURY firemen, "He is so thick he wouldn't notice his wife being screwed, even if it was being done in front of him."

No story of station life within the Fire Service would be complete without some stories of the clothing stores etc.

There was an excellent newspaper article many years ago in which the reporter slated the emergence of the P.P.O. — Petty Public Official

— who had been created by an unknown masochist and unleashed on the public at large, like traffic wardens. These men and women of inconsequential lives suddenly found themselves wielding great power — classic grown-up bullies.

The Fire Brigade stores are no exception to these rules with each employing its own brand of 'Petty Dictator'. We were fortunate at LITTLE SNOBSBURY Fire Brigade in the fact that the stores and clothing came directly to us so therefore the men on the ground never visited the suppliers.

Kit checks within MAMMOTH COUNTY were rather lax affairs compared to the attitude of the hierarchy at LITTLE SNOBSBURY. At the former it was a brief look at kit and if any items needed replacing it was up to the O.I.C. to condemn the same. In LITTLE SNOBSBURY there was a picture hung up in the dormitory in which it detailed, in a set way, how to lay out kit in readiness for inspection — blankets on the bottom with every item of gear right down to a locker key laid out in a ritualistic order and God help the fireman who had anything out of place.

With the inception of MAMMOTH COUNTY when kit was required appliances were despatched to the central store. Once inside the men had to wait for the stores officials to come to them and by the entrance to the same was a dividing line. If any fireman crossed this line without permission, P.P.O.s would descend on him as if he were trying to break into Fort Knox. On one particular occasion we had an A.D.O. with us, but he too was treated like a potential criminal and eyed with suspicion when he tried to cross the line.

The disadvantage of the old LITTLE SNOBSBURY system was often

high-lighted by not only the wrong sizes of kit being issued, but faulty kit as well. One fireman was issued with a shirt which was perfect in every sense of the word with the exception of the collar which must have been designed for a man with a size 30 neck. Another man was sent a pair of trousers with one leg six inches shorter than the other. At least by going to the stores one would eventually be given kit which actually fitted.

Once MAMMOTH COUNTY got into top gear, old Emergency Tenders were converted into clothing vans until the Brigade had enough finances to purchase the custom built vehicles. Instead of firemen having to travel to the stores, the stores were brought to the firemen on a rota basis. To describe the visit of such a fine band of men I will once again call upon the excellent wit of INCOGNITO PRESS.

'Making preparations for a visit of the clothing van involves careful planning on the part of the O.I.C.s. Time has to be found for a kit check of all Watch members. Lists of requirements are drawn up and stores demands made out for each member of the Watch, ensuring, in order to comply with the stores department requirements, that all stores code numbers are correct, a time consuming operation in view of the complicated layout of the stores book'.

'On the day of the projected visit, the van is eagerly awaited by firemen walking round the station with little piles of condemned kit. Thirty minutes pass, but still no sign of the stores departments travelling circus. A quick check of the relevant Routine Notice is made to make sure the mistake is not the O.I.C.'s, then an enquiry to stores to find out the reason for the hold-up'.

'He is told, "You should have known the van cannot come today because it is in workshops." How could he have known? On it's last visit, amongst the many items not available were 'Crystal Balls'. Perhaps he will be able to get one on the next re-arranged visit and also a pair of shoes that will allow him to walk on water'.

If one was lucky enough to actually be on the station when a stores van arrived he would join the queue waiting his turn to be served. Condemned kit would be handed in and slung to one side. If the van official had his back turned the condemned kit would be snatched back and handed in again on another visit thus enabling the 'thief' to gain an extra pair of shoes or trousers etc., for use with his 'fiddle'. Eventually the geniuses within the hierarchy worked out what was going on and condemned kit was placed out of the reach of the men.

Fm. "Angry', by now a Station Officer in Fire Prevention, got wind of the arrival of the stores van and needing a replacement I.D. card he made his way down to the appliance bay. As has been mentioned before, we know that Fm. 'Angry' was not the most patient of characters. By the time most of the men had been issued with new kit he was coming to the boil. When the last man had been dealt with he stepped forward with his old card only to be confronted by the van driver who was shutting up shop to go for his dinner and he refused to see his card. The driver walked away and Fm. 'Angry' (sorry) Station Officer 'Angry' vented his pent up rage by hurling his I.D. card to the ground, jumping up and down on it, bawling, "F*!K THE CARD — F*!K THE FIRE BRIGADE — F*!K THE STORES VAN AND F*!K EVERYONE," before angrily stomping off to his office.

If we were unable for some reason to make the appointed time with the clothing van, frantic calls would be made by the O.I.C. to Brigade stores via the 'Big House'. The appropriate paperwork would then be despatched with the person who needed the item or items of clothing.

Gordon, who had missed the van by minutes, travelled to where the van had its next appointment. Upon arrival he gave the stores official his stores order form and waited expectantly for the pair of sheets he had ordered. The official emerged from the van and gave Gordon one sheet. "What's this?" asked Gordon, "I have a pair on order and you have only given me one." Consulting the stores code book the official exclaimed, "Sheets — *pair* — issue — *one.*" "But how can a pair of sheets be one?" retorted Gordon in disbelief. "Because it says so in the book," remarked the unmoved official. "The book must be wrong then." — "The book is never wrong."

There then followed a furious argument between Gordon and the clothing man. "IF YOU ASKED FOR A PAIR OF TROUSERS, HOW MANY WOULD YOU GET?" asked the smirking official. Gordon countered by saying, "ONE, BUT IT IS CALLED A PAIR BECAUSE THERE ARE TWO LEGS IN IT, UNLESS ORDERED SPECIALLY FOR A ONE-LEGGED MAN," adding sarcastically, "AND THERE AREN'T TOO MANY OF THEM IN THE FIRE SERVICE, ONLY ONE-EYED ONES." His comments fell on

255

stony ground so he continued, "WHAT ABOUT A PAIR OF GLOVES THEN? WILL YOU ONLY GIVE ME ONE?" Gordon was wasting his time for whatever he said the official was not to be moved and he had to be content to return to his home station with his one (pair) of sheet(s).

Whilst still on the subject of sheets, not long after 'Frankenstein' was based on my Watch he was asked by the Station Officer, "How many sheets have you been issued with?" After several minutes of blank thought 'Frankenstein' replied, "Urrmmm ..... Urrmmm..... Tut-Tut ..... Urrmmm ..... Them, them white things?" The Station Officer nearly fell over at his reply.

Every item of kit which a fireman is issued with has to be marked or stamped with his personal Brigade number. If on an inspection kit was unmarked the miscreant was for the high jump. INCOGNITO PRESS describe the ACME WHISTLE TEST as follows:

'Wouldn't it be nice to find out the name of the man at the Home Office who first had the idea that all operational firemen should be issued with whistles. If I knew his name I would organise a kidnapping squad to take him into custody and imprison him in the appliance room so that he could suffer the ear rending noise as firemen test their new toys at the change of shift'.

'Talking about whistles, did you hear the one about the ex. Training School inmate (instructional staff), who, on being issued with his whistle, was informed by one of his colleagues that his whistle had to be marked with his Brigade number using the metal stamp. He will remain anonymous to save any embarrassment, however, if anyone has a use for a flat ACME THUNDERER whistle, please contact Fireman ....'

One 'Tin-Pot' dictator had his come-uppance during a visit to Brigade

256

stores by a MAMMOTH COUNTY Councillor, who's favourite 'Quango' organisation was certainly not the Fire Brigade. Moving round the rows of clothing he came to several racks containing fireboots. He halted at a section which contained size 15 boots and posed the question, "How many firemen are there in the Service who are actually wearing such massive boots?" — "Errmmm ..... Errmmm..... I will have the computer check this out sir." The Councillor, aware of the rife wastage of public funds, retorted, "You do that." Within minutes the reply came back, "None sir." "Then get rid of them — sell them," snapped the Councillor to the red-faced 'Hitler'.

To complete this chapter there was an occasion when 'Billy J' was dumping some household items in the large external rubbish bin at LITTLE SNOBSBURY Fire Station. Included was an old carpet, but before he could sling it in the bin, 'Pierre' intervened. He had noticed a parked and unattended van from another station in the yard and persuaded 'Billy J' to put the carpet in the back, just for a laugh. Several shifts later the same van was once again at the station. With the driver nowhere to be seen they opened the back door out of curiosity and lo and behold the carpet was still there.

'Pierre' rushed to the office and returned with some string and a label. He wrote on the label — 'TO BRIGADE STORES' and attached it to the carpet. They learned later that the said carpet had been taken to and been accepted without question at the stores. Considering nothing was allowed in or out of the stores without the appropriate paperwork, the acceptance of such an item, which wasn't on their books, was rather strange to say the least. Similar pranks to this certainly helped to relieve the boredom of 'Station Life'.

Visits from the Hierarchy

In LITTLE SNOBSBURY days it was rare for the hierarchy, A.D.O.s upwards, to interfere with the operational workings of the station, leaving the day to day running of drills and lectures in the 'capable' hands of the Sub and Station Officers. The exceptions were test turnouts, probationary/promotion drills, visits from the Mayor etc., and the annual Home Office Inspection.

The idea of 'test turnouts' was to test and time the reactions of crews responding to the 'bells' going down. These were done at random, mostly during the day, but sometimes in the evening — never in the early hours. A fictitious address would be given to the O.I.C. who would inform his crews of the same. The clock would only be stopped by the overseeing officer once the last fire engine had cleared the engine house and come to a halt on the station frontage, with the respective crews lined up for inspection in their fire kit.

The O.I.C. would either be given a 'bollocking' or praise for the standards reached — usually the former. On one such occasion Station Officer 'Red-Cheeks' chose a real address instead of a fictitious one and he stood there in amazement as the fire engines disappeared into the wide blue yonder. "WHERE THE F*!*!*G HELL HAVE THOSE CLOWNS GONE?" he roared. "But sir," interjected the Control Room man, "You gave them a proper address." "GET THEM BACK."

Aside from the random test turnouts, Sub-O 'Squirrel' suggested to the hierarchy that each Watch should compete for a 'test turnout' cup. This was accepted and 'Squirrel', at great personal expense, bought a 'trophy', a cup — no larger than an egg-cup.

During one of these 'championship' runs I was riding in the back of the Pump. We rushed downstairs and whilst donning our kit it became more than obvious our appliance wasn't going to start. The driver even tried using the starting handle, but to no avail. Eventually we had no alternative but to push the appliance out of the bay under the 'glaring' eyes of 'Glarer'. Big 'Jock', the 'Death Grip' Leading Fireman who was in charge of the Pump, muttered to us as we pushed and pushed, "This is f*!*!*g ridiculous." The hierarchy made no allowances for the breakdown of the appliance and as a result we were placed last, well behind the other Watches — there was no room for excuses in LITTLE SNOBSBURY.

Station Officer 'Red-Cheeks' decided to get the annual 'test turnout' cup out of the way within a few days. All three Watches achieved a time of seventeen seconds, truly remarkable, until another Station Officer examined the stop-watch and discovered it was faulty. Each time he started it, it stopped on seventeen seconds!!! There of course had to be a re-run after a reliable stop-watch was purchased.

After the take-over the test turnouts ceased, along with the 'cup' competition. The 'egg-cup' disappeared, eventually turning up years later in some obscure cupboard on the station. The person who found it asked one of the former LITTLE SNOBSBURY firemen what it was. When the purpose was explained he couldn't believe his ears. There were a lot of things which happened at LITTLE SNOBSBURY which had to be seen to be believed!!!

Whenever the Mayor, Aldermen and Councillors put in an official appearance at the station, we had to 'cow-tow' to them and perform the usual 'Punch and Judy' show in the drill yard. One regular dignitary, a highly respected Alderman, suddenly disappeared from the scene after his less than respectable antics in a public toilet with a fellow male were 'exposed' in the local rag.

Prior to a Home Office Inspection, set drills would be practised for weeks and weeks, as we did for 'Open Days', and everything possible was covered to minimise 'balls-ups'. We would be paraded in the yard whilst the Home Office Inspector, the Chief Fire Officer, his cohorts, officials from LITTLE SNOBSBURY Council and wives were seated on the podium prior to the main show.

By the time the Chief etc., had finished thanking each other and their respective wives for attending the annual inspection, a good hour had passed by and many of us who had stood on parade were on the edge of wilting.

Many 'Inspections' passed without a hitch, mostly due to the fact that for a number of years the Home Office Inspector was from the 'old school', a hardened drinker. Upon arriving at the station this particular gentleman, who had a large 'bulbous' boozer's nose, was almost immediately escorted to the bar by the Chief and his entourage. "You must be tired and thirsty after your lengthy journey sir." In 'Pierre's' words, "He didn't walk up the stairs to the bar — he floated up". By the time the drills were being performed he hardly took any more than a passing interest in the proceedings.

Then, one year, the inevitable happened, the 'boozer' retired, being replaced by a 'keen' representative of the new 'super-breed' of Inspectors. He was a teetotaller to boot — horror or horrors. One can imagine the scene, "Would sir like a drink before the drills?" "No thank you, I don't drink — let us get on with my inspection." Once the initial introductions were over — "I would like the thank the H.M.I. and his wife," etc., the H.M.I. was informed of the set drills, for which we had been training for weeks. After listening, he turned to the Chief and said, "I do not like what you have arranged for me. What I require is . . . . . " The hierarchy of LITTLE SNOBSBURY were stunned and flabbergasted as were ourselves.

As the new drills were detailed each member of the fire crews, including your's truly, thought to himself, 'Which is the easiest task to perform'. As we stood there in a panicky haze, the final command was shouted, "GET TO WORK". (The easiest appliance to hide away from the Inspector was the Hydraulic Platform, with the cushiest job being that of the pulpit operator.)

Two qualified operators were detailed to take charge of the H.P. with 'Q.P.R.' on the pulpit and another man on the cage controls. Part of the drill was a rescue from the top of the tower, 'Building heavily smoke-logged — persons trapped'. With the carefully planned 'unit' drills gone out of the window, along with any semblance of teamwork, it became 'every man for himself'. At least six men donned compressed air B.A. sets and rushed to the cage of the H.P. where they were joined by the O.I.C. of the 'rescue', who also had a set on.

Bearing in mind that there is a weight of limit of five adults in the cage at any one time, there were at least eight men assembled near to the same, seven of them with bulky sets on. The O.I.C. climbed into the cage, followed by the other B.A. wearers. By the time there were three or four men with sets on crowded into the cage it became all but impossible for anyone to move, including the operator, and still the remaining B.A. wearers tried to get aboard.

The O.I.C. went crackers and threw two of the men out of the cage, but it still contained five wearers, including himself, plus the operator, so he threw another two off in an effort to alleviate the cramped conditions. What he was unaware of was the fact that as he was throwing them off, they made their way to the other side of the cage and clambered on once more, like a merry-go-round. Whatever the Chief and the H.M.I. thought of this fiasco they kept to themselves.

261

At the sight of this never ending farce, 'Q.P.R.', on the pulpit, was reduced to tears of helpless laughter and was bent double over his controls. He said to us, after the drills were eventually completed, "All I could see were men crowding into the cage. Compressed air bottles were clanking against one another as each man tried to obtain a prime position whereby he wouldn't be thrown off. The O.I.C. was purple in the face as he threw them off and when they went round and round and climbed back on I cracked up. If the Chief had come up to me and threatened me with the sack if I didn't stop laughing, I would have been sacked."

This fiasco reminds me of the story Gordon once related about the time he was in the Royal Air Force Fire Brigade. He said, "For some reason the hierarchy kept on picking on our station for monthly inspections. There we were on parade, surrounded by senior officers with handlebar moustaches, when, from over the horizon an aircraft appeared, trailing smoke from the engines. I thought, 'This is rather realistic, even for a monthly inspection'. As it passed overhead the officers looked up in disbelief and then I realised it wasn't part of the drill. We all watched as it disappeared over some trees, then there was a 'crump', followed by an explosion."

Those of us who were listening were just about regaining our composure when Gordon continued, "After the explosion we were ordered to take our appliance to the scene of the crash, but there was a slight snag. The fire engine had been based at the camp for many years and due to the fact that the camp had its own maintenance facilities there were no reasons for it to travel beyond the main gate. Over the years, however, the camp perimeter had been modified, mostly for security reasons and the entrance had been fortified with brickwork. When we reached the entrance the fire engine was too wide for the gap and by the time we reached the scene of the crash, after a wall had been demolished, there was nothing left, apart from some smouldering wreckage."

Within weeks of MAMMOTH COUNTY being formed details were forwarded to each station of the impending visit of the new Chief Officer's representatives. Apart from a Divisional exercise, which is the 'norm' in large Brigades, various stations would be subjected to a 'visit', some only fleetingly (tea and toast), but others were chosen for station drills. As we at LITTLE SNOBSBURY hadn't long belonged to an independent Brigade, we were chosen for the 'full treatment', involving the whole of the morning up to dinner time.

Prior to their arrival we were paraded by a panicking Station Officer 'Red-Cheeks', who said, "Whatever happens lads, don't say you don't know to any of their questions. Bull-shit often baffles brains, even the brains of the hierarchy." As it happened this advice was to stand us in good stead, but during the entire drill session our 'Fearless Leader' was nowhere to be seen, making himself scarce within the confines of the station.

Generally speaking all went well, but there were the usual spate of 'cock-ups'. One fireman, taking part in a B.A. drill, ran past an 'inspecting' senior officer trailing a guide line behind him. This was correct procedure, but the man concerned had the ill fortune to have a line which contained a 'bird's-nest' within the bag and his progress came to an abrupt halt when the bulk of the line jammed in the bag.

'Frankenstein' was so keen to make an impression he almost ripped hose-lines in half as he ran them out. The average length of standard hose is 75', but instead of slowing down as he came towards the end he carried on running until the hose would stretch no longer, pulling him backwards.

One fireman, in an effort to gain a few moments respite from the grilling, thought he had gained sanctuary behind a stationary fire engine. Keeping an eye on the MAMMOTH COUNTY officers he backed out of their sight and muttered to himself, "I will be glad when these w*nk*rs have gone." He continued backing up until he 'backed' into another of the senior officers who was facing in the opposite direction. Fortunately the latter hadn't heard his disparaging remark, but far from gaining a respite the fireman was subjected to an instant 'question and answer' session.

'The Goalkeeper' and 'The Lancastrian' were detailed to carry out a drill involving the use of hydraulic equipment, Epco gear, under the watchful gaze of one of the Chief's officers. During the drill he requested the use of a 12″ extension tube. Between them the two fireman selected an appropriate section, but before they could use it they were asked,

"How do you know it is 12" long?"

There was silence, so 'The Lancastrian' was detailed to fetch a ruler from the office. He rushed off and returned with the same. Bearing in mind that most rulers are 12" long the extension tube was measured, taking up the entire length of the ruler. The Chief's 'man', satisfied with the measurement, moved on to another drill, leaving them in peace. It was only after he had gone that 'The Goalkeeper' took a closer look at the ruler and discovered it was 18" in length, not 12". A perfect example of Station Officer 'Red-Cheeks' maxim — "Bull-shit baffles brains."

MAMMOTH COUNTY Fire Brigade had several Chief Fire Officers during my time in the regime. One of the new ones was paying a courtesy visit to several stations in my Division following his appointment to the Brigade. I met him whilst on standby duty at a station which once belonged to the 'Big City Brigade'. Accompanying the new Chief was a member of the Fire Service Watch Committee, once part of the 'Big City' Council.

The Councillor looked dreadful, health-wise, as he passed along the ranks of men who were being introduced to the Chief and him. After they had departed I found out why the Councillor looked so 'out of sorts'. One of the longstanding 'Big City' firemen explained. "The former Chief of the 'Big City Brigade', who was MAMMOTH COUNTY'S first Chief, used to like a 'tipple' or two whilst visiting stations, but the new one doesn't drink. The Councillor, who used to accompany the first Chief likes a 'tipple' or two as well. I would imagine by the time he visited our station the Councillor was 'cracking up', having to remain 'dry' for so long."

During one of the first visits to LITTLE SNOBSBURY Fire Station by one of the MAMMOTH COUNTY Chief Officers, the men were lined up and introduced to him, one by one. When he came to 'Pat', the conversation went something like this. "What is your name lad?" — "Fm. 'McMurphy' sir." — "Ah. You are Irish then!" — "No sir." — 'Where are you from then?" — "I transferred to LITTLE SNOBSBURY from Glasgow sir." — "Ah. You are from Scotland then!" — "No sir". By now the Chief was becoming perplexed and he became even more so when 'Pat' tried to explain further. It transpired that his parents were of different nationalities — 'Irish/Scottish' — and he had been born in England, but lived in Ireland before moving to Scotland, or something very similar.

In the end the Chief gave up the ghost and moved on to the next man, who happened to be 'Pierre'. They chatted for a while and when the Chief asked 'Pierre' how many Brigades he had been in, he answered, after some thought, "Now there was YOKEL COUNTY, LITTLE SNOBSBURY AND MAMMOTH COUNTY — three sir." Impressed, the Chief said, "How many stations have you served from?" He was not so impressed when 'Pierre' replied, "Just the one sir."

Many of the junior officers, including myself, were sent to the 'Big House' on an internal 'Get To Know You' course, which in theory sounded excellent, but in practice was an absolute waste of time. We were crammed within the cramped confines of a little room which was situated immediately next to a busy elevated dual carriageway. If the 'Head of Department' spoke softly it was all but impossible to understand what he or she was saying, thanks to the traffic noise. It was also rather obvious that the majority of these 'Top Persons' had little time for us either.

One of my former Divisional Commanders was the D.C. of the Division into which we had been sent on the course. His 'scenario' (where have I heard that before?) was on the theme of free speech — no holds barred. We looked at each other in amazement and 'freed' of our 'men to officers' relationship (temporarily) one Leading Fireman really went to town.

During an earlier part of his speech, the D.C. had emphasised the importance of the men checking the equipment on appliances at the change of each shift. To prove his point he often removed the odd piece of small gear and waited for it to be reported missing — sometimes days later. The L.Fm., who originated from the Black Country, said to the D.C., "Are you sure we'me can speak freely sir?" There was a nod from the D.C. "Youm mean theyr'e be now comebacks?" more nods of approval from the D.C. "Roight then. With reference to the men not checking they'm apployences properly, yow think it's moused important to catch they'm out?" Yet more nods from the D.C. "Well, oi think that if yow ave nothing better to do with yower toime, then yow shouldn't be a Divisional Commander." The D.C. was stunned and I think this was the first and last time one of the lower ranks was allowed to express his 'open' opinion without being placed on a charge for insurbordination.

A particularly nasty senior officer arrived at one station and for some reason he wasn't happy with the man at the top of a turntable ladder during drills. On the pulpit of the T.L. was 'Dave Rainbow' and the officer strode up to 'Dave' and grabbed the internal phone. "Which w*nk*r is on the phone?" he demanded. (Meaning the firemen at the top of the ladder.) "Which end sir?", replied 'Dave Rainbow'.

The A.D.O. who decided 'the mirror on the bed in November' had started the fire in an earlier chapter, constantly harangued the lower ranks and would appear without notice on different stations within our Division. He recently turned up at one station and having poked his nose into the B.A. room he observed a cylinder which he immediately assumed belonged to another Division. Collaring a passing fireman, he took him into the B.A. room and pointed to the cylinder, saying, "What is that cylinder doing here?" The fireman replied, "Because it's ours A.D.O." "No it isn't, it belongs to another Division." "I can assure you it's ours sir." The A.D.O. strode to the cylinder and said, "Then why does it say A1 R? It says A1 Reserve. This cylinder belongs to A Division." The firemen turned to him and said, "That doesn't say A1 R — it says AIR — it is an air cylinder." End of story!!!

During a visit to the station by a Mayor of LITTLE SNOBSBURY the bulk of our Watch were lined up outside the rear of the appliance bays. As the Mayor was being introduced to our 'Gaffer', Roger, by one of the senior officers, 'Pierre' who was standing next to me, whispered, "I know what I would do if I became the f*!*!*g Mayor, I would ask if the senior officers were firemen as well and insist they join the rest of the men on the drill ground." It was all I could do to stop myself from having a giggling fit.

On yet another 'Mayoral' visit, we were once again lined up in fire kit, prior to the 'Punch and Judy' show. The Mayor, along with his 'boggle-eyed' wife, was working his way along the line of firemen being introduced to each and every one by our 'Gaffer'. I was at the end of the line with 'Taffy'. As the Mayor came within earshot we could hear him saying, "And what is your name?" 'Taffy' whispered to me, "If he asks me my name I will tell him to mind his own f*!*!*g business." At that I couldn't resist a snigger and was glared at by the Divisional Commander. Thankfully the 'bells' went down and saved the day for me.

We often had 'visitations' from an Assistant Chief Fire Officer. According to the Chief's dictat these were supposed to be 'get to know you' informal meetings, but nine times out of ten we would first of all be run ragged round the drill yard, prior to the 'informal' chat.

One such A.C.F.O. had a speech impediment (drink?) problem and it was difficult to understand his lack of coherent instructions at the best of times. But what could we do against such a high ranking officer? We had little choice but to obey his orders when he took personal command of a drill session. Gordon and 'Pierre', who were on the H.P., noticed him going from machine to machine, questioning all and sundry on a host of subjects connected with the appliance they were working from.

'Pierre' said to Gordon, "Just keep the H.P. rotating, he will never climb aboard whilst it's in operation and ask stupid questions." In this they totally succeeded. Throughout the entire session they went round and round in pointless circles and at the end of the drills they were doubled up with mirth. They were not to know the A.C.F.O. didn't possess enough knowledge about the H.P. in the first place to even dream of grilling them about it.

Officially, catering men were not allowed off the station prior to an impending visit from the hierarchy. However, our 'Gaffer' used to let a man out as he considered (rightly) that the ingredients for lunchtime were far more important than a Fire Service visitor. During a drill session being overseen by the Deputy Chief Fire Officer ('Darth Vader'), Gordon managed to sneak into the kitchen without being noticed with his box of groceries. As he placed the box on the floor he heard someone in the corridor speaking to the Dep. "The phone call for you is in the mess sir." With seconds to spare Gordon managed to dive on the floor, out of sight, near a row of cupboards.

The Dep. was on the phone for ages, but despite the cramp afflicting his legs Gordon was unable to move for fear of being discovered. As some of the conversation between the Dep. and the caller was of a 'Top Secret' nature, he would have been for the high jump. Thinking he was on his own, the Dep. had been passing comments similar to, "Get that man on a charge. So and so will be sacked if found guilty. I will be over to give such and such a dressing down later." Gordon could hardly move by the time the conversation was over.

One final story concerning an impending visit from a Mayor which occurred at LITTLE SNOBSBURY sums up the attitude of some members of the hierarchy within the Fire Service. The fire engine I was in charge of 'broke' down on the way to a job. Having informed Fire Control of the problem another machine was mobilised and we managed to limp back to the station. With the first line appliance (a spare) having taken our place the appliance bay was all but bereft of fire engines apart from an elderly Driving School appliance and a reserve H.P.

After booking in to Fire Control I was joined by 'Smoking Joe'. This D.O. took me into the appliance bay and said, "What a shambles! All we appear to have on show for the Mayor is a selection of reserve and broken down fire engines. We will have to bring some new appliances in from other stations, otherwise he won't be very impressed." I commented, "Why not show him what we have to put up with? Perhaps it might do us some good." The D.O. was not to be moved. He appeared to be more concerned with creating a favourable impression with the Mayor than with the realities and needs of the crews on the ground floor — the ones YOU rely upon in your hour of need.

In more recent times there has been much talk about the merits of females joining the Fire Service, something which has become a reality in many Brigades, often with disastrous results. At a 'get together' at my old station I was informed of a story which concerned the employment of female firefighters. During a tea break one of the firemen passed the general comment of, "What do you lot think of 'split-arses' joining the Fire Service?" This was overheard by an A.D.O. (the one with a face like a melted wax candle) and fearing possible future problems he decided to use his rank and authority to clamp down on the offending fireman. He tore into him. "If I ever hear you make a comment like that about females again, within this Brigade, you will be out of the job before your feet touch the ground."

At that he calmed down, no doubt filled with smug self-importance at having been able to use his 'authority' so effectively. During the same tea break one of the few decent officers within the Division, a Divisional Officer (who outranked our melted wax candle friend) arrived. He acquired some tea and toast and joined the table where the others were seated and said, "Well lads, what do you think about 'split-arses' joining the Fire Service?" I need comment no further!!!

And so we come to the end of my story and bid farewell to the likes of Gordon, with his 'Up the Fire Service' motto, our 'Gaffer' and his "Well.....Errmmm.....Errmmm.....Errmmm" approach, and 'Pierre' with his 'Harry Growlers', 'Harry Spiders' and 'Torf*!*!*gpedoes' linguistic approach to descriptions in the English language.

I will leave the last word to the latter with his recent overall observation of life in the Fire Service, after 28 years in the job.

"Do you know?" he said, "After all the 'Hi-Tec' equipment we have been supplied with over the years and the intensive training, little has really changed since the day I joined. One exception is that we are now 'Glorified Water Squirters' instead of 'Simple Water Squirters' — so much for progress."

Postscript One — Circa 1900

(photograph courtesy of Peter Hay)

"I wonder what the Fire Service will be like in the eighties?" asked the first man on the left. "I dread to think," replied his partner. "I expect the officers, like them standing there, will be just as idle and bombastic as they are now." And do you know, he was . . . .

Postscript Two — Circa 1990

Not so long ago I was standing by some shops in LITTLE SNOBSBURY High Street, when a fire engine went racing by with headlights blazing, sirens blasting and blue flashers turning.

A mother turned to her youngsters and said, "Look, there goes a fire engine, off to someone's house," and I reflected on the fact that nothing had changed since the beginning of this book.

Hopefully, if she reads it, she may be more enlightened.